Contents

Playing with Identities
in Contemporary Music in Africa

Editors
Mai Palmberg
Annemette Kirkegaard

Published by
Nordiska Afrikainstitutet, Uppsala 2002
in cooperation with
The Sibelius Museum/Department of Musicology
Åbo Akademi University, Finland

Indexing terms

Cultural identity
Music
Popular culture

Africa
Cape Verde
Ivory Coast
Nigeria
Senegal
South Africa
Tanzania
Uganda
Zimbabwe

Cover photo: Zach's Productions, Lagos, Nigeria.
Lágbájá, the Masked One, Nigerian musician of a new style and stage personality.
Language checking: Elaine Almén

Editorial assistance: Pia Hidenius

@ the authors and Nordiska Afrikainstitutet, 2002

ISBN 91-7106-496-6

Printed in Sweden by Elanders Gotab, Stockholm 2002

Foreword

In 1995 the Nordic Africa Institute launched a research project on culture, "Cultural Images in and of Africa", which functions as a complement to the studies on economic, political, and social problems and developments in Africa.

Although culture can certainly be entertaining, the aim in including cultural studies in the Institute's research profile is not to convey the message that culture shows the bright side of Africa, but rather to highlight the important role of cultural aspects of development and change.

One aim for the project "Cultural Images in and of Africa" is to analyse and increase awareness of the sources of the images of Africa in the Nordic countries. The publication of the anthology *Encounter Images in the Meetings between Africa and Europe* in 2001 was one outcome of this, as was the book in Swedish by the project coordinator, Mai Palmberg, on the images of Africa in Swedish schoolbooks (*Afrikabild för partnerskap. Afrika i de svenska skolböckerna*, 2000).

Another aim is to encourage studies of how culture and cultural creativity in Africa contribute to self-images, that is, to building identities, and expressing the agonies, visions and endeavours in society. In 2001 the project published a first book on these issues in the anthology edited by Maria Eriksson Baaz and Mai Palmberg entitled *Same and Other. Negotiating African Identity in Cultural Production*. The present book is the second publication on this theme, with a concentration on music.

The Nordic Africa Institute wishes to thank the co-sponsors of the conference in Åbo, the Sibelius Museum/Department of Musicology and the Centre for Continuing Education at Åbo Academy University for their decisive input into the preparation and organisation of the conference, from which the chapters in this book have been selected. We particularly wish to thank professor Pirkko Moisala, curator Johannes Brusila, programme officer Eva Costiander-Huldén, and assistant Henrik Leino.

The African presence at the conference was impressive. Perhaps this is not surprising, given the pivotal role of music in African societies. But it is noteworthy, given the fact that research into this and other fields of the humanities, is suffering greatly in the crisis for higher education and research in Africa, and many African researchers in cultural studies have joined the diaspora.

We wish to thank the Division of Culture and Media of the Department of Democracy and Social Development in the Swedish International Development Cooperation Agency (Sida) for contributing additional funds to make it possible to strengthen the African presence at the Conference.

Uppsala, April 2002
Lennart Wohlgemuth
Director

Introduction

Annemette Kirkegaard

> I believe that it is often the case that the musical practices and the
> musicians that we study are more sophisticated than the theories we
> apply to them, and, further, that African popular music can itself be
> engaged as embodied theory, as illuminating thought-in-action, rather
> than mere empirical grist for the metropolitan mills of academia.
>
> (*Waterman*, in this volume)

This statement by Chris Waterman in many ways mirrors the difficulties of theoris-
ing music, and an attitude like this could possibly deter some students and scholars
from venturing into academic contact with African musics. Nevertheless, it is very
clear that thoughts about the music, its roots and its meanings are there all around
us, and it would be highly annoying if researchers did not try their hand at the
debate.

In November 2000 a conference was held in Åbo (Turku) in Finland dealing with
the role of music in modern Africa—and the agenda directly asked for the way in
which identities were played with in contemporary musical cultures both in and outside Africa.

Many different issues were touched upon during the three days of meeting, and
a general and fruitful discussion over the topics of the conference took place in the
halls and lobbies of the Sibelius Museum: itself so rich in connotation and imaginations over a specifically Finnish tone in musical work as for instance expressed in
Jean Sibelius' national-romantic symphonic poem, Finlandia from 1899.

The conference was arranged in cooperation between the Nordic Africa Institute,
the Department for Musicology/Sibelius Museum and the Centre for Continuing
Education, both of the latter situated at Åbo Akademi University in Finland. It was
proposed within the project "Cultural Images in and of Africa" of the Nordic African Institute, and the idea to hold a conference had emerged out of several meetings
and seminars within its framework.

The Åbo conference initially aimed at stimulating the interest in and enhancing
the knowledge of African contemporary music in a societal context, and it further
wanted to reflect on and bring out the discussions and views held by African scholars
and musicians themselves. The articles in this book represent a choice of the many
papers presented, and even if very different in style and content, they all reflect the
overall theme of identity and music of the conference.

Some years ago one of the authors in this book, John Collins, in a Danish produced video describing African cross rhythms, proposed that African music was to
become the music of the 21st century. According to Collins this was partly due to
the high musical quality, and the notion that the complexity often experienced in
drum orchestras and larger types of ensembles represented the right music to match

the philosophical, emotional and cultural demands of the citizens of the global culture of the next millennium.[1] But it was also—I think—a statement, which tried to pay respect to the immense importance African music has played in the global imagination and the role of black culture in the actual historical development of music not least in the cross-Atlantic exchange, which has so deeply affected all the popular musics in the world.[2]

The idea that African music could become a global asset is oddly enough also continued by a more unexpected ally, i.e. the World Bank. Apart from minerals the music industry is the only area in which Africa as a continent seems to have an opportunity to make money at present. Because of this the World Bank has launched a programme on commercial music development as it realised that the music, so vibrant and alive in spite of the downfall and economic depression of most African nations, formed a market in which Africa had a potential for making money.

We have already now seen that African musics have very different connotations and meanings. In the following I shall try to trace the scholarly background to this situation.

African music seen by musicology and ethnomusicology

African music studies, like the general study of the musics of "the other", have been confined to the realms of ethnomusicology—or comparative musicology—as it was originally called. Initially the discipline was tied up with the study of folkoristics[3] and only gradually did it develop into a discipline of its own.

An evolutionistic view of musical cultures dominated comparative musicology, and prior to the 1950s an interest in musical sound and the recording and registration of its melodic and rhythmic patterns and structures, rather than a concern for its meaning, marked the field. Especially African music of what was believed to be precolonial time was collected and analysed according to these ideas since it provided a direct counterpart—or put more bluntly the complete "Other"—to the civilised high cultures of the colonising European nation states.[4]

After the Second World War with the beginning of a new scientific and scholarly paradigm, the study of music also changed dramatically. Now the point of departure was not so much an investigation of the melodies, metres and sonoric physicalities as the meaning of the music and the role it played in the society to which it belonged. Musical anthropologist Alan P. Merriam termed this turn of interest the call for a "study of music in culture".[5] Ethnomusicology gradually was understood as a method rather than as a discipline defined by its object or geographical distance. Foreignness and otherness remained important points of discussion, and have accompanied the field until today, as is evident in the debate over the concept of World Music, to which I shall return later. This change of focus, however, also made it possible for the researchers to view even their own cultures. The dichotomy of insiders versus outsiders was brought to the fore, together with a renewed and diverse interest in fieldwork and its implication for the study of music.[6]

1. Bishoff 1994.
2. The origins of jazz—though thoroughly disputed, is but one of the many examples of how the transatlanic exchange has made its mark on Western music.
3. Kirschenblatt-Gimblett 1995.
4. Examples are for instance the early ethnographic work done by anthropologist Clyde Mitchell, who later produced the book "The Kalela Dance" in 1954.
5. Merriam 1960, p. 109.
6. One general discussion has been whether the researcher should and could participate directly in the musical performance, and learn the musical language so to speak, which was the idea behind the launching of the term bi-musicality by Mantle Hood. See Cooley, 1997.

The development thus had a specific meaning to the role of the African research-ers. Throughout the process of independence—and particularly during the struggle for liberation—a whole generation of African scholars had been educated in West-ern, primarily European universities and schools. These people were of course insid-ers, as they had been born and raised in African surroundings, but they had possibly also become outsiders precisely due to their education and knowledge of non-African norms and values and their sometimes prolonged stay in the European metropoles. It soon became a question whether an African studying African musics could be called an ethnomusicologist.[1]

Music and identity

The above dilemma of insiders and outsiders touches directly on the theme of the Åbo conference and the subject of this book—i.e. music and identity. In recent years the discourse over identity has increased in the ethnomusicological literature, and the general concern for understanding and defining how borders between the "us" and the "them" are established, has been at the fore in many writings and current debates. This concern is shared with other branches of cultural scholarship, but in musicology—and particularly in ethnomusicology—the question of identity has focussed on the discussion of whether music should be viewed as having embodied meaning (as essentialistic) or as referential, "in which music's significance is tied to its more overtly extra-musical associations with such entities as rituals, religion, nationalism, specific occasions, personal memories and the like".[2]

The question whether music can represent something more than itself is an old one in musicology going back a long way, but being most vehemently debated in the 19th century. There were those who regarded music as absolute music, which could only be interpreted as musical waves of sound with no extra-musical meaning, a view held by, for instance, German composer Johannes Brahms and the critic Edouard Hanslick. Others regarded music as programmatic, which can be under-stood to represent non-musical meaning and convey specific, even if sometimes un-conscious messages. This view informed the music used in opera and symphonic poetry, and Richard Wagner and the philosopher Friedrich Wilhelm Nietzsche were among the strongest advocates of this perspective.

The debate is still running, and I shall not try to solve an ongoing controversy, but when the question of identity is involved, it is at least important to be aware of the distinction.

Modern ethnomusicologists like Martin Stokes and Mark Slobin have fought the idea that one particular music could represent one particular group of people,[3] a fea-ture very well known in ethnomusicological works on African music, and sometimes bordering on a racist ideology for instance in the effort to stereotype and stylise *yoruba* music.[4] This is not to deny that a particular often traditionally organized grouping—and especially the so-called "fourth worlders" are the favoured ones here—relies on specific musical norms and ideas, but rather to stress that these are almost always a result of a conscious attitude towards the norms and values of neighbours and visitors sometimes resulting in acceptance of new musics and at

---

1. Artur Simon 1978.
2. Manuel 1995, p. 230.
3. Stokes 1994 and Slobin 1993.
4. The stylised and frozen image of *yoruba* is present in many writings on transatlantic musics like the Santeria cult of Cuba.

other times causing rejection.[1] In other words: there is no original core music belonging to a specific ethnic group or a national entity. Instead musical sounds are chosen for the purpose of setting up necessary boundaries and accordingly the musical performance is often the exact spot in which this can take place.[2] Therefore it cannot be reduced to plain musical analysis of why, how and where a people or a group want to depict themselves in music. Scholarly works must address both the social and the musical layers of performance in order to understand the overall meaning of the music culture. In this way identity is negotiated, often constructed and sometimes stylised in music—a point highly relevant in understanding the idea of musical revival.

What then is playing? Well, that is of course simply what musicians do—they play the music and the instruments. Some would add that in music there is always play, that it is always transforming space and that it always displays an aspect of non-seriousness of ideas—different from the earnestness of other cultural forms. This is not altogether true, and debates, discussions and controversies are abundant in the history of the field, but it is true that music creates a lot of fun, it inspires collective joys and somehow above all it has a special capacity to represent and recalibrate time.[3]

But it is also a way of living for many—combined with the hardships of making ends meet and its performers are often met with the double sword of both being needed and respected and at the same time deeply feared and mistrusted. This is most clearly demonstrated in the attitudes towards the traditional African *griots* and other heritage singers and performers, but it is also a feature known for modern musicians: in Africa as in the West the mistrust towards the musician as a person making his living from an improper walk of life, is prevalent. Here, from a more practical and less romantic point of view the term "playing" can also be used. Musicians play instruments, but they also play with images and expectations in order to draw attention to their skills. I shall return to this special element of musical life in relation to the discussion of World Music and its affiliation with the music industry and the global cultural economy.

The debate over change and continuity in music

One of the major points of discussion both in ethnomusicology as such and in African music studies in particular has been the distinction between or the adherence to either a static or a dynamic view of the music culture. As related above ethnomusicology in the days of comparative studies primarily held a static view of music cultures based on an evolutionistic line of thought, and even if this view in recent scholarly work has been rejected and proven absolutely false, it nevertheless still haunts the imagination and dreams of audiences, performers and producers of African music.

Music has been examined on both theoretical and analytical grounds for its relation to development, and the dilemma between change and continuity in Africa has been on the agenda at least since Bascom and Herskovits' groundbreaking book of 1959.[4] The terms "premodern—modern—postmodern" have been employed by, for

1. It is well known from linguistics that the generic term or name of the people or ethnic group is often just the generic term for 'people' or even 'human' and that the often exotic names of neighbours often just mean 'those from the north'.
2. Stokes 1994, p. 3.
3. Bohlman 2002, p. 4.
4. Bascom and Herskovits 1959, p. 2ff.

instance, Peter Manuel[1] in order to bring the discussion further. In a simplified version, the premodern is interpreted as synonymous with the precolonial or even authentic music. The modern is represented by the fused, urban musics of the 20th century, while the postmodern—although the definitions are diffuse—signifies the highly hybridised musical forms of the mediascape and global imaginations. Manuel and Erlmann both point to the fact that in the postmodern interpretation it is important to make a distinction between Western music culture and its way of using the musics of the "other", as opposed to the systems of meaning and function of the same musical styles and patterns in their "homeground" so to speak.

It is important to reflect on this division, but at the same time it should not be overemphasized. The dichotomy of global versus local is a major key to the understanding of these issues. In other words the whole world is tied up in the proceedings and happenings of the global arena, while at the same time—and with sometimes very different results and outcomes—the music makes a statement on the local ground. In this way the postmodern condition is present in all cultures and much of what is normally discussed as postmodernism actually deals rather straightforwardly with the experience of living in a world in which distance and presence are locked together with each other in quite a historically new way.[2] A direct result of this situation is that playing with identities and establishing images becomes a very important feature to the musicians and performers of music and culture.

In a recent book on multi-culturality in contemporary Sweden, ethnomusicologists Dan Lundberg, Krister Malm and Owe Ronström with reference to Mark Slobin propose the concept "visibility" to deal with the new implications for identity.[3] This concept signifies the importance of being seen in the postmodern world, and as the disembodying of time and place is one of its markers, cultural expressions are also marked by disembedding mechanisms, which in some ways make them free floaters in the overall global mediascape.

As a result of the new orientation and understanding of these theoretical implications, the scholarly debates instead of speaking about African music now talk about African musics in the plural.

Revival

As a direct answer to the cultural and music repression which many colonial powers had exercised, African scholars in music and culture felt the need to reclaim the values of their culture and accordingly a huge momentum of revival and even invention of some musical traditions occurred. The Christian churches had in many places forbidden the use of drums and sometimes even participation in communal musical performances as such, and in many African states ministries of culture wanted to collect and save the music, which was believed to have survived the oppression. Revivals have recently been the subject of a number of articles and writings in ethnomusicology and many interesting findings have surfaced.[4] It is a difficult area to define precisely, and the major reason is that the concept and terms it builds upon depend largely on a "handful of the most potent and powerful concepts of modern Western civilization: nation, tradition, identity, ethnicity and culture".[5] Of these the greatest

---

1. Manuel 1995.
2. Lundberg et al. 2000 interpreting Anthony Giddens, p. 401.
3. Lundberg et al. 2000, p. 25.
4. See for instance, Kirschenblatt-Gimblett, Tamara Livingston, and Owe Ronström.
5. Ronström 1996, p. 7.

difficulty is caused by the dominance of the concept of tradition within revival movement. The concepts of tradition, change and continuity are in the foreground of this discourse.

In revival movements there are generally two attitudes towards the material. Either it is formed by the dichotomy puristic versus syncretic—as it was formulated by John Blacking in the 1970s[1]—or termed as a search either for authenticity (object-oriented) or as an investigation of processes (process-oriented), as proposed by Ronström.[2] The two ideas are somewhat overlapping in that the puristic, as the object-oriented attitude, relies on an essentialistic view of the role of the revival, bordering on the static freezing of a particular moment in the life of a musical form, while the other, syncretic, as the process-oriented view, adheres to a dynamic view of culture. The latter attitude seems to be the winning one, and generally the development goes from dealing with a tradition to traditionalisation, and accordingly the process implies an abandonment of "the notion of tradition as the handing down from one generation to the other of bounded cultural or natural entities". [3]

The revival thought is important to this debate, as it both represents a cultural production—closely related to the heritage production which is a increasing part of the tourist industry[4]—and as revival movements tend to homogenize their object. In this way it leads us on to a more modern but in some ways similar phenomenon—that of the late 20th century World Music Business.

World Music

Since the 1980s the concept of world music has also made its entrance in both scholarly and more popular writings on African musics. Being the initial field of interest, Black music both in Africa and in its diasporic areas for some years held the priority in the field. Styles like *soukouss* and *mbalax* from Africa and *samba* and *salsa* from the Americas dominated the World Music arena. Not much music under this label originated from Russia or Japan. By the end of the millennium the concept of World Music had been substantially broadened. Even if it has by many researchers and scholars been rejected because of its unclear categories and the impossibility of defining the concept on a theoretical and musical level, it is nevertheless a fact in popular global music culture.

Bohlman discusses the exoticism, which is regarded as a more conspicuous thread in World Music—and I believe that this is so because World Music has an aura of *ecumene*, of doing well and showing solidarity with the poor.[5]

It is as Veit Erlmann has shown closely related to the more down-to-earth elements of music making, i.e. the connection of the music culture to the business or music industry, and the undeniable fact that musicians always and everywhere have struggled to make a living from their competence and expertise.[6]

Also the connection to both local and global Mediascapes is quite evident,[7] and as more than any the Swedish ethnomusicologist Krister Malm has shown this relationship is a crucial, thorough and very real factor in all thoughts on world music.[8]

---

1. Blacking 1995, p. 155 ff.
2. Ronström 1996, p. 6.
3. Lundberg, Malm and Ronström 2002, p. 13.
4. Kirschenblatt-Gimblett 1995.
5. Bohlmann 2002.
6. Erlmann 1993.
7. Erlmann 1993, Slobin 1993.
8. Malm and Wallis 1993.

For musicians and agents of music in Africa the presence of world music has influenced their creative making of new musics.

In African music the presence of the world music issue has meant that it is in the mind of the musicians and agents of music in such a way that it influences their creative making of new musics. A direct result is that the global imagination created by this situation strengthens the importance of the Western and European metropoles as for instance Paris, and thus it puts the musicians at the risk of being exploited by the music industry.[1]

These relatively disturbing aspects of the presence of the global World Music, are, however, balanced by an until recently unknown possibility for African musicians to find a niche in the global commercial music life, and even more importantly, as emphasised by Jocelyn Guilbault, the postmodern disembeddedness also gives to African musicians and other world music stars the chance of escaping a stereotyped and essentialistic imagination of tradition and purism.[2]

So, World Music is both local and global. Even if it is a truly Western phenomenon, it makes a strong impact on African cultures and it matters to the musicians, it both helps them promote their music, and it sometimes represents an obstacle, if for instance the music is not regarded as truly "world" which often happens. Here the concept of authenticity appears again. Both in revivals and in World Music there are important limits drawn and they are often assumed to happen on the basis of an ascribed authenticity.

Authenticity in music studies

In contemporary African music authenticity has been renegotiated. In earlier ethnomusicological works from the first half of the 20th century many cried over the apparent loss of authenticity in so-called modern or urban musics. The introduction of popular or Western musical elements such as electric instruments, harmonic progressions in major/minor keys with few—well-known—chords and foreign lyrics were seen as contaminations of authentic traditional music. These changes are unfortunately not given any attention by early researchers and collectors of African music, who preferred the more true or authentic traditional or folk music of the rural areas.

The paradox between the traditional and the modern is well known. In many ways music demonstrates very clearly and more illustratively than many other art forms how impossible it is to distinguish between the two in living cultural products. Urban musics in the academic discourses have been understood as westernised at least to the extent that western or global musical material like scales, chord progressions and simplified rhythmic patterns has often made its impact in the very well known imitation of Western or Caribbean popular musics.[3] Today we know and we have seen proof that the modern musics are not at all only a feature of foreign influences, but that structural musical elements are transformed and moved from older and traditional instruments like the *likembe* of Zairean music and the *mbira* of Zimbabwe, both of which have resulted in modern electrified musics like *soukous* and the so-called *chimurenga* music of Thomas Mapfumo.[4] In this way the music plays an equally important part in the countryside as well as in the urban and in diasporic

---

1. For more detail on this see Kirkegaard 1996.
2. Guilbault 1997, p. 32 ff.
3. Imitation being a very logical and necessary tool in oral transmission (Kirkegaard 1996).
4. Turino 1998, p. 92.

centres around the world. This is, of course, partly due to the spread of the modern media, primarily the radio, but it is also a continuation of the exchange between migrating peoples and in this way it displays the dynamics of musical culture.

Special attention has been given to the period following independence in African states and a whole branch of studies has surfaced under the heading of postcolonial studies.[1] In these the discourse over authenticity is a major issue of discussion. One of the most important findings and statements within this discourse—resembling the dichotomy of distance and presence in the postmodern condition—has been the realisation that the colonial setting not only and obviously influenced the areas that were actually colonised, but that also the coloniser was deeply affected by the power structure, the exchange relations and the cultural complication and implications of the strategies and morals and values of the colonial situation. This means that even the centre was deeply affected and in my view it is clearly demonstrated in music.

Music is different from other art forms in a number of ways. For one, music is a free floater, which in that it is aurally transmitted and easily dispersed is there to be used and misused quite free of all the thoughts and ideas of the academic world. Artists, musics and not least audiences use music and make it their own disregarding all fine thoughts. This is the essence and the quality of being a popular art form, so to speak. But one of the pitfalls of the condition is that it is open to misuse, mis-interpretation and broad generalisations.

Popular articles, magazine essays and radio broadcasts on African music abound in generalisations, and African music is described and denotes everything "other" than Western. In this way the difference is overemphasised and enhanced and even imagined. The ensuing image of the happy and naive African musicians is in total accordance with most other images of Africa: i.e. poverty, corruption and natural catastrophes. The gap is never bridged, but in real life the role of African music is very different. Its impact has been large: Western popular musics, *jazz, soul* and lately *rap* music is still closely tied up with the musical influences and ideas brought to the Americas and the Western world by black people.

The discussion is complicated and complex and even the learned debate over influences, survival and authenticity is enormous. Yet too many scholarly books, articles and essays have drawn too harsh or strong conclusions on too weak evidence and knowledge—hence the generalisations—also many writers on African musics have looked after number one and simplified complicated relations in order to meet their own desire and wishes.

Some brilliant studies, however, have stood out in order to try to do away with or eradicate the generalisations: writers like Chris Waterman, Veit Erlmann, David Coplan, John Miller Chernoff and a few older ethnomusicologists like John Blacking have paved the way for a new generation of scholars. In the context of this book not least the pioneering work on popular African musics, its Atlantic transfer and its Round Trip by John Collins has provided unique reorientation of the field.

Perhaps in the future some more of this material can be published and this volume—we hope—emphasises that not only geographically, but just as much musically, Africa is a vast continent.

---

1. See Baaz 2001 for a discussion on postcolonial studies on African culture.

The chapters in this volume

In everyday life music can be hard to distinguish from other cultural elements. In Africa, as in most other continents, it is hard to talk about music without taking into consideration how the dance is performed, how the lyrics relate to social, cultural or political events and happenings. Accordingly this is not a music book in the sense that it will tell you about the notes, the sounds and the harmonic progressions of a piece. It is trying to be multidisciplinary.

At the presentation of the programme for the Åbo conference a number of issues were listed to which the papers were addressed. The theme sessions were directed through the following titles: Music and ethnic identity, Music and gender, Music and globalisation, Cultural identities and music in South Africa; Music and political identity; Music and resistance; Religious music.

Many different views on these issues can be seen in this book. For African scholars—working in their own culture—the use, relevance and meaning of ethnomusicological study are somewhat different from those of affluent and theoretically concerned scholars from the Nordic countries. The learned debate over the distinction between musical history and the ethnographical present as highlighted by Philip Bohlman is apparent here.[1] Many African researchers are concerned with recording the past, with doing historical musicology with a direct and political aim, as opposed to the Western ethnomusicologists' interest in meaning and interpretation. This difference is at the same time a mirror of the dynamics and diversity of musicological research in African music and it depicts the pluralism of theoretical and scholarly work at the beginning of the 21st century.

The book opens, as did the conference, with the paper of the keynote speaker Chris Waterman (USA). In his opening address to the conference he introduced the question of identity in Nigerian popular musics by referring to three levels of identity in music. His paper follows this line of thought and by examining the exciting artist Lágbájá—the Masked One, he emphasises a new trend in the displaying of and playing with identity, that of a new awareness of self. Through a juxtaposition of the two more renowned styles of *jùjú* /*fuji* made famous by King Sunny Adé, and *Afro beat* almost exclusively ascribed to the late Fela Anikulapo-Kuti, Waterman in his paper develops an interesting perspective on how the present day musician is negotiating both time and identity on fairly new grounds.

* * *

Several papers address in a more general way the role and function of African musics in their specific environments.

Mai Palmberg (Sweden/Finland) in her chapter "Expressing Cape Verde" takes the presence and dominance of *morna* and *funaná* and their meaning to the construction of national identity in the Cap Verde islands as a point of departure for a discussion of identity formation on a national basis. The dichotomy of African versus European in cultures is contested, as is the concern for mapping roots instead of looking at the ends the music serves. As an illustration at the end of the paper the expressive longing and nostalgia found in the musical styles is compared to the somewhat similar musical mood of the Finnish tango.

The issue of gender is addressed most strongly in the paper by Sylvia Nannyonga-Tamusuza (Uganda) in her paper, which analyses the text and the subtext of the

---

1. Bohlmann 2002.

dramatised song *Kayanda*, a piece of *Kadongo-Kamu* music of Uganda. Nannyonga-Tamusuza draws conclusions on the functions of the song both in political, social and gendered ways and she calls for a new and dynamic understanding of popular music in the political and historical interpretation of ethnicity.

Simon Akindes (USA/ Côte d'Ivoire) in his paper on "Post-Democracy" Popular Music in Côte d'Ivoire sees the emergence of the musical styles *zoughlou* and *mapouka* in the Ivory Coast in relation to political-cultural factors in the society such as ethnicity, class struggle and migration. Via a discussion on the presence of *reggae* music Akindes goes on to explore the introduction of styles like *zoughlou* and *mapouka*, and the controversial aspects of the *zoughlou* and *mapouka* dance and music forms. The paper concludes that music in this respect—drawing on local humour—is rewriting the people's history.

Jenks Okwori (Nigeria) examines the role and function of music in the resistance movement of two oppressed ethnic groups, the Ogoni and Idoma in Nigeria. Here the meaning and use of tradition plays a major part, and Okwori emphasises and highlights how older ritual musics are transformed and used dynamically in the contemporary struggle. Also gospel music is touched upon, and the author concludes that what is happening to the use of music in this particular case is not a game but a battle for survival.

John Collins (Ghana) addresses the generational conflict within the West African societies and beyond, and claims, with rich documentation, that this has always been an agent in developing and shaping the popular and traditional musical styles, while Siri Lange (Norway) explores the dance and *taarab* competitions in Dar es Salaam from the point of view that competition has increased and that the political impact of multipartyism has sparked off a fierce struggle over visibility and access to the important medias and stages in Tanzanian cultural life.

* * *

Another trend in the present papers is represented by the increasing scholarly interest in the global relations between Africa, its diaspora and the West: here authenticity and the importance of the global imagination are major points of departure.

In a historically based excavation Ndiouga Adrien Benga (Senegal) examines the role of urban musics and identities from the 1950s to the 1990s in order to highlight the way in which these have resulted in new musical products. Recently rap music has begun to play an important part in the African cultural landscape of today, and its emergence is interpreted as a protest of the powerless against the deteriorating economic and social conditions.

David Coplan (South Africa) relating to the new ideas within the identity discourse also touched upon by Chris Waterman, proposes a third way in the reception and theory of contemporary African musics. By discussing South African popular musics Coplan finds this third way by giving the music the seemingly paradoxical label modern-traditional.

Johannes Brusila (Finland) much in the same vein mixes the local and the global in his discussion on tradition versus development in Zimbabwean popular music. He dismisses the essentialistic interpretation of music cultures and in his analysis of Virginia Mukwesha's modern *mbira*-based music, he relates to the possibilities in the modern musical media and their ability to "play" with real or artificial sounds in order to reach a specific goal—in this respect the re-established negotiation over tradition.

My own paper, which discusses a Norwegian cross-over album of techno and Tanzanian *taarab*, "Tranzania", opens up to the direct use of African musics in Western productions. The recording is a clear-cut example of how music today can be seen as a global pool of sounds and how meaning, identities and values are negotiated, exchanged and dramatised in the musical products. Hereby the playing with identities is brought to the fore in a quite different way from its direct cultural political functions within the African nation states.

* * *

As this short summary of some of the issues and all of the chapters in the book hopefully demonstrates, the scope is wide and the issues many. We hope that it will also contribute to a further discussion and bringing out of stories from the vast African musical landscape, which deserves and needs proper/scholarly attention to be given to its strong and beautiful musics.

References

Baaz, Maria Erikson, 2001, "Introduction—African Identity and the Postcolonial", in Baaz, Maria Eriksson and Mai Palmberg, *Same and Other: Negotiating African Identity in Cultural Production*. Uppsala: Nordiska Afrikainstitutet.

Bascom, William R. and Melville J. Herskovits, 1959, "The problem of stability and change in African cultures", in Bascom, William R. and Melville J. Herskovits, *Continuity and Change in African Cultures*. Chicago: University of Chicago Press

Bishoff, Peter, 1994, *African Cross Rhythms: As seen through Ghanaian music*. VHS, Loke Film, Mellemfolkeligt Samvirke, Copenhagen.

Blacking, John, 1995 (1977), "The Study of Musical Change", in *Music, Culture and Experience, the Selected Writings of John Blacking*. Chicago: University of Chicago Press.

Bohlmann, Philip, 2002, "World music at the 'end of history'", *Ethnomusicology*, 46/1, Winter.

Cooley, Timothy J., 1997, "Casting Shadows in the Field: An introduction", in Cooley, Timothy J. and Gregory F. Bar, *Shadows in the Field: New Perspectives for Fieldwork in Ethnomusicology*. Oxford: Oxford University Press.

Erlmann, Veit, 1993, "The Politics and Aesthetics of 'World Music'", *The World of Music*, 35(2).

—, 1997, "How Beautiful is Small? Music, Globalisation, and the Aesthetics of the Local", *Yearbook for Traditional Music*, Vol. 30.

Garafaro, Reebee, 1993, "Whose World, What Beat? The Transnational Music Industry, Identity, and Cultural Imperialism", *The World of Music*, 35(2).

Guilbault, Jocelyn, 1997, "Interpreting World Music: A challenge in theory and practice," *Popular Music*, 16(1).

Kirkegaard, Annemette, 1996, *Taarab na Musiki wa densi*. Unpublished Ph.D. thesis, Copenhagen 1996.

—, 1999, "Exodus—men hvorhen? Hvad er baggrunden for reggaens enorme popularitet i Afrika?", *Musik & Forskning*, 24, 1998–99.

Kirschenblatt-Gimblett, Barbara, 1995, "Theorizing Heritage", *Ethnomusicology*, 39(3).

Lee, Pedro van der, 1997, "Sitars and Bossas: World Music Influences", *Popular Music*, 17 (1).

Livingston, Tamara E., 1999, "Music Revivals: Towards a General Theory", *Ethnomusicology*, 43(1).

Lundberg, Dan, Krister Malm and Owe Ronström, 2000, *Musik Medier Mångkultur: Förändringar i svenska Musiklandskap*. Stockholm: Gidlunds Förlag.

Malm, Krister and Roger Wallis, 1993, "Patterns of Change", in Frith, Simon and Andrew Goodwin (eds), *On Record*. London: Routledge.

Manuel, Peter, 1995, "Music as Symbol, Music as Simulacrum: Postmodern, Premodern, and Modern Aesthetics in Subcultural Popular Musics", *Popular Music*, 14(2).

Merriam, Alan P., 1960, "Discussion and Definition of the Field", *Ethnomusicology*, IV(3).

Mitchell, Tony, 1993, "World Music and the Popular Music Industry", *Ethnomusicology*, 37(3).

Ronström, Owe, 1996, "Revival revisited", *The World of Music*, 38(3).

Simon, Artur, 1978, "Probleme, Methoden und Ziele in der Ethnomusikologie", *Jahrbuch für Volks- und Völkerkunde, 9.*

Slobin, Mark, 1993, "Micromusics of the West: A comparative approach", *Ethnomusicology*, 36(1).

Stokes, Martin, 1994, "Introduction: Ethnicity, Identity and Music", in Stokes, Martin (ed.), *Ethnicity, Identity and Music: The Musical Construction of Place*. Oxford: Berg.

Turino, Thomas, 1998, "Mbira, Worldbeat, and the International Imagination", *The World of Music*, 40(2).

Big Man, Black President, Masked One
Models of the Celebrity Self in Yoruba Popular Music in Nigeria

Christopher Waterman

> I wanted to depict that facelessness,
> that sense of not having an identity anymore,
> of the faceless masses ...
> (*Lágbájá*, June 4, 2001)

In seeking to explicate the social role of music in colonial and postcolonial Africa, ethnomusicologists have in recent years frequently invoked the concept of identity.[1] The concept of identity played an important role during the 1960s and 1970s in problematizing the received definition of ethnomusicology as 'the study of music in cultural context,' a formulation which too often reduced the complexities of history, ecology, culture, and society to a generalized backdrop for the technical analysis of musical sound. Scholarly monographs of the time often had separate sections for cultural and musical analysis, reflecting a bifurcation of anthropological and musicological perspectives and methods.[2] During the late 1960s the notion that music could be analyzed as a particular form of cultural practice began to appear in the literature, and the concept of identity played a crucial role as an analytical lynchpin between music and culture. Similarly, attempts to study linkages between music and society often relied on homologies between reified musical and social forms.[3] Here too, the move toward analyzing music-making as a specific type of social action depended to an important degree on placing 'identity' at the center of the ethnomusicological equation. By the 1980s and 1990s the notion that one could *explain* particular musical practices and forms by specifying their role in expressing or enacting identity had become commonplace in the ethnomusicological literature.

In its crudest form the analytical strategy flirts with tautology. Why does she sing like that? She sings like that to express her identity. Why does she express her identity through music? Because music is intimately bound up with memory, the emotions, and other foundations of identity. This is admittedly a bit of a caricature, but I do think it is fair to say that the initial burst of insight occasioned during the 1970s and 1980s by the introduction of 'identity' analysis into ethnomusicology has to some degree waned.

The very ubiquity of the concept—with its alluring juxtaposition of the public and the private, the social and the psychological, the cultural and the iconoclastic—

---

1. See, for example, Coplan 1985; Waterman 1990; Turino 2000.
2. For example Alan Merriam's *Ethnomusicology of the Flathead Indians* (1967).
3. This is true to a certain degree, in Alan Lomax's cantometrics project; see Feld 1984.

suggests that 'identity' is in some danger of being transformed into a taken-for-granted analytical lynchpin between the musical and the social. Of course, it is typically at the point where such explanatory concepts take on an aura of 'common sense' that they begin to limit our thinking, and to short-circuit all sorts of interesting questions. I am not arguing that we should abandon 'identity' in our attempts to understand music, music-making, and musical experience. Rather, I think that developing approaches which problematize not only the category 'music' but also our own unexamined assumptions about the nature of 'identity' (and related concepts such as 'the self' and 'the person') can help us to better understand music as a technically, cognitively, and perceptually specialized cultural practice.

In western intellectual traditions philosophers and psychologists have long raised questions about the unity and stability of both the self (commonly represented as the internal face of identity—subjective, psychologically unified, essential, and real) and the person (the external, socially constructed, represented and enacted identity of individuals). Since these theories have typically focused on language, rather than embodied practices such as speech, music, theatre, and ritual, they tend to be phrased in terms of grammatical categories. At the center of many such arguments lies the linguistic convention of the first-person subject pronoun, the "I".

Theorists of identity have made much of the fact that Nietzsche, back in the 19th century, argued that the internalization of the pronominal logic of a given language conditions us, as native speakers, to believe in our own subjectivity. From this point of view, one's experience of an integrated, stable 'self' is dependent on a suspension of disbelief made possible in the first instance by language. According to the psychoanalytic theorist Jacques Lacan the subject

> ... is originally an inchoate collection of desires ... and the initial synthesis of the ego is essentially an alter ego, it is alienated. The desiring human subject is constructed around a center, which is the other in so far as he gives the subject his unity.[1]

Here the self appears as a fiction, constructed around a core that is not "I", but Another. Elsewhere Lacan uses the metaphor of the mirror to point out that although we learn to 'identify ourselves' by gazing at the reflected image of our face, we in fact always see ourselves reversed, not as others see us. This shift away from essentialized models of the self and toward a focus on difference and reflection, leads to the linked propositions that one's sense of self is to a significant degree constructed through others, and that the privately experienced 'self' and the publicly enacted 'persona' are mutually and dialectically (i.e., often contradictorily) implicated.

In anthropology, systematic consideration of these issues dates back at least to Marcel Mauss's classic essay on notions of the person and the self, first published in 1938.[2] As it happens, cross-cultural research has also undermined the putative universality of the distinction between subjectively-experienced, interiorized selves and socially-constructed, externalized persons. For example, the scholarly literature on Yoruba expressive culture supports the claim that the ultimate goal of performance is to intensify experience and enhance the prospects and image of local actors. But these 'local actors' are not stable, already fully-constituted entities; rather, the process of performance involves the consolidation of persons out of diverse, multifarious, overlapping materials, materials often borrowed from beyond the bounds of the Yoruba-speaking world. This process suggests a sophisticated conception of personality as an assemblage of traits, made coherent and sustained by the attention

---

1. Lacan 1985, p. 39.
2. Mauss 1985.

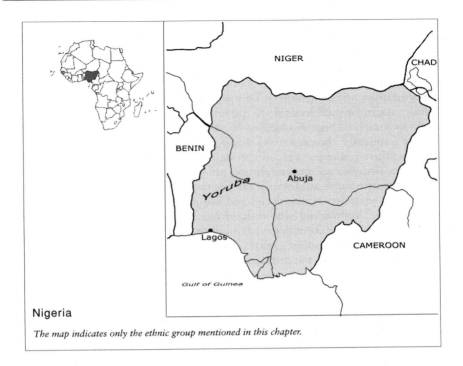

Nigeria

The map indicates only the ethnic group mentioned in this chapter.

of others.[1] Persons, from this perspective, are the products, as well as the agents, of performance.

This vision of identity as a multidimensional product of interaction between destiny (*orí*), character (*ìwà*), circumstances, and purposive action in the world (work, ritual sacrifice, hustling) is also registered in the Yoruba lexicon. One of the primary anatomical metaphors for the mutually constitutive interaction between self and society is *ojú*, a Yoruba term designating "face" or "eyes". In its external aspect, *ojú* is the primary social organ, the locus of self-expression and the tactics of self-construction through sentient interaction with others. In its inward-facing aspect *ojú* (more specifically, *ojú inun*, the "inner eye") is the locus of contemplation, imagination, and creativity. These two dimensions of the Yoruba metaphor *ojú* point toward a conception of identity which indeed recognizes 'inner' and 'outer' dimensions of the self, but nonetheless does not map neatly onto the western bourgeois notion of an essential, autonomous, subjective interiority which 'expresses itself' in the world. Instead, the face and eyes are configured as portals between society and the self, crucial synapses in the process of personhood. Even this brief sketch of Yoruba concepts which appear to cluster around the translation term 'identity' is enough to suggest that ethnocentric generalizations about the nature of 'selves' and 'persons' are problematized by cross-cultural research.

The point I am making here is that contemporary western philosophies of the subject and the cross-culturally comparative study of self and person point us toward broadly similar conclusions. First, identity—even the seemingly elementary grammatical concept of the pronoun—is not as well-bounded, unitary, or determinate as we sometimes claim, particularly when our arguments depend on fitting mu-

---

1. Barber and Waterman 1995.

sical genres and human subjects into boxes labeled with standardized rubrics of ethnicity, race, gender, generation, nationality, and class. Second, it is clear that the distinction between 'self' and 'person,' or the 'inner' world of subjective experience and the 'outer' world of social action, is neither completely stable nor universal. It turns out that, as the musicologist Robert Walser has succinctly put the matter, "interiority is anything but private".[1] This insight is of crucial importance for understanding enactments of identity in popular music, where the construction of celebrity is so often a central aspect of the social logic of performance.

It has frequently been observed that African popular musicians serve as 'role models' for their audiences, a thesis that deserves more detailed exploration. Enactments of the celebrity self in performance are publicly articulated models of subjectivity, multidimensional images of what it is to be a person, to inhabit the world in a certain way under particular social and historical circumstances. In postcolonial Nigeria the State has worked hand-in-hand with the extractive machinations of transnational capitalism; 'government' has neither exerted moral suasion nor created sustainable public institutions; global media peddle images of the self-as-consumer and strive to penetrate (or to create) local regimes of representation; the intersubjective norms that govern economic and political life have become radically enervated, and civil society itself appears as "a fetishized sphere of circulation within the national economy".[2] Under such conditions, popular musicians' public enactments of interiority-in-performance may have profound consequences indeed for the imaginative modeling of social identities and the creation of new publics. It is therefore important that we explore the possibility that celebrity can serve progressive, humane ends. This is an approach that runs in the face of Cultural Studies' jaded view of celebrity qua Madonna, and of the 'Afropessimism' prevalent in current scholarship about Nigeria—precisely because the charismatic suasion exercised by popular musicians has the potential to shape ideas of selfhood, moral community, and citizenship. As John and Jean Comaroff have suggested, such ideas are "complex, resonant historical constructions ... grounded not only in political ideals and formal institutions, but also in public manners and personal dispositions, in conventions of taste and style, in carefully attuned sensuous regimes".[3]

The Big Man

The substantive basis of my paper is a comparison of three distinctive models of celebrity in Yoruba popular music, each a complexly distributed field of representations embodied in specific musical practices, tactics, discourses, and images; each traversing, in its own way, the distinction between 'inner' and 'outer,' 'private' and 'public' dimensions of identity. The first of these models is what I am calling The Big Man, a celebrity persona cultivated by performers of Yoruba-language popular music genres such as *jùjú* and *fújì*. Polished to a fine gleam by the competitive friction of the marketplace, sustained by complex patron-clientage networks, and wielding the formidable rhetorical resources of Yoruba praise poetry, proverbs, and social dance drumming, superstar musicians such as Alhaji Dr. Sikiru Ayinde Barrister and King Sunny Ade project a contemporary, dazzlingly syncretic vision of the praise singer as wealthy merchant chief, a charismatic market-being constructed,

---

1. Walser 1997, p. 271.
2. Apter 1999, p. 302.
3. Comaroff and Comaroff 1999, p. 32.

*King Sunny Ade
and the African Beats*

through performance, out of the magnetic accumulation of people, cash, and other symbolic resources.

The intensive hybridity of *jùjú* and *fújì* music, and their seemingly voracious appetite for stylistic difference, is related to the conception, discussed above, of 'the person' as an agglutinative configuration. In Yoruba-language music videos, played in homes and viewed publicly in bars, restaurants, and barber shops, the superstar musician is projected as a diversely-constituted hyper-ego who draws exotic commodities and styles into a discursive field grounded in local ideologies and social relations . Constantly in motion, he appears in a succession of lavish *mise-en-scènes*, clothed not only in gorgeously varied costumes, but also in layers of people—his friends, employees, patrons, and fans. In these videos, the *gbajúmòn*—a big-shot, etymologically speaking, someone known by a hundred pairs of eyes—commands attention by capturing and domesticating difference, and in so doing produces both his own celebrity and the mass audience upon which it depends.

Although *jùjú* and *fújì* performance rely heavily on the expansive corpus of 'deep Yoruba' verbal lore, there are some crucial differences between the socio-poetic logics of popular music and long-standing genres such as *oríkì* (praise poems or epithets).[1] In *oríkì* performance the ultimate subject of praise is someone other than the performer. In *fújì* and *jùjú* music, on the other hand, the singer has become the subject of his own panegyrics. His continually shifting attention to others is primarily a strategy for reproducing his own celebrity. Although all Yoruba performers have means of calling attention to themselves, this degree of self-aggrandizement is a new thing. The Yoruba superstar—praise singer, master of commodities, and 'plenipotentiary of enjoyment,' as one *fújì* video proudly proclaims—collapses the contrast between patron and client, a fundamental semiotic and social distinction around which the economy of praise singing, and the careers of big men and big women, have long revolved. This conflation of roles in turn allows him to transcend traditional limits on the praise singer's ability to accumulate wealth and to exercise power. As such, it could be argued that the *fújì* or *jùjú* star also embodies, in highly stylized form, the vanished middle of the Nigerian socioeconomic order, and the collapse of many Nigerians' dreams for the future, precipitated by kleptocracies private and public, and by the IMF-mandated devaluation of the naira.

Identity and alterity, intimacy and distance, sincerity and fakery are all mutually implicated in this mode of cultural production. The well-established social *raison d'être* of Yoruba musical and verbal performance—the representation and activa-

---

1. Barber 1991.

Alhaji Dr. Sikiru Ayinde Barrister

tion of vertical client-patron linkages and the redistribution of capital—now coexists with a new social-ideological formation, the mass-mediated star-fan relationship, couched in the language, images, and affective textures of patron-clientage (just as patron-clientage has for centuries clothed itself in the idioms of kinship).

The Black President

A contrastive model of the celebrity self is embodied by the late Fela, Olufela (Ransome) Anikulapo-Kuti, founder of Afro-beat music, 'Black President,' and Emperor of the "Kalakuta Republic" that also functioned as a marijuana market and a social security center for Ikeja neighborhood 'area boys'. In comparing the persona of Fela with that of mainline Yoruba pop stars such as Alhaji Barrister and King Sunny Ade, one difference stands out immediately—while *jùjú*, *fújì* and other mainline Yoruba praise-pop genres are performed by thousands of musicians, Afro-beat music was associated almost exclusively with one charismatic figure. Fela's popularity rested largely on the lack of perceived distance between the private self and the public persona—Fela was Fela, whether you encountered him on stage at the Shrine or in the confines of his Kalakuta Republic, and this conflation of the 'inner' and 'outer' surfaces of his identity was central to his authority as a musician and political icon.

Fela's core audience was heterogeneous, yet very particular. It included the radical Nigerian intelligentsia, the street-smart youths of Lagos, members of the urban working-class, and, in Europe and the U.S., a mix of black nationalists and white college students, a subset of the same uneasy coalition that played an important role in Bob Marley's international success. To be sure, Afro-beat music has never been as popular among the mass of Yoruba listeners as *jùjú* and *fújì*, performed by scores of bands each weekend at the weddings and funerals of the wealthy. In the end, it is hard to know if it was Fela's increasingly experimental *music* that held his fan's affections, or his charismatic aura and talent for hurling *yabis* (verbal abuse) at the succession of corrupt regimes who stole Nigerians' civil rights and, through incompetence and collusion, ran the economy into the ground.

One of Fela's many nicknames among the dozens of 'area boys' who clustered around his home in the Ikeja area of Lagos was *Abami Eda*, Yoruba for "mysterious one". Certainly, Fela's personal conduct was enigmatic. He celebrated African tradition by his mini-dictatorship (the Kalakuta Republic). He touted the virtues of African polygyny by wedding twenty-seven young women, and then had them dance

Fela Anikulapo-Kuti

in cages at his nightclub, The African Shrine. Later, after a bout in prison, Fela came to the conclusion that marriage was a western contrivance, and summarily divorced them all. And he spent much of his creative energy mocking the colonial Afro-Christian culture that birthed him, and that implanted in him early on a stereoscopic view of Yoruba tradition.

Fela's Gentleman (1973)

Unlike the rhetoric of mainline Yoruba pop music, where the singing and drumming of contextually appropriate praise epithets and proverbs is central to the social and economic logic of performance (and to the public construction of the musician persona as a master of deep lore), the use of 'folklore' in Afro-beat is typically somewhat distanced. In many of his recorded performances, Fela in fact seems to maintain an insider/outsider relationship with 'deep Yoruba' poesis—he cites oral tradition as a category, rather than mobilizing it as a technology for the amassing of patron-clientage networks and the agglutinative construction of self. I would argue that this insider/outsider relationship to Yoruba tradition, forged during his childhood in the Afro-Christian world of Abeokuta—and reminiscent of Lacan's claim that "the initial synthesis of the ego is essentially an alter ego"—was an important dimension of Fela's complex performative persona.

Photo: Leni Sinclair

Fela Anikulapo-Kuti

The celebrity personas of the mainline Yoruba pop stars Alhaji Barrister and King Sunny Ade on the one hand, and Fela Anikulapo-Kuti, on the other, may be read as contrastive fields, each comprised of multiple layers of stylistic, social, and historical relationships. The identity projected by Yoruba praise-pop practitioners is not only a *representation* of the Yoruba-speaking public, but is in a sense also *constituted out of* this public, out of the millions of fans and patrons who are drawn inward by the magnetic force of the superstar's performances and charisma. Like the kings and chiefs represented in centuries-old sculpture, the mainline Yoruba superstar 'wears people like cloth'.[1] Afro-beat music, on the other hand, was focused—in the tradition of bourgeois revolutionary expression—on a charismatic, hard-headed iconoclast, whose art was inseparable from his life, and whose ambivalent relationship to tradition was publicly negotiated through performance. Fela presented himself as a *model for*, and not an *embodiment* of his audience, the heterogeneous social formation which formed the basis of his celebrity.

The Masked One

I turn now to Lágbájá, a contemporary Yoruba musician whose performative projection of self both incorporates and resists the praise singer *cum* big man identity of mainline Yoruba *jùjú* and *fújì* stars and the Afro-bourgeois radical charisma of Fela Anikulapo-Kuti. Lágbájá—a Yoruba term meaning 'somebody,' 'anybody,' or 'nobody'—is the creation of a graduate of Obafemi Awolowo University in Ile-Ife, Nigeria.[2]

Lágbájá's musical career began in the early 1990s, when he played electric bass with the jazz quartet Itan (Yoruba for history, or historical narrative), and tenor and soprano saxophone with the Colours Band, which performed both original material and covers of John Coltrane recordings such as "My Favorite Things". In 1993— just as the election of M.K.O. Abiola as President of Nigeria was annulled by the military, plunging the country into its worst political and economic crisis since Independence—Lágbájá established his masked alter-ego, and released his first album, entitled *Lágbájá*. Lágbájá's first hit recording was "Coolu Temper", released in 1995. In 1996 he was one of six African artists who participated in an International

---

1. This sartorial metaphor for charisma appears often in Yoruba popular discourses. On one of his records, King Sunny Ade pleads with God not to let the 'agbada (sumptuous gown) of popularity be torn' from his body. Another of his songs is entitled "People Are My Garments".
2. There are musicians who quite consciously have chosen to emulate Fela's style, including not only his son Femi, but also Kayode Olajide (whose most popular album is *Once Upon a Time*), Olaitan "Heavywind" Adeniji (*Ibadan*), and Dede Mabiaku, who leads The Underground Sound, a Fela cover band.

Red Cross-sponsored concert tour of the continent's war zones, was featured on an consciousness- and fund-raising LP entitled *So Why?*, and appeared in a 1997 video documenting the tour, called *Music Goes to War*. In 1999 Lágbájá released a set of three CDs onto the Nigerian market: *We, Me,* and *Abami (A Tribute to Fela)*.

The most striking aspect of Lágbájá's carefully crafted celebrity persona is his use of cloth costumes based upon the *Egúngún* ancestral masquerades, the power of which is bound up with the purposive concealment of the masquerader's face. Lágbájá explained his performative strategy in an interview with Jon Kertzer and Francis Bensignor:

> Lágbájá itself is a Yoruba word that existed before I borrowed it. And the young kids now don't know the history—they think that Lágbájá is a brand new word that came from me … so we are gradually starting to change the history of the word itself … the new generation didn't even know there was a lágbájá before this Lágbájá! … It's a Yoruba word that means nobody, somebody, anybody, everybody. It depends on the context in which it's used.

> I picked that word, because I wanted to depict a concept, a word to communicate the essence of the millions of people, so-called "masses", the "common man", the people with no voice, that don't have a face, just one in a million—in our society. You find lots and lots of them back home. I wanted to depict that situation, that was strange—because many years ago, everyone had an identity—not like everyone was a king, or princess—but everyone was a part of a bigger whole. The biggest thing about our society was that we had a sense of community; we took care of each other. Everyone belonged one way or the other. It didn't have to be myself—to discipline you, everyone took care of your education, informally, your growth, economic needs—we depended so much on each other. That has changed in what we call the modern world of today. So I wanted to depict that facelessness, that sense of not having an identity anymore, of the faceless masses, the voiceless people in Africa.

> The mask was the perfect thing to communicate that … [and] the music itself played a role, because the whole idea was to send a message to all parts of society. One to the leaders, who control—to talk about the problems of society [and] to the people who are being led themselves, that is, all of us together, to give encouragement [and] essential social, political messages.[1]

Ologunde identifies himself at press conferences as "Bisade Ologunde, representing Lágbájá", and credits "Lágbájá and Bisade Ologunde" as co-composers and co-arrangers on his recordings, maintaining a clear distinction between the public icon and the private subject. The distinction drawn by Lágbájá between the public face (*ojú*) of celebrity and the inner eye (*ojú inun*) of the artist's creative imagination is crucial to understanding his ability to project a multivocal public identity which draws upon, yet implicitly critiques, the models of celebrity discussed above.

Lágbájá's recordings can be heard on the streets of Lagos, in marketplaces and bars, elbowing in among the energetic rhythms and Muslim-inflected singing of fújì music, the ecstatic clamor of contemporary Gospel music, and the swaggering reggae/hip-hop recordings of the self-styled "Ghetto Soldier of Ajegunle" [neighborhood], Daddy Showkey. On his recordings and in performance at his Ikeja-neighborhood nightclub Motherlan', Lágbájá's performative map of contemporary Nigerian identity extends down into 'deep' traditions such as *bàtá* and *dùndún* drumming, folk tales, and proverbs, and outward to incorporate aspects of jazz, soul music, hip-hop, and even kletzmer music. This progressive traditionalism is complemented by a keen interest in contemporary slang from various regions of Nigeria, and in the arche-

---

1. *An Interview with Lágbájá*. Conducted by Jon Kertzer and Francis Bensignor in Angouleme, France, 6/4/2001. http://www.rakumi.org/archives_lagbaga.htm. There is an alternative popular account of his decision to choose a 'stage name' that circulated in Ibadan in the summer of 2000, according to which he chose the name Lágbájá when his parents, who are devout Christians, objected to his experiments with 'pagan' music and images, worrying that they would ruin the family name—and so he reportedly said, "Don't worry, I'll just call myself 'Somebody'."

ology of older cosmopolitan traditions such as palmwine guitar, *agidigbo* music, and *highlife*. Lágbájá freely incorporates grooves, textures, and melodic 'hooks' from *jùjú*, *fújì*, *àpàlà*, and Afro-beat (the genre with which his music is, perhaps unfairly, most commonly associated by the Nigerian public).

Evoking the transformational powers of the *Egúngún*—acrobatic masked figures whose channeling of ancestral potency is predicated on a strategic effacement of the dancing subject—Lágbájá's vocal performances mutate from supple, soul-influenced crooning to the rough voice of a Lagos motor tout, the abusive taunts of a drunk at a soccer match, the chicken-like clucking of a verbose politician or tongue-wagging gossip, the whining tone of an old man begging for the attentions of a young woman, and the tense, quavering, other-worldly quality of Yoruba *oríkì* chanters and masquerades. This flexibility of vocal quality allows him to create a veritable aural diorama of familiar personality types, and in so doing to create a diversely-voiced image of Nigerian civil society. The aural surface of Lágbájá's recordings is complex and shifting, with pungent horn lines and the sharp tone of *bàtá* drums penetrating the polished surface of synthesizer-based pop production and melismatic soul singing. At his concerts the impossibly tall Lágbájá rises magically from beneath the stage, or climbs down a wall, tenor sax suspended around his neck, dressed in a multi-colored masquerade costume, and always covering his face, protecting the man behind the mask from the public gaze that has the power to construct or destroy Big Men.

Lágbájá's corpus of recorded work deserves detailed musicological analysis—for the moment, however, a brief description of representative tracks from his 1999 CD trilogy *We/Me/Abami Eda* will have to suffice. The track "Put Am Well Well" from *Abami Eda*, opens with the sound of talking drums and the shouting voices of market women and their customers. As a loping groove is established, Lágbájá uses digital sampling to open a channel of communication with Fela, the strange one, and engages him in posthumous dialog over the meaning of African language traditions and food ways. In the opening sequence, Lágbájá invokes several types of food strongly associated with the Yoruba kingdoms of Ijebu, Kwara, and Ekiti, while Fela extols the virtues of toasted cassava meal and maize porridge, foodstuffs found throughout Yorubaland, and often associated with the poor, who cannot afford more expensive comestibles such as pounded yam or European-style prepared foods:

> *Lágbájá*: Ijebu, omo alare, dem no dey joke with ikokore [cassava]
> [The Ijebu Yoruba, they don't joke around with cassava]
> *Fela*: Gari [toasted cassava meal], morning, noon and night
> L: Kwara, dem no dey joke with wara [a local type of cheese]
> F: And Eko [maize porridge]
> L: Ekiti, hali moni uyon [name of local Ekiti food]

As Lágbájá expresses his preference for "bread and butter" over African food, partly on the basis that the more weighty traditional foods tend to induce noontime somnolence, Fela protests vigorously:

> F: Ah, you don't know!
> L: Hali moni uyon, count me out
> F: Eh, what are you talking about?
> L: Count me out, count me out...
> F: Try!!
> L: Try wetin? [Try what?]
> F: Try!!

> L: Look am dey sleep for work [Look at them sleeping at work]
> F: No, no be that...
> L: When bread and butter dey [When they could have had bread and butter]
> F: No, excuse me....
> L: Ahh..

As the argument progresses, Fela accuses Lágbájá of 'colonial mentality':

> F: You see, colonialism makes you think that bread and butter...
> L: Ah-ah!
> F: ...is better than gari
> L: Me, I no be colo [colonial]! Bread and butter get i' [has its] own advantage
> F: Lailai [never]
> L: I' get..
> F: Lailai
> L: I say i' get...
> F: Lailai!
> L: Oh, baba, you no go wan' hear...
> [Oh, baba, you don't want to listen...]
> F: Okay, go now...
> L:Bread and butter no go weigh you down..
> F: Dat one no concern me...
> L: Ah-ahhh...
> F: No concern me
> L: Uh...
> F: You see now, educated men will eat sausage and bread every morning. They forget that ewa [beans] and moinmoin [bean pudding] taste better.

After a vigorous exchange on the merits of *moinmoin*, the Afro-beat rebel proclaims "My name is Fela", his voice echoing hauntingly across the break before the choral refrain begins. As Fela's voice fades, the chorus sings a refrain based on a Pidgin English phrase commonly used by customers of food vendors in Lagos: "Put am well-well!" (i.e., "Fill the plate very well!").

Toward the end of the track, Fela's sampled voice advances the quasi-racialist arguments that increasingly dominated his thinking (and lyric-writing) throughout his career:

> *Fela*: Hm-hmm...Okay, now look: You see, me I know one thing. You see, human beings may seem to be the same. But African is different from Europeans, in the inner and cultural structure, from the Creative Ascendancy
> *Lágbájá*: Baba! [chuckling]
> *Fela*: So, white man's food is white man's way, you know. The African way gon-gon-gon [the real African way], hmm, is different from white man's system

If Fela's statement is ambiguous as regards the relative contributions of 'race' and 'culture' to a putative ontological gap between Europeans and Africans, Lágbájá complicates matters further by letting Fela have the last word. By positioning Fela's posthumous statement within a larger musical work (the *We/Me/Abami Eda* trilogy) that includes explicitly anti-racist songs like "Me and You No Be Enemy (We Are Family)", with its refrain "all tongue is red" (an anatomical metaphor for a unified human nature underlying phenotypic diversity), Lágbájá simultaneously entrains and destabilizes the late Afro-beat rebel's discursive authority.

The track "Enún Dùn Ro'fó" is another example of Lágbájá's nuanced juxtaposition of selected aspects of the diverse verbal codes, registers, and discourses, poetic images, character prototypes, and musical styles that circulate in contemporary

Nigerian civil society. The title phrase, a Yoruba proverb, can be roughly translated as "It is easy to say to *others* that they should prepare vegetables" (i.e., "it is easier to tell others to accomplish a task than to do it yourself"). Once the groove is established, Lágbájá's voice begins in a rough deep timbre:

Sá ba'lè	Just get down (cool down?)
Tó bá ta féle-fèle	If you exceed your authority
Sá ba'lè	Just get down (cool down?)
To ba ta fele-fele	If you exceed your authority
Sa	Just ....
Enún dùn ro'fó	It is easy to say to *others* that they should prepare vegetables

This first enunciation of the song's central proverb is followed by detailed instructions for cooking a Yoruba meal:

Gb'omi le'na, f'epo si	Put water on the fire, put in oil
F'ata si, fi tomato si o	Put in pepper, put in tomato, oh
F'alubosa, F'atarodo	Put in onion, put in pepper (*capsicum chinense*)
Fi iyo si, f'egusi si o	Put in salt, put in ground melon seed, oh
Eja gbigbe, t'ori t'ori	Fried fish, complete with head
Oya f'efo si, se o de ti te e l'orun	Now put in vegetables, are you full now?
So de ti jinna o	Are you completely satisfied, oh?
So de ti ro efo niyen, sebi?	You have cooked vegetables for them, isn't it so?

As the talking drum and electric bass-driven groove intensifies, Lágbájá's cooking lesson mutates into instructions for dancing:

Okay maa ro! Maa yi po!	Okay, cook! Stir it!
Maa ro! Maa yi po!	Cook! Stir it!
Oya chop am	Go ahead, eat it
Abi it no sweet for your mouth?	Doesn't it taste good?
Sebi na you cook am yourself?	Didn't you cook it yourself?

The song's second core metaphor is now introduced—the image of the braggart as an 'empty barrel' (*agba ofifo*), a discursive figure accompanied by the sound of a beaten oil drum, a sonic image which in turn evokes Nigeria's precarious petro-economy and the corrupt wealth which it has engendered:

Empty barrel, empty barrel
Àgbá òfifo [Empty barrel]

After a repetition of the title proverb (reinforcing the link between the arrogance of one who attempts to manipulate others to cook for him and the hollow bravado of the corrupt businessman or politician), Lágbájá extends the empty barrel metaphor:

When people dem they try, working hard day and night
Empty barrel go sit down, he no go do anyt'ing at all
But the louder the noise, the emptier...
Nothing better for dey eye [Nothing is good enough for them]
But na them sabi everything for theory [But it is they who understand everything in theory]
Everything he must yab one by one [He must insult everything]
Everybody, dem must yab one by one [He must insult everybody, one by one]

The track continues with a personification of the metaphor of the pretentious hollow man, a *tour de force* evocation of two drunks at a soccer match, heaping invective upon the players on the field, and touting the 'good old days'. The metaphors of cooking as self-reliance, on the one hand, and of arrogance as an audible hollowness of character, on the other, are alternated as the supple funk-influenced dance rhythm gradually fades.

Other examples of the diversely constituted public self projected by Lágbájá can only be noted briefly here. The song "A o M'erin J'ba" (We do not appoint the Elephant as King), the refrain of which evokes a Yoruba folk tale in which the clever tortoise (Ajapa) humbles the giant elephant (Ajanaku), includes the following stanza, in which the link between praise-singing and sycophancy, so evident in *jùjú* and *fújì* music, is explicitly identified:

> But when praising too much o
> Na dat is advertisement for paper
> Rankadede (Corrupt people)
> Na sycophancy o (It is sycophancy)

Here Lágbájá simultaneously signals his knowledge of Yoruba oral lore and critiques its contemporary excesses. In the track "Simple Yes or No" Lágbájá parodies the truth-twisting speech of politicians, likening it to the meaningless clucking of chickens. The track "Agidigbo" celebrates the Yoruba bass lamellaphone ('thumb-piano"), an instrument no longer in common use in popular music, and associated by older listeners with pre-Independence genres such as palmwine guitar music, *konkomba*, and *àpàlà*.[1]

Space does not permit a more thorough analysis of Lágbájá's trilogy, but I hope that these examples convey some sense of the range and subtlety of his allusions to (and invocations of) diverse historical periods, 'local' cultural practices, *dramatis personae*, and global popular styles. In order to better understand Lágbájá's performative tactics, and his construction of a polyvocal celebrity self, it is necessary that we return briefly to his use of the ancestral masquerade tradition as an instrument of social critique.

In Yoruba *Egúngún* performances, the cloaking of the individual masquerader's facial features allows him to embody the life-force of an ancestral spirit, usually associated with a particular patrilineage. Masking is a tactical effacement of the self, a technique for bringing the otherworldly and the social into active (and sometimes dangerous) communication. In Lágbájá's performances the sacred power of masking is self-consciously displaced into the contemporary socio-political realm, enabling the performer to embody diverse stylistic references, discourses, and voices, and even—via the 'magic' of digital sampling—to hold conversations with the ghosts of celebrities past. In much of traditional Africa masks are used at one and the same time to conceal the human face of generalized ancestral power and to reveal the faces of spirits. Lágbájá, on the other hand, uses his concealment to reveal a *public*, a social body made up of vividly diverse individuals, despite its representation as a faceless collective by the Nigerian State, mass media, and well-meaning development agencies. While *Egúngún* masqueraders traverse the boundary between earth (*aiye*) and heaven (*orun*) in order to reaffirm community through public manifestations of ancestral power, Lágbájá uses the technology of masking to transform himself into a kind of negative celebrity, a pop star with no face. The critical distance created by

---

1. See Waterman 1990.

masking allows Lágbájá to project shape-shifting, polyvocal images of a Nigerian 'public' made up of real people with distinctive voices.[1]

And unlike many 'progressive' musicians in Nigeria and elsewhere, Lágbájá practices what he preaches. Lágbájá's band is a more-or-less egalitarian social unit—quite the opposite of *jùjú* and *fújì* hierarchy or Fela's autocratic modes of governance— and his arrangements and studio mixes provide privileged space for women's voices, particularly the brilliant singer Ego Ihenacho. The covers of recent albums feature not only photographic and graphical images of Lágbájá—masked or covering his features with bare hands—but also a verbal declaration of ideological and artistic intent: *Society blossoms when each of its members learns to place the group's interests above his individual interest.* Lágbájá's work projects a utopian, but at the same time eminently down-to-earth, version of the loftier aspects of African socialism, indigenous capitalism, and musical syncretism.

Although it has been suggested that fandom and objective popular music scholarship are inimical, I must admit that I am a Lágbájá fan, in part because I find the music, the public icon, and the broader social and artistic project in which both are embedded so interesting; in part because the future of civil society in Nigeria hangs in the balance, and I believe that musicians could play a central role in this future; and in part because I believe that Lágbájás work sketches an imaginative 'third way' for Yoruba popular music, a rhetorical path between praise-song patronage and windmill-tilting, grounded in a vision of a moral economy that "celebrates diversity" in a critical way.

Conclusion

What is the relevance of this comparison of three models of musical celebrity in Yoruba popular culture for our understanding of the 'play of identities' in contemporary African music? To begin with, I would argue that there are, here and there, performers in Africa whose work in some fundamental (though perhaps not imme-

---

1. It should be noted that certain types of Egungun masqueraders also often portray caricatures of social 'types', including prostitutes, hunters, hicks, and members of non-Yoruba ethnic groups.

diately familiar) manner engages questions about 'identity,' about what it means to live in the world today. Their imaginative manipulations of texture and timbre, tune and tone, speech and bodily practices (dance, costuming) can create imaginative 'quality spaces'[1] within which received dichotomies between self and other, modernity and tradition, the public and the people are neither defended nor demolished. Rather, these oppositions are digested and transformed into the very stuff of which performance is made, and from which the public image of the musician is constructed.

© Communicart Nigeria Ltd.

As the cases of Fela and Lágbájá remind us, this has much to do with representations of the relationship between the private self and the celebrity persona. In the case of Fela, the two were conflated into a charismatic whole. In the case of Lágbájá the two aspects of identity are quite self-consciously held distinct from one another, establishing a series of critical distinctions between the public face (*ojú*) of celebrity and the 'inner eye' (*ojú inun*) of the artist's experience; between the ancestral force revealed by masking and the critical leverage of public self-concealment. Recall Lágbájá's testimony—"I wanted to depict that facelessness, that sense of not having an identity anymore, of the faceless masses." Faceless, perhaps, but definitely *not* voiceless. Like the ancestral *Egúngún*, Lágbájá channels others' voices, creating a resonantly invisible celebrity identity, and projecting visions of a heterogeneous, incorporative, and humane civil society into popular discourse in contemporary Nigeria.

I believe that it is often the case that the musical practices and the musicians that we study are more sophisticated than the theories we apply to them, and, further, that African popular music can itself be engaged as embodied theory, as illuminating thought-in-action, rather than mere empirical grist for the metropolitan mills of academia. Musicians such as Lágbájá clearly have much to teach us about the complexities of performed identity. But more importantly, amidst all of the pessimism surrounding the postcolonial African state, music like this—socially committed, pulsing, nuanced, good-humored, and humane—holds out the hope that elements of the precolonial and colonial past can be mobilized in the interest of a future in which colonialism finally proves irrelevant.

---

1. Fernandez 1974.

References

Apter, Andrew, 1999, "IBB=419: Nigerian Democracy and the Politics of Illusion", in Comaroff, J. and J. (eds), *Civil Society and the Political Imagination in Africa: Critical Perspectives*, pp. 267–307. Chicago: University of Chicago Press.

Barber, Karin, 1991, *I Could Speak until Tomorrow: Oriki, Women and the Past in a Yoruba Town*. Edinburgh: Edinburgh University Press for the International African Institute.

Barber, Karin and Christopher Waterman, 1995, "Traversing the global and the local: Fújì music and praise poetry in the production of contemporary Yorùbá popular culture", in Miller, D. (ed.), *Worlds Apart: Modernity through the Prism of the Local*, pp. 240–62. London: Routledge.

Comaroff, John and Jean Comaroff (eds), 1999, *Civil Society and the Political Imagination in Africa: Critical Perspectives*. Chicago: University of Chicago Press.

Coplan, David B., 1985, *In Township Tonight: South Africa's Black City Music and Theatre*. London and New York: Longman.

Feld, Steven, 1984, "Sound structure as social structure", *Ethnomusicology*, 28(3):383–409.

Fernandez, James W., 1974, "The Mission of Metaphor in Expressive Culture", *Current Anthropology*, 15(2):119–45.

Lacan, Jacques, 1985, *Book III: The Psychoses 1955–1956*. Translation Greg Russell. New York: Norton.

Mauss, Marcel, 1985, (1938), "A category of the human mind: The notion of person; the notion of self", in Carrithers, M., S. Collins and S. Lukes (eds), *The Category of the Person*, 1–25. New York: Cambridge University Press.

Merriam, Alan P., 1967, *Ethnomusicology of the Flathead Indians*. Chicago: Aldine.

Turino, Thomas, 2000, *Nationalists, Cosmopolitans, and Popular Music in Zimbabwe*. Chicago: University of Chicago Press.

Walser, Robert, 1997, "Deep Jazz: notes on interiority, race, and criticism", in Pfister, J. and N. Schnog, (eds), *Inventing the psychological: Toward a cultural history of emotional life in America*, pp. 271–96. New Haven, CT: Yale University Press.

Waterman, Christopher A., 1990, *Jùjú: A Social History and Ethnography of an African Popular Music*. Chicago: University of Chicago Press.

"Modern Traditional" Music from Zimbabwe

Virginia Mukwesha's Mbira Record "Matare"

Johannes Brusila

The increasing human and musical global mobility has led to readjustments in the relationships between the performer, the industry and the consumer. The changes are not only practical and for example related to the flow of recorded music or immigrating people. Instead, the development also has more intellectual and ideological consequences. Music becomes reconstructed as an object of new forms of knowledge, meanings and ways of thinking. This reconstruction does not mean that old conceptualisations will die out, but their interpretations can vary during the continuous reinterpretations of identities and histories that currently are happening at increasing speed.

In order to highlight how the new cultural situation can affect the construction and interpretation of concepts such as "traditional music" and "modernization" and how these aspects are reflected in the creative work of the contemporary artist, I have chosen to focus on one *mbira* recording in my article, namely *Matare*. On this CD Virginia Mukwesha is playing with the group "Gwenyambira". On the back of *Matare*'s CD-cover Mukwesha has summarised the nature of the record in the phrase "modern traditional meditation music from Zimbabwe/Southern Africa". Mukwesha's way of explaining the record, which contains music that is connected to the Shona spirit possession ceremony, in a seemingly paradoxical expression "modern traditional" offers an opportunity to study how our conceptualisations and ways of understanding cultural heritage and identity in connection with African music can vary.[1]

Virginia Mukwesha and the *mbira*

Virginia Mukwesha was born in Zimbabwe, where she grew up first in the rural areas of Mashonaland and later in the capital Harare. Mukwesha's mother, Stella Chiweshe, is an internationally recognized *mbira* player and she became Mukwesha's first teacher. Thus, Mukwesha already had at an early stage the opportunity to follow her mother to performances of *mbira* on different occasions, including the Shona spirit possession ceremonies called *bira* (plur. *mapira*) where *mbira* plays a central part.

The *mbira* that Mukwesha heard when living in rural districts of Masimbura and Mhondoro and then learned to play herself, is the specific type of instrument associated with the Zezuru people. In the musicological literature this lamellophone is

---

1. This article is based on my dissertation project, in which I study "world music" as an industrial and cultural phenomenon. The dissertation project is based on material that I have gathered during four trips to Zimbabwe in the 1990s, lately working mainly with three cases: The Bhundu Boys, Virginia Mukwesha and Sunduza.

usually known as *"mbira dzaVadzimu"*, although many musicians, Mukwesha among them, mostly only call it *mbira*.[1] This type of *mbira* consists of twenty-two to twenty-eight keys made of flattened iron, mounted on two manuals to the left (bass and middle registers) and one (the highest register) to the right.[2] A characteristic feature of the *mbira*'s sound is its buzzing tone quality, which is produced by attaching bottle caps, or formerly pieces of snail shells, to the instrument and its gourd resonator.

The word *"mbira"* in Shona is plural, even when referring to one instrument (therefore in English: a *mbira* and many *mbira*), and it refers both to the instrument, the lamellae, or "keys" of the instrument and the philosophy and law surrounding the instrument.[3] American ethnomusicologist John E. Kaemmer has summarised the position of the *mbira* in the conceptual framework of Shona musical thinking by stating that "as the piano provides a conceptual basis for the Western musical system, so the *mbira* provides a conceptual basis for the Shona, which is primarily an improvisational tradition, with both vocal and instrumental performances based on recurring harmonic and rhythmic cycles".[4] Using European terminology, the music can be explained to be based on a 12/8 metric-rhythmic structure and repeated four phrase harmonic-melodic cycles, which are based on successions of two-tone chords. *Mbira* music is essentially not linear, but cyclical in all formal aspects, and a *mbira* piece is not a fixed musical structure with a specified beginning and end, but a composition of certain characteristic repeated patterns that provide a framework for the creative expression of the performer.[5]

A common feature of all Shona music is that it is based on at least two contrasting and often interlocking parts or patterns, which together form cross-rhythms and counter-melodies.[6] The interrelationship of melodic and rhythmic patterns is more important than are these patterns alone. *Mbira* compositions contain at least two basic patterns: the *kushaura*, which is the "leading" pattern and contains much of the melodic essence of the piece, and the *kutsinhira*, which "follows" and provides an interlocking, contrasting rhythmic part.[7] Together the two interlocking patterns form the basic structure of the song.

The role of women in *mbira* music has been touched upon in academic literature over the years.[8] It seems that although some women also used to play *mbira* earlier, it was not until the 1970s that they became more common on the professional circuit.[9] According to Mukwesha it was however very rare in the places where she toured with her mother Stella Chiweshe and their performance was often met with astonishment especially as she as a young girl played in a *mbira* group.[10] The career of her mother was important for Mukwesha's development because it offered both practical guidance and a strong role model. Besides performing with her mother as a young girl in Zimbabwe, Mukwesha also performed on her mother's recordings. It was not until Mukwesha moved to Berlin at the age of 21, that she started her own career as a performer and recording artist. When living in Germany, Mukwesha

---

1. Cf. Goddard 1996, p. 86 and Turino 2000, p. 74.
2. For overviews see e.g. Tracey 1969; Kauffman 1970, pp. 77–81; Berliner 1981, pp. 29–34; and Kaemmer 1998, p. 745.
3. Goddard 1996, p. 85.
4. Kaemmer 1998, p. 747.
5. Berliner 1981, pp. 52–53; Tracey 1988, p. 52; and Maraire 1990, pp. 292–95.
6. Kauffman 1970, passim.
7. E.g. Berliner 1981, p. 73.
8. See e.g. Berliner 1981, p. 17; Goddard 1996, pp. 80–81; and Kaemmer 1998, p. 753.
9. See particularly Impey 1992, pp. 112–13.
10. Mukwesha, interview March 14, 1997.

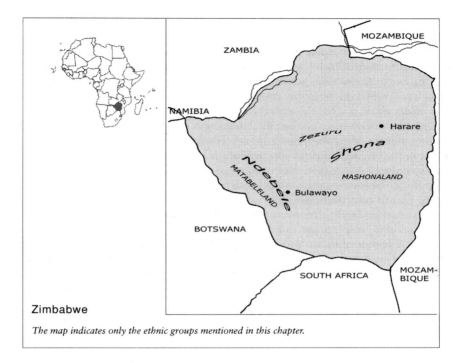

Zimbabwe

The map indicates only the ethnic groups mentioned in this chapter.

started cooperating with some Zimbabwean musicians and formed a band, which specialised in performing Zimbabwean *jiti* with an electrified instrument set-up. Besides performing, Mukwesha started teaching and working, together with her German husband Florian Hetze, at the family record company Shava. She also continued to perform with her mother on international tours and records, but the CD *Matare*, released in 1997 by Shava, was the first time Mukwesha made a *mbira* record of her own.

Mediaization of *mbira*

One of the factors which motivated Mukwesha to make a *mbira* record was her wish to utilize the new technology, which, in her opinion, made it more possible than before to truthfully reproduce the music of the *bira* spirit possession ceremony. The recording of *mbira* has a relatively long history, but according to Mukwesha few productions had fully taken into consideration the nature of the music. From the 1940s onwards the mobile studios of the local radio companies, first Central African Broadcasting Station and later Rhodesia Broadcasting Corporation, recorded African music for their programmes.[1] Also South African record companies and later their Zimbabwean subsidiaries released *mbira* music. In the 1960s and 1970s many *mbira* players, such as Hakurotwi Mude, Cosmas Magaya, Ephat Mujuru, Beauler Dyoko and Stella Chiweshe, managed to acquire national fame with the help of such recordings.[2] This media dissemination of *mbira* led to a faster and wider spread of formerly local styles, younger players already learnt different interpretations and techniques at an early stage by copying the music they heard on recordings, and re-

---

1. See Fraenkel 1959 and Woods 1995 for descriptions of these activities.
2. See Berliner 1981, pp. 212, 218, 230 and Impey 1992, p. 206; also Chiweshe, interview March 15, 1997.

puted players could get professional engagements in a much wider area than before because of the media exposure.[1]

The process of recording *mbira* for the electronic media required a certain adaptation of the music, which had functioned as an integral part of the spirit possession ceremonies or leisure time activities of the rural society. Roger Wallis and Krister Malm have coined the term "mediaization" to describe how music is adapted to the mass media when it is fed through the music industry pipeline such as the recording studio and a distribution system involving radio broadcasts and record shops. The different aspects of mediaization can, according to Wallis and Malm, range from a change in the original cultural performance context or instrument setting to a deliberate attempt to recast the lyrics or musical structures in an attempt to mould the music for an international market.[2] In the *mbira* recordings made by both the radio and the record companies the most notable aspects of the mediaization process are the shortened musical form, caused by the 45 rpm format and the modest tape reserves and equipment. Sometimes the sound of the *mbira* was adapted to suit the technical demands of the recording and playback equipment, and also to the sound ideals of the production staff, which consisted of European expatriates. Many *mbira* players (e.g. Stella Chiweshe, Virginia Mukwesha and Chartwell Dutiro) still speak about the way the buzzers of the *mbira* were dampened for the recording sessions so that the buzz would not be too dominating. In the 1980s and 1990s the buzz has usually been greatly reduced on records that were aimed at an international market, which, according to Turino is a consequence of the North American audience's aesthetic preferences.[3]

It is partly against the earlier mediaization of *mbira* that Virginia Mukwesha's decision to record *Matare* should be seen. A second, equally important factor is the larger musical changes that had occurred in the musical life of Zimbabwe. Since the 1960s many musicians rearranged older *mbira* music for band instruments and managed to achieve such great popularity that the acoustic *mbira* ensembles found it hard to break through in the media.[4] This in turn made Mukwesha's mother Stella Chiweshe amplify her *mbira* at the end of the 1980s and add electric instruments to her group so that she could reach the younger urbanised audience for whom the acoustic *mbira* ensembles sounded old-fashioned. Virginia Mukwesha, however, was not interested in these new ways of combining *mbira* with electric instruments. When she decided to record *Matare* she took as her starting point firstly the possibilities offered by the new technology in recreating the music of the spirit possession ceremony on CD in what she felt to be a truthful way, and secondly her preference for acoustic *mbira* and her dislike for rearranging the old music. Mukwesha says that she understands her mother's efforts to renew *mbira*. According to Mukwesha changes in instrumentation are acceptable as long as the old musical structures and melodies, which are the basics of *mbira*, are not changed. However, when Mukwesha herself recorded *Matare* she wanted to avoid both new instruments and such rearrangements that incorporate new melodies:

> Because if you change the melodies to compose a song and you do it with *mbira*, then the originals will be always wiped away and there are no footsteps anymore for the younger generation. So I thought I'd preserve *mbira* as it is and leave it how it is.[5]

---

1. Berliner 1981, pp. 139, 175, 244.
2. Wallis and Malm 1984, pp. 278–81 and Malm and Wallis 1992, pp. 24, 241–45.
3. Turino 2000, pp. 345–46.
4. For a thorough analysis of the development of "*mbira*-guitar" music see Turino 2000.
5. Mukwesha, interview March 14, 1997.

For Mukwesha the *mbira* is an instrument which she prefers to use only for what she calls "the original music" whereas her electric band and the *jiti* format offer her more freedom to create, rearrange and play with both older and newer elements. The fact that Mukwesha wanted to preserve *mbira*, as she explains her motives, while her mother was a key innovator in the genre could be interpreted along the generation and migration axes. Chiweshe directed her music to the Zimbabwean audience, whom she saw turn away from the *mbira*, whereas Mukwesha, who also performed on her mother's ground-breaking electrified *mbira* recordings, made her solo career after she had moved to Europe. For Mukwesha the idea of preserving the music in what she saw as an original form for the coming generations had become important, much in the same way as ethnomusicologists have noted how immigrants often emphasise preservation of their cultural heritage rather than innovation.[1]

"Traditional modern" music

Matare was released with a European audience in mind. According to the general opinion in the Zimbabwean music industry *mbira* does not sell on the domestic market if it has not been rearranged and adapted to the electric pop band format. Only one Zimbabwean record company, Africa Sounds, which has concentrated on the tourist market and sells at airports, hotels, art galleries and other places where the tourists move, releases *mbira* records. After having released *Matare* in Europe Mukwesha also licensed the record to Africa Sounds, but with little hope of any real economic gain due to the small Zimbabwean tourist market. Thus, the main market of Mukwesha's record is in Europe, the United States and maybe also Australia and Japan.

On the CD-cover Mukwesha has summarised the music for the consumer in the marketing slogan "modern traditional meditation music from Zimbabwe/Southern Africa". The same wording can also be found in the CD-booklet, where Mukwesha's and her husband Florian Hetze's record company Shava advertises its records with the sentence: "We release modern traditional music from acoustic civilisations where cultural meaning is formed through the union of bodies and rhythms in motion".[2] The paradoxical expression "modern traditional" has its explanation in Mukwesha's wish to emphasise how the music is ancient but at the same time also very viable. According to her expressions like "traditional", "folklore" and "ancient" connote something "which is dying", "which existed", "is forgotten about", "out of fashion" and "doesn't matter now", or that Europeans think that "there is still a small group of people practising this thing but they will also die out soon".[3] This is especially critical for her, because she feels that people might also believe that *mbira* and its spiritual context do not mean anything to her after she has lived in Europe for so many years. Therefore she wanted to point out how "it's something which still has a function in today's life" and that "it's up-to-date".[4] This is crystallised in the seemingly contradictory description "modern traditional music".

Mukwesha's interest for this modern tradition is of both a musical and spiritual nature. The Shona concept *matare* (sing. *dare*) refers to the latter part of the *bira* spirit possession ceremony. In the traditional Shona belief system the world of the living is seen as a function of the workings of the ancestral spirits, which in Shona

---

1. Compare e.g. Nettl 1983, p. 227.
2. *Mukwesha nema Gwenyambira: Matare* (1997), CD-booklet p. 22.
3. Mukwesha, interview March 14, 1997.
4. Ibid.

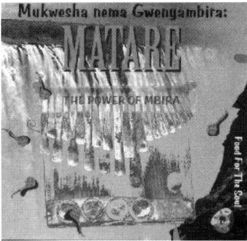

are called *mudzimu* (plur. *midzimu*). It is possible to communicate with a *mudzimu* at a spirit possession ceremony. Various members of the community are known as spirit mediums (*homwe*) and as he (or she) goes into a trance during a ceremony, the spirit enters into him and speaks through him.[1] During the *matare* part of the ceremony the *mudzimu* can give advice about matters concerning the family. Maraire uses the expressions "counselling, investigation, post mortems, diagnostic sessions" to describe the activities taking place during *matare*.[2] In the beginning of the *bira*, which starts after sundown, the music can be very dominating and important because of its power to bring about the *mudzimu*, but when the ceremony reaches the matare part, which usually occurs in the early morning hours, the music fades into the background and the dancing stops. It is the music of this particular moment that Mukwesha chose to record on the CD. This spiritual connection also increased her motivation to record the music in a form which would be "original", because playing any other type of *mbira* music, be it re-arrangements or some completely other songs, would not make the spirit come: "It's like drinking beer without alcohol—the taste is there and everything, but it doesn't have any effect".[3]

The recording

Despite Mukwesha's wish to be truthful to the original way of performing the music, the instrumentation and the musical structure she did not record the CD "in the field" during a *bira*. Instead she gathered a group of musicians with whom she recorded the music in a studio. Mukwesha's leading idea was to use the full one-hour playing time of the compact disc so that "people really listen once to what it's like" and so that the music on the record corresponds to "how it really is".[4] This is also emphasized in the CD-booklet, where the spiritual nature of the music is brought up "because *mbira* music unfolds its psychic power only in time".[5] The one hour format

---

1. See Maraire 1990 and Berliner 1981, pp. 186–206 for descriptions of *mudzimu* possession.
2. Maraire 1990, p. 354.
3. Mukwesha, interview March 19, 1997.
4. Mukwesha, interview March 15, 1997.
5. *Mukwesha nema Gwenyambira: Matare* (1997), CD-booklet p. 6.

was a reaction against earlier *mbira* releases which contained only short musical excerpts, which had been adjusted to fit the music industry's and radio's three minute format. The wish to be truthful to the original way of making the music and the choice to work in a studio could of course be called a paradox, but for Mukwesha the studio technology offered a way of controlling the process of playing and recording within the one hour time limit so that the outcome would fulfill her expectations both with regards to the truthful reproduction of the music of the *matare* and her own creative interests.

Mukwesha had lived in Berlin for many years when she decided to make the record. Hence she did not have any stable group of *mbira* musicians with whom she would have performed regularly at *mapira*. Instead she contacted Zimbabwean *mbira* players Chinembiri Chidodo and Otari Chidembo, whom she had got to know through her mother, and Leonard Ngwenya, who plays *ngoma* on *Matare* but also performs in her *jiti* group. Mukwesha also got in touch with Sidney Musarurwa, a *mbira* player whom she had heard of from a German ethnomusicologist, and after meeting and getting to know Musarurwa in Zimbabwe she decided to add him to the group. These *"gwenya mbira"*, [1] or musicians who "scratch" the *mbira*'s keys with great finesse, then assembled in Harare and rehearsed together for two months under the supervision of Mukwesha. This rehearsal time was indispensable not only for making the group musically closely knit but also to make it prepared to realize Mukwesha's musical vision. Mukwesha did not want to simply let the musicians improvise freely for one hour in the studio. Instead she carefully planned a structure for the recording session and rehearsed it with the group in advance.

Mukwesha divided the one-hour session in five shorter sections, lasting ten to fifteen minutes each. The recording session, which was carried out in Shed Studios in Harare, started with four *mbira* playing through the whole one-hour piece of music. Mukwesha, who played the leading, so-called *kushaura* part, directed the ensemble from one section to the other. After Mukwesha, Chidembo, Chidodo and Musarurwa had laid the basic structure by playing their *mbira* parts, the session continued with a second recording in which three *mbira* were added on top of the first take. The additional *mbira* lines, improvised by Chidembo, Chidodo and Musarurwa, were responding and adding variations to the first ones, thereby making the texture even more complex. On top of the in all seven *mbira*, Mukwesha played *hosho*, which is the main rhythmical accompanying instrument of the *mbira* ensemble made of a hollowed gourd with dried seeds inside it. After the *hosho* part two more tracks were laid on top of the earlier ones. First Ngwenya played a *ngoma*, which is a Shona cylindrical drum with a single membrane attached by pegs. Finally Musarurwa whistled a free improvisation on top of the *mbira*.

The recording session with its many stages and uncommon procedures was stressful for the older *mbira* players who had never worked in a studio before. Playing first *mbira* tracks without the *hosho*-accompaniment, which usually marks the basic beat for the musicians, was already hard. This was further complicated by the strictly pre-planned structure with sections and bridges, which Mukwesha led the ensemble through. Also the technological requirements like avoiding coughing and sitting firmly in a fixed position in relation to the microphone, were according to Mukwesha "tough" and the musicians "were really sweating".[2]

It is basically impossible for a listener to hear how the session was structured and put into practice by simply listening to the record. First of all the partition of the

---

1. From Shona *kukwenya*, to scratch, see e.g. Berliner 1981, p. 44.
2. Mukwesha, interview March 15, 1997.

music was never done sharply. Instead both Mukwesha and the rest of the musicians always performed the transitions gradually, and all *mbira* lines were built on constant variation. Secondly the complexity of seven musicians playing *mbira* simultaneously makes it impossible to single out a *mbira*, instead a listener picks out smaller elements or hears melodies which can be created by several interlocking instruments or their overtones.[1] A key factor affecting the listening process is also that the final auditive form of the record was worked out in the mix, which was done by Mukwesha in a studio in Berlin. The CD starts with the gradual fade in of seven *mbira*, after eleven minutes variation is achieved by fading out five *mbira* and then fading them in again, the whistling has been added at times, the *hosho* and *ngoma* is audible only in some sections and the whole record ends with the gradual increase of echo and fade out of the *mbira*. The variations which have been produced in the mixing also form the basis of the partition on the record, which is also reproduced on the CD-cover, thereby strengthening the mixing's role in the final auditive formation of the music.

Reception

Matare could in many ways be called a very personal work of art. The work process behind the CD reminds one of the approach commonly used in the production of popular music, where an artist collects a group of musicians for a recording session and the music is constructed by adding several tracks step by step on top of each other, after which the final version is created in the mixing. This could of course be called mediaization, but in all instances Mukwesha motivates her artistic choices along the lines of the preservation aspect. Mukwesha for example chose to dampen the bottle cap buzzers of the *mbira* because she felt that their metallic ring "disturbs the ear" and becomes too dominating when it is picked up by a microphone and amplified. This could of course be explained as a further step in the mediaization direction, but Mukwesha motivates her choice by saying that the original *mbira* had snail shell buzzers with most likely a smoother sound than the bottle caps and the dampened bottle caps in fact come closer to the original than the sharper unaltered bottle cap buzzers.[2] Preservation is also emphasised in the CD-booklet and promotional material in which the spiritual and musical context is described thoroughly and where the record is explained to be groundbreaking as a truthful reproduction of the ceremonial music.

The way in which the record manages to reproduce the ceremonial music was also brought up when the record was reviewed in the Western world music media. For example in The Beat the record was described as a "curative web of shamistic rhythm" and "the first time a full cycle of Shona healing music has ever been recorded"[3] and Folk Roots' reviewer Rick Sanders gives credit to the Shava label "for delivering it so closely to the way it happens in real life".[4] The question of how the recording process was carried out and how these practices were related to the original *bira* context is not mentioned. However, Sanders' way of comparing the recording with "how it happens in real life" is interesting because his comment suggests

---

1. The analysis of the music required that the different tracks were separated from the 16-track master tape by mixing—in fact without this it would also have been impossible for the contributing musicians to be able to single out the different parts and elements of the music.
2. Mukwesha, interview March 15, 1997.
3. Poet 1997, p. 39.
4. Sanders 1997, p. 83.

that the way it was done on the record and the way it is transmitted by way of a CD is not representative of "real life", although it might come close to it. This is of course true because it can be argued that no merely auditive media in itself would be able to do it. From a more philosophical point of view it might even be asked whether all media, which are used to re-create something existing outside the media, can at most only come close to "real life". Also a field recording of the music of a *matare* would have given only one possible version of its music, and it would also have been influenced by the producer's choices of using stereo or multi-track technique, mixing the music or not, editing the music for the record format etc.

In the Shona performance context *mbira* music is not written down or played from a score. The music is transmitted from one generation and one musician to the other by playing from memory, as part of an oral transmission of culture. The freedom to interpret and create is great within the general framework of the composition. The structure of the *matare* part of the spirit possession ceremony also offers variation, as it does not have any precisely fixed time limits or sharply defined sequences. The crucial point about the CD *Matare* is that the record is a realization of Virginia Mukwesha's vision, or her version of how the music can be mediaized. Her wish to be truthful to the original music at a *matare* means that the record for her is a reproduction (and in that sense not "real life" in itself), but at the same time it is also a personal creation. She has made the choices, from the production process to the decisions regarding the CD's cover. Therefore it is also natural for her to call herself the composer, arranger and producer of this "modern traditional" music on the CD-cover.

Concluding remarks

Mukwesha's approach highlights the problems of the bipolarisation traditional-modern, which is common for much writing about African music and can be found in both older folkloristic literature as well as in later writings on musics from other cultures. The dividing line between what should be considered traditional and modern cannot always be drawn sharply. This is so for many reasons. One is the nature of oral cultures, where tradition changes while being transmitted. A second reason is the fact that musical genres that are called modern in fact often have a long continuous history.

A key problem is that in the European context traditional music is usually understood as a fixed body of music, inherited from the timeless past where it was created by a collective community, whereas the term modern connotes an artistic creation by a particular contemporary person. This problem becomes even more complex when the European ethnocentric ideas of musical structure, creation and composition are combined with ideas of tradition and modernisation in other cultures. Andrew Tracey has described the tendency to try to distinguish what proportion of a performance of so-called African music is "traditional" and what is "modern" as "one of those cases where if you ask the wrong question you get the wrong answer: If you ask the African performer 1) if what he plays is traditional, and 2) if he composed the song himself, you often get the answer 'Yes' to both questions". According to Tracey this mistake is born out of ethnocentric thinking which fails to understand that what is "paradoxical in the Western frame of thought" is not necessarily the same in African thinking. African composition is based on a collective musical process which creates structural opposition between several parts and this processual nature of the music makes it very different from the European idea of music as fixed songs, made up of a unique melody and its accompaniment.[1] Tracey could be blamed for strengthening a simplistic dichotomy between the West and Africa, but his general observation offers a fruitful approach to, for example, Mukwesha's work. It is for example very hard to single out one melodic line from *Matare*, which could be called a composition, or *the* composition *Matare*. Instead, the record *Matare*, as all *mbira*, could rather be called a compositional process, which is based on the structural oppositions that the different *mbira* parts create together as they are improvised within the framework of *mbira*'s musical rules and codes. The African conceptions of composition and originality are therefore also seldom congruent with the European copyright legislation, which is based on the idea of traditional music as collective and modern music as a product of unique creativity.[2]

Mukwesha's way of describing *Matare* as modern traditional music can be said to crystallize a very central feature of her approach to *mbira*. For Mukwesha *mbira* is not built on a contradiction, but rather on a continuous interplay between her cultural heritage and life today. Both aspects are always present, be it in the thematic musical details or in the choice of the whole work process. Yet, the fact that she feels a need to explain her CD by using the expression "modern traditional" tells how she has become aware of the perception of her music, which is so common in Europe and nowadays visible in for example the world music discourse, and the contradiction that this perception involves. She has, in fact, not only become aware of it but also feels a need to explain her position with these concepts (which would hardly appear on any of the old Zimbabwean *mbira* records). As a musician from Zimbabwe, who has lived both in the rural areas and the capital of her home country, and who is now living in Berlin, Mukwesha could be said to have entered the modern and become aware of her distanced position to the traditional, but in a way which incorporates both aspects in her identity. Thus, it is also natural that this dualism is negotiated in her creative work in a manner that both preserves and creates her musical heritage.

Interviews

Chiweshe, Stella, March 15, 1997 in Berlin.

Dutiro, Chartwell, February 18, 1997 in London. Musician (Spirit Talk *Mbira*, former member of Thomas Mapfumo's Blacks Unlimited), and *Mbira* teacher.

Mukwesha, Virginia, March 14, 1997; March 15, 1997; March 17, 1997; March 19, 1997; March 20, 1997 in Berlin.

Records

Mukwesha nema Gwenyambira, 1997, *Matare*. Shava, SHAVACD004-2.

References

Berliner, Paul F., 1981, *The Soul of Mbira: Music and Traditions of the Shona People of Zimbabwe*. Chicago/London: The University of Chicago Press.

Eriksen, Anne, 1993, "Den nasjonale kulturarven—en del av det moderne". Kulturella perspektiv, *Svensk etnografisk tidskrift*, No. 1, 1993, pp. 16–25.

Fraenkel, Peter, 1959, *Wayaleshi*. London: Weidenfeld and Nicolson.

---

1. Tracey 1995, pp. 57–58.
2. For *mbira* and ideas of original composition, see Turino 2000, pp. 281–83.

Giddens, Anthony, 1979, *Central Problems in Social Theory: Action, Structure and Contradiction in Social Analysis*. London: Macmillan.

Goddard, Keith, 1996, "The Soul of Mbira Twenty Years On: A Retrospect", *African Music*, Vol. 7, No. 3, pp. 76–90.

Impey, Angela, 1992, *They want us with salt and onions: Women in the Zimbabwean music industry*. Ph.D. dissertation, Indiana University (unpublished).

Kaemmer, John E., 1998, "Music of the Shona of Zimbabwe", in Stone, Ruth M. (ed.), *The Garland Encyclopedia of World Music*, Vol. 1, pp. 744–58. New York & London: Africa. Garland Publishing.

Kauffman, Robert A., 1970, *Multi-Part Relationships in the Shona Music of Rhodesia*. Ph.D. dissertation, University of California (unpublished).

—, 1975, "Shona Urban Music: A Process Which Maintains Traditional Values", in Kileff, Clive and Wade C. Pendleton (eds), *Urban Man in Southern Africa*, pp. 127–44. Gwelo: Mambo Press.

Malm, Krister and Wallis, Roger, 1992, *Media Policy and Music Activity*. London and New York: Routledge.

Maraire, Dumisani A., 1990, *The Position of Music in Shona Mudzimu (Ancestral Spirit) Possession*. Ph.D. dissertation, University of Washington (unpublished).

Nettl, Bruno, 1983, *The Study of Ethnomusicology: Twenty-Nine Issues and Concepts*. Urbana: University of Illinois Press.

Poet, J., 1997, "All Over the Map: Björn Again", *The Beat*, Vol. 16, No. 2, pp. 38–39.

Rosenberg, Neil V., 1993b, "Starvation, Serendipity, and the Ambivalence of Bluegrass Revivalism", in Rosenberg, Neil V. (ed.), *Transforming Tradition: Folk Music Revivals Examined*, pp. 194–202. Urbana and Chicago: University of Illinois Press.

Sanders, Rick, 1997, "Mukwesha nema gwenya Mbira", *Folk Roots*, Jan/Feb 1997, Nos 162/164, p. 83.

Tomlinson, John, 1991, *Cultural Imperialism: A Critical Introduction*. Baltimore: The John Hopkins University Press.

Tracey, Andrew, 1988, "The System of the Mbira." Paper presented at the 7th Symposium on ethnomusicology, Department of Anthropology and Ethnomusicology, University of Venda, 3–5 September 1988, pp. 43–55.

—, 1995, "Structural Opposition as Composition", in Muller, Carol (ed.), *Papers Presented at the Eight Symposium on Ethnomusicology (Music Department, University of Durban-Westville, 1989) and Ninth Symposium on Ethnomusicology (Music Department, University of Namibia, 1990)*. International Library of African Music, pp. 56–63.

Tracey, Hugh, 1969, "The Mbira Class of African Instruments in Rhodesia (1932)", *African Music*, Vol. 4, No. 3, pp. 78–95.

Turino, Thomas, 2000, *Nationalists, Cosmopolitans, and Popular Music in Zimbabwe*. Chicago and London: University of Chicago Press.

Wallis, Roger and Malm, Krister, 1984, *Big Sounds from Small Peoples: The Music Industry in Small Countries*. London: Constable.

Waterman, Cristopher A., 1990, *Jùjú: A Social History and Etnography of an African Popular Music*. Chicago and London: The University of Chicago Press.

—, 1997, "'Our Tradition Is a Very Modern Tradition': Popular Music & the Construction of Pan-Yoruba Identity", in Barber, Karin (ed.), *Readings in African Popular Culture*, pp. 48–53. The International African Institute, Indiana University Press and James Currey.

Woods, Gurli, 1995, *Zambian Heritage of Sound: Znbc Transcription Service*. SIDA Project Description (unpublished).

"Tranzania" – A Cross-Over from Norwegian Techno to Tanzanian Taarab

Annemette Kirkegaard

In 1998 a CD was released which featured the Norwegian techno group, Acid Queen, who had been on a visit to Tanzania and there met with two Tanzanian *taarab* groups. One was the Egyptian Musical Club, a band playing classical *taarab*, which is orchestral and features prominent singers and instrumentalists in organised performances. The other was Sisi Kwa Sisi, who play so-called *Kidumbak-taarab*, which is more informal, simpler in sound and closer to a rural traditional musical sound.

The result of the encounter is a very remarkable and highly provocative album. Recordings with the *taarab* groups were made in Dar es Salaam, but after the return of Acid Queen to Norway the recorded music was mixed with modern sampling techno-procedures to form a product which is clear *cross-over*. The CD was called *Tranzania* and according to one of the key initiators of the project, radio-producer Siegbjørn Nedland, the project had a strong political motive.[1] The Norwegians found that due to very poor legislation on copyright and musical piracy the Tanzanian musicians—like so many other African artists—were subject to very poor economic conditions. Consequently they embarked on the project to draw attention to these questions and to contribute to improving the situation.

The production was supported by The Norwegian Agency for Development Cooporation, (NORAD) the Norwegian Radio, (NRK P2) and the Norwegian organisation "Kirkelig Kulturverksted" (The Church Culture Workshop) a church-aid organization with a record company. To illuminate the questions this project raises, I will make use of some of the conceptualisations of the World Music issues, which are based both on ethnomusicological and popular music theories.[2] I will at the same time develop my thoughts on the musical forms of *taarab*, which I have been studying for some years. I will explain the definition of musical features in *taarab*, but also linger on its very prominent openness to renewal and innovation. Some key questions are: Does the merger of techno and *taarab* represent just one further step on a continuing ladder of innovative processes? Is the merger compatible with the usual contexts of *taarab*? What use did the musicians in Egyptian Musical Club and Sisi Kwa Sisi make of the encounter with the Scandinavians? Are the *taarab* musicians in other words playing consciously with their identity or are they victims of an ever growing Western domination of African musics? I intend to view the issue as a complex, modern phenomenon both from the point of view of the Norwegians, but just as much from that of the Tanzanians.

---

1. Interview with Siegbjørn Nedland at Womex in Berlin 1999.
2. See the introduction to this book for a definition of some of these terms.

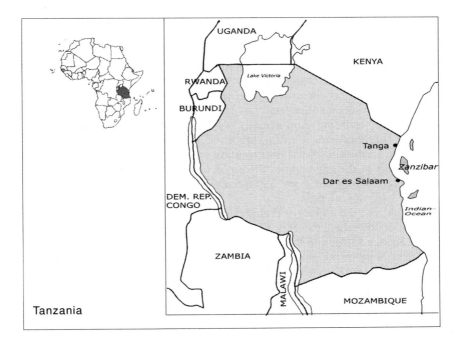

Tanzania

Let me also state from the start that I have not had the possibility to do proper field-work on the making and release of this record. My observations are thus based on my previous studies in the field—which has been Zanzibar and Dar es Salaam—and on my more overall knowledge of *taarab* and its relationship to the World Music setting. Accordingly, the discussion should be seen as tentative and probing.

Music, identity and the negotiation of culture

Music can be interpreted in a number of ways. As a piece of art, as a part of an overall cultural identity, or as a highly individual way of positioning oneself into societies and surroundings. In this chapter I will not so much address the discourse on music as art, but rather look at the implications and reflections of popular music studies seen as a society-related issue.

Formerly, music culture was viewed as a reflection of the proceedings in the social life. Now we have come to understand that music not only reflects what is happening beyond the immediately visual or aural, but rather is the particular space of negotiation over identities, ethnicities and human relationship. This is a view strongly advocated by Martin Stokes in his groundbreaking book on the relations between ethnicity, identity and music.[1]

My analysis of the CD *Tranzania* will also be informed by studies in ethnomusicology on the strengthening and apparent increase of the forces of cultural globalisation and its very conspicuous relationship to economic globalisation. Music is and has been for a long time a commodity, but the presence of modern media, the amount of money put into the production and marketing of the albums and the as-

---

1. Stokes 1994.

symmetrical flow of power and knowledge, takes the phenomenon to a hitherto un-precedented level.

Cultural products including music from the South are left with the almost im-possible task of making it through the cultural, economic and political (de)fences of Western societies. More than maybe any other area of the non-Western world, Africa is at risk, precisely because of its general poverty rates, its poor infrastructure, and its very wanting technical facilities. These matters combined lead to very little power in music recording. And actually only after the Tranzania-project was con-cluded, did Tanzania get a recording studio of its own.[1]

Taarab in relation to this is no exception and since its entrance into the World Music business in the mid-eighties the problems of cultural exchange and domina-tion have been highlighted. Some key questions are the position of the music indus-try and the issue of copyright.

The scope and the impact of the modern media are described by James Clifford in his work on 'travelling cultures',[2] and they have been analysed at length in several works by Krister Malm and Roger Wallis.[3]

The hegemony of the global media situation intensifies the debate on diversity versus homogeneity. The concept of 'otherness' in music has within the new cultural situation of postmodernism taken on new meaning. Constantly Western listeners are exposed to both known and unknown features. The music we hear from 'out there' is very often a mixture of strange and unfamiliar sounds combined with the globally well-known and transculturated patterns of music-making. This is very prominent in the use of instruments, where, for instance, electric guitars and increasingly elec-tronic keyboards can be heard everywhere.

In the periphery, reversely, non-Western citizens also know of Western music through a similar mix of otherness and the well-known. The African audience will recognise many elements familiar to them, because of the paradoxical way in which Western culture has accepted African-American music as its own.

Within this interconnected cultural situation of late modernity often character-ised as 'complex cultures' [4] we can find a clear heroisation of "otherness" both in the superculture of the musical industry and media on a global scale, and also in the local subcultures all over the world.

But what does the use of 'other' musics mean in the Western cultures? And does the process represent anything new? Certainly musical borrowing across borders and between peoples has been an integrated part of music history, also within Euro-pean high cultures. Although it is hard to determine and categorize about the estab-lishing and crossing of cultural boundaries, in the musical grey-zone or *cross-over* phenomena, we come across some of the clearest expressions of and attitudes to-wards the distinction. In the *cross-over* zone a blend of formerly incompatible ele-ments of black and white, the first musical *cross-over* to be recognised,[5] and high and low, a standard quality distinction within musicology, are matched and mixed and here, for better or for worse, the borders between otherness and the well-known are suspended or neutralized.

Cultural and musical pluralism are closely related to the definition of *cross-over*, and it must be understood as a postmodern construction—often based in the ideas

---

1. Womex, Berlin.
2. Clifford 1992.
3. Malm and Wallis 1984 and 1992, and diverse articles and papers.
4. Hannerz 1992.
5. The crossing was between the music charts and labels of blacks and whites in the US, which in the first half of the 20th century were totally separated.

of either the 'imagined communities'[1] or 'the global village'.[2] Both the global village metaphor and the reference to imagined points of reference, are strongly connected with the spread of modern media, and they invoke a global community on a rather optimistic level. It is, however, important to realize that the cultural encounter takes place in a situation that Erlmann has called a 'complete commodification' of our cultures and an 'unprecedented acceleration of transnational movements of people'.[3] Erlmann also posed the question:

> How do we account for the fact that we can no longer meaningfully talk about the music of a West African village without taking into consideration the corporate strategies of SONY, U.S. domestic policy and the price of oil?[4]

Yet even within the music business the important niche production of the *indies* (independent record companies) gradually makes its mark and annihilates completely the horror scenario of the 70s of a cultural grey-out, in the shape of a complete homogenisation, or a 'Michael Jackson world take-over'. This emerging pluralism is closely related to the development of the media. The CD was introduced in the 1980s, and at first it was feared that it would destroy the music market because of its high price. Today the price has gone down. CD production has turned out to be less complicated than the production of LPs, which were too technically difficult to make, and therefore produced only in a limited number of places. For these reasons even industrially strong Denmark by the 1980s did not produce its own LPs. In comparison the CD is now considered a more democratic medium.

Homogeneity and diversity are still negotiated and contested, but it seems as if the diversity gathered and collected in World Music products assists in undermining the threat of homogenisation.

World Music/Beat

World Music—or World Beat by its American name—is very clearly rooted in the same mould as the many other popular music cultures at the end of the 20th century and is very closely related to globalisation. The World Music concept originates from the 1980s, when the record companies of the West turned to Third World musics in a more systematic way. Previously a number of artists within the popular music business had visited the Third World and had integrated local musicians or sounds in their products. Prominent examples are the involvement of *The Beatles* in classical Indian musics and the more Africa-oriented search for interesting musics by *The Rolling Stones*. Guitarist Brian Jones went to Morocco to record and perform with the *Master Musicians of Jajouka*,[5] *The Rolling Stones* in the late 1960s invited the Nigerian master drummer Ginger Johnson and his *African Drummers* in order to bring spirits and colour to their live concerts.[6] Generally in the 1980s record companies and radio stations developed a consistent strategy involving Third World musics for a new market-oriented niche.

The musics which were hosted on the Western stages and arenas were both the so-called traditional, acoustic musics of rural Africa and the highly electrified urban

---

1. Anderson 1996.
2. McLuhan and Powers 1989.
3. Erlmann 1993, p. 4.
4. Erlmann 1993, p. 4.
5. Today this recording counts as a clear copyright violation case, because no reference was made to the Moroccan musicians when the tapes were later used by the heirs of Brian Jones. Wallis 2000
6. Collins 1985, p. 87.

musics of modernised and creolised fusions. Both were considered authentic musics in different ways expressing collective values. A huge celebration of the exotic and the marvels of afro-related rhythms and sounds followed.

African or Afro-American musics were the first to be celebrated in radio pro- grammes, in the recording business, and not least on the emerging live-music scene, which was initiated by the big stadium concert LiveAID in Wembley, London, in 1985.[1] Eastern or Asian musics have only recently been addressed and as yet with rather poor results in commercial terms.

Many musicologists have examined the World Music issue, but none quite as sharply as Veit Erlmann, whose harsh critique of the phenomenon has influenced many. His point of departure is sceptical and generally he finds that the concept is misleading and that it invokes unfair expectations.

On the one hand Erlmann views World Music as a commercial phenomenon in which the Third World artists are exploited by the business. As the search for a new Bob Marley was at its highest in the mid-eighties, the record companies and their scouts went around the world to find another possible superstar with unheard sounds—and this is what much World Music is about—i.e. searching for new sounds for a bored Western audience who found the rock music scene stagnating and the new hip-hop and techno arenas too specialized and artificial.

On the other hand the musical aesthetics on a global level also offer a new ecumene: "... a possible totality long deemed lost by contemporary critical thought",[2] but it is a simulacrum because in the words of Jean Baudrillard: "... we simulate and dramatize in an acrobat act, the absence of the Other".[3] It is an artifi- cial dramaturgy and the subject accordingly becomes 'the other of nobody'. It be- comes a value without reference and remains fractal.

But if the ideal and spirit of the World Music of the 1980s was pluralism, the movement and the *cross-over* of the 1990s can possibly be seen as a new attempt at getting diverse and exotic musical features and traits together in a new and com- pletely different synthesis.

No longer can we talk of mere fusion, rather what is taking place is fission. Many musical products display this same quality: for instance, the Norwegian singer and folk music expert and entrepreneur Kirsten Bråten Berg released a CD in 1999 called *From Senegal to Setesdal* and it featured two Norwegian and two West African tra- ditional musicians. Most of the tracks on the album consist of the putting together of two different songs—lyrics as well as melodies. In this way the musicians use their traditional or ethnic roots and musical identities as a take off point. The only appar- ently uniting force is the use of a mouth harp (jewsharp), which is said to have been used in both Norway and Senegal. The instrument dominates the sound-scape in most tracks and by the way carries the same drone[4] effect as often heard in other *cross-over* products. The musics from both sides are non-diatonic—even modale at some points—and the instruments used are *djembe* (drum), *kora* (chordophone) mouthbow and mouth harp.

In many ways it is an irresistible musical encounter. All through the album Nor- wegian traditional songs are combined or grouped with lullabies, or genealogical and religious songs from West Africa. All are older songs, which have been orally

---

1. Garofalo 1993, p. 22.
2. Erlmann 1993, p. 7.
3. Erlmann 1993 referring to Baudrillard, p. 8.
4. A drone can be described as a tone or a tone cluster held continuously throughout a musical piece, thus pro- viding a bordun base for melody or song.

transmitted through generations. The sounds of the voices are distinctively kept apart, and the pronounced and overtone-rich Norwegian woman's voice with its prominent ornamentations is contrasted with the African male singer and his some-what hoarse and typically nasal vocal style.

The lyrics, equally sound constructing in this relationship, are in Norwegian, in Mandingo and in other West African languages. Sometimes the Norwegian singers shift to the African melodies—and accordingly the sounds are changed.

The most interesting feature, however, is that the two musical idioms are kept apart in such a way that they face each other without any seeming intention to mix or blend the music in creolization. As audience we are kept in the belief that what we hear are two separate traditional forms juxtaposed and that they are authentic in the oldfashioned way (i.e. "they have sounded like this since time began").

One wonders about the aim of this album. Are we to marvel over the coinciden-tal similarity of the two clearly separate musical styles, or are we on a more general level being instructed that there are common and possibly universal musical forms beyond the unifying and domineering embrace of Western classical art music?

From Senegal to Setesdal is a very typical *cross-over* product within the World Music aesthetics of the 1990s, but in contrast to earlier strategies, it does not bring about a fusion of the musical traits, rather is keeps them apart in a new kind of fission.

World Music as a Trope of the new Cultural Situation

World Music is in many ways both a means and a result of the complex music situ-ation described above. It encompasses the ethnic and even exotic over-tones of the discourse and it comments on the aesthetic distinction of high/low cultures and the tendency to romanticise the exoticism of the music. In these respects the elements of World Music are shared with other *cross-over* products—for instance contemporary art music. However, the dichotomy of high and low is based on a different assump-tion in World Music than in Western art music. Where Western art music ranks great complexity and development of the musical material highest, the tendency within World Musics is that the purer and simpler—that is, older and more original—the better. This is the background to the static and conservative tendencies, which flow back and unfortunately influence the living cultures by imposing new standards for music making [1]. The prerequisite for the creation of a product like *From Senegal to Setersdal* is as mentioned above the imagining that what we hear is the 'real thing'. Accordingly the music is made to assist in the celebration of interhuman relations and eucumenical cultural traits in music, in Erlmann's terms referred to above. In this way universalism is invoked.

Neither World Music nor *cross-over* can in musical terms be labelled 'a style'. All the categories are expressions of a cultural condition. It is very close to the nostalgic pastiche, as described by Veit Erlmann: "I take pastiche and its central role in the postmodern global culture as an index of the rapid loss of referentiality".[2] Again we are close to the simulacrum of Baudrillard and the postmodern nostalgia.

The taarab scene—openness to innovation and renewal

The story of the origins of *taarab* music contains many questions and until now few answers. The style is known along most of the East African coast, being today pop-

---

1. Kirkegaard 1996, p. 343 ff.
2. Erlmann 1993, p. 11.

ular from the south of Somalia over Kenya and Tanzania down to Mozambique and it stretches into the hinterland as far as Rwanda and eastern Congo as well. It is a result of the continuous cultural encounter between Arab, African and European influences brought to Africa in the wake of the Arab presence since around the turn of the first millennium. The musical style as we know it was apparently founded in the latter half of the 19th century, after the Omani Sultan Seyyid Said settled in Zanzibar and his successor Seyyid Barghash (1870–1888) developed a grand court with an abundant cultural life and a strong representative music culture.[1]

Zanzibar was a safe harbour used internationally for travellers into the African interior, and accordingly many visitors stayed in the exuberant palaces and houses of the Omani rulers. This period is musically very sparsely documented, but from after the turn of the 19th century we have more solid information.

In 1906 the sultanate, which was now under British dominion, started a male social and cultural club, with the Muslim male clubs known all over the Arab world as its model. To play and enjoy music there you had to be a member. According to the Muslim conventions concerning culture and music, being an amateur was ranked the highest. However, the musical idioms of the clubs were very innovative and open-minded, and accordingly new ideas and musical influences were easily—and readily—adopted into the overall fabric of the music in the first decades of the 20th century. One such ideal model was the popular Egyptian music of the *thakt* and later *Firquah* ensembles, which had evolved together with the development of the radio and the gramophone.

In Zanzibar the legendary singer Siti Binta Saad (1880–1950) had made her own contribution to the musical development when she in the early years of the 20th century had emerged from the position as a street vendor singing out her bargains, to eventually take the whole of the Zanzibari aristocracy by the heart. She became the most popular singer not only in Zanzibar but of the greater part of the Indian Ocean area; she recorded 78rpms in Bombay in the 1920s and she was a much-admired entertainer both on the visiting dhows of the wealthy merchants and in the salons of the sultan's palace, where she sang every Thursday evening. Her success is the more remarkable since she was a daughter of freed slaves, a woman in a male dominated culture and she was a professional in a world where amateurism was the best. She was in many ways a Zanzibari forerunner of the Egyptian icon Umm Kalthum, who decades later enjoyed a fame remarkably close to that of Siti.

By the mid-20th century *taarab* had settled as an important cultural marker of identity in the East African coastal areas, and its relationship to the wedding ceremonies was quite prominent. In addition to the blend of African and Arab musical features, Caribbean dance styles and Indian film songs had influenced the *taarab* style heavily since the 1930s. Both styles were introduced via film and radio.

In the turbulent days of independence and revolution in Zanzibar in the early 1960s *taarab* with its inter-ethnic qualities was again to become a direct battleground and a strong mouthpiece of the cultural and political negotiation for the different forces within the region. The most conspicuous Arab elements, for instance language and names, were forbidden and Swahili and African *ngomas* (that is, dance songs) got a stronger foothold.

Due to a number of differing reasons the *taarab* environment at the beginning of the 1980s was in a crisis. Suddenly and seemingly randomly, however, the music was adopted by the World Music business and several high quality recordings were

---

1. The sultans from Oman controlled the trade routes, and in the 1840s moved their court to Zanzibar.

made. It meant a boost and a much-longed-for foreign interest in *taarab*, but not much money came from the effort.

The Dar es Salaam and Tanga scenes in *taarab*—or *tarabu* as it is often termed on the mainland—both share and differ from the Zanzibari story. Generally Zanzibaris regard themselves as the true *taarab* artists, as they believe the style originated with them. This local appropriation of the style is often contested, and some good music also came out of the mainland groups. These however, have not had the same international appreciation as the islanders. This could be due to the more exotic surroundings in Zanzibar, which attract even researchers, and the only Western produced recording from the mainland was for a long time an album recorded in Tanga in the early 1980s. In Dar es Salaam, however, *taraab* has recently seen a renaissance as it has become an integrated part of the performances of cultural groups like TOT (Tanzania One Theater) and Muungano.[1] This trend however, is quite different from the Zanzibari setting both in musical and ethical ways, because it embarks on an integration of dance music, partly unfamiliar to classical *taarab*—and it also involves other quite non-Muslim ways of life.[2] Still the musical style is easy to recognize, and some of the melodies are re-used for the new songs.

The difficult economic situation is shared by all the *taarab* groups whether on the main land or in the islands. But by now *taarab* is actually also a showpiece in the big international hotels, and thus provides a way of living for the musicians.[3]

The economic situation of Third World musicians

Musicians and composers in the Third World are generally facing a very difficult economic situation. Even though music is considered an important element of African culture when identity and self-respect is debated on the national and political level, it often gets a very low priority when more serious issues like health care, deforestation and debts are decided upon. It is more often than not considered a luxury, which is not affordable in times of general economic stress. In most African countries culture in general, and music in particular is left to take care of itself. This means that the performers are in a difficult financial situation. They have to make their own way in order to get their music out and this leaves them at the mercy of the market forces, be they club and hotel owners or recording companies from the North. In itself this is not unique, and it is a situation facing many Western musicians, too. However, the size of the problem is bigger in Africa, and no social security provides for the striving young musicians to make their way into the business.

One particular element in this situation is the discussion over copyright and intellectual property rights. This has been at the front of the awareness of the world community for some years. Under the auspices of the World Trade Organisation (WTO) intellectual property rights have been examined and negotiated under the heading of the agreement on Trade-Related Aspects of Intellectual Property Rights, TRIPS.

Basically copyrights are held in the West, and it is a system invented in the West to protect and provide for artists and their livelihoods. It is a complicated system with much fine print and generally the Third World musicians have often been cheated of the rights. The stories are many: one is about the popular song *Malaika*, to which these rights were first given to Western artists recording the song with the

---

1. See the paper of Siri Lange in this volume.
2. For more descriptions of the style of *taarab*, see Kirkegaard 1996.
3. Kirkegaard 2001, p. 59.

argument that it was traditional. After its worldwide success a Kenyan songwriter and singer called Fadhily William claimed to have composed the song in the 1950s.[1] And in the 1990s Tanzanians are again claiming that Malaika is a traditional Tanzanian song exploited by Fadhily William.[2] Another example is *El Condor Pasa* recorded by Simon and Garfunkel in the 1970s, and yet another striking story is the quite disagreeable sampling by the group Deep Forest of a Solomon Island female singer for the million seller *Lullabye*. The original recordings were made as ethnomusicological research for the huge collection of UNESCO, which is a tempting pool of sounds for samplers to use, and which they choose to see as a free for all source.[3]

These cases of critical borrowings are quite easy to have an opinion on, but some other issues within the debate are much harder to solve. The general problem is that in order to claim the rights, the performer must be recognised as an individual person and the authorship must be proved. Most music in third world countries however has a more or less collective origin, and the concept of authorship is unfamiliar. There are some attempts to increase the scope of the copyright laws, in order to make some of the money earned through album releases go back to the communities from which they originated. Also the debate over the presence of collective authorship has started.

This is however, also a tricky matter as a strengthening of copyright laws will also increase the amount of money Third World countries will have to pay for Western music and television, and also because much of the development of for instance African popular music initially came about as an imitation of foreign idiom—above all Caribbean musics.[4] The World Bank is now taking actions to support indigenous musical industries in Africa, as they see a possibility for the music business to become profitable. This might strengthen the awareness of the copyright issues. It is in this respect very interesting that the "Tranzania" project is directed towards bettering the copyright situation.

The "Tranzania" project and what it represents

The CD *Tranzania* is situated in the middle of the discourse mentioned above. It was initiated by the Western partners in cooporation with the Tanzanian musicians. The style was probably selected because of the relatively high rate of interest in *taarab* music in the West particularly since the recordings of the prominent Zanzibari *taarab* groups like *Ikhwani Safaa Cultural Club* (aka. *Malindi*) and *Culture Musical Club* (aka. *Utamaduni*) in the 1980s and the general demand for new sounds within the Western musical culture of techno and other computer mastered genres. The album nevertheless represents a unique meeting between Norwegian techno musicians and the Dar es Salaam based *taarab* groups Egyptian Musical Club and Sisi Kwa Sisi.

On the record the techno techniques can be spotted quite clearly, as in the many incidences of "real-sound", for instance take-off, flight announcements, and a Dar es Salaam backtape with tropical noises of bush babies, mosquitoes and engineered *taarab* radio-broadcasts. Here is a combination of good technical facilities and

---

1. Malm and Wallis 1984, p. 138 ff.
2. Wallis 2000.
3. For this story of *Lullabye* see Hugo Zemf 1996.
4. For a differing yet related angle to this problem see Steven Feld 1996, where he marvels over the procedures of jazz improvisers and their closeness to copying.

strong interest in otherness and strange music cultures, a clear example of heroisation of otherness.

What is most striking when listening to the album is the total domination of the techno-sound. The *taarab* elements are merely a spice to the overall Western dominated style. *Taarab* music which puts a premium on the personal rendering of a specific song is only granted sampled utterances, in which the same expressions are repeated over and over—very much against the live principles of *taarab*.

To present how the record is put together let me present a rather detailed description of one of the representative tracks. The song *Sema*—a title very often used in *taarab*—can serve as an example. It consists of both "real sound", taped *taarab* singing and technically mastered samplings mixed with studio based production. At first we hear a distinctive "tropical" sound of cicadas and night-time noises so familiar to everyone who has been in tropical Africa. This sound is mixed with a faint airplay of the *taarab* song; an equivalent to the first impression a visitor is most likely to get of the style, as the radio transmitted recordings very often pour out of the open windows of private Swahili houses or tea parlours. After approximately one minute of this exotic soundscape, a distinctive techno drum gradually develops. The modern equipment imitates the ornamentations of *taarab* with vibratos and trills, and suddenly the female *taarab* voice is raised to the fore of the sound formation and the first verse is rendered.

The computers also imitate vibes and later the violin—so prominent in instrumental *taarab*—is copied on the keyboard, and functions as a call-response maker in relation to the voice.

The vocal lines are clearly sampled and all through the track the female voice has exactly the same expression whenever the lyrics of *Sema* appear. Later again, a vocal response with a rising melodic contour is heard. This is also sampled to be used as a standardized element over and over in the progressing mix.

After approximately six minutes the track ends, and we are left with the exotic sound of the introduction; the cicadas and the imaginary radio transmission of the song.

What is remarkable and what makes this version of *Sema* very different from the live *taarab* performances is that the lyrics are limited to a very few words, whereas *taarab* songs generally have an elaborate poetic line and great attention to the particular performance of the individual singer. The other songs on the CD bear the same traits. It seems that the producers anticipate that the audience for this record will not know the setting—except for the imagined tropical night—and do not understand the Swahili language.

The aim of the project

The project was launched in order to use the platform of Norwegian musicians and well-off institutions like NRK (Norwegian state television) and NORAD to do something for hardworking and poor fellow musicians in Tanzania.

For the specific aim and the spirit of the project, let me quote the cover notes in full:

A musician's life in Africa may be very different from a musician's life in Europe. While the Norwegian participants in this musical collaboration have a well established system of organisations and rights to rely on, the Tanzanian musicians have had to face a situation where the music they create is often exploited by pirates, where the copyright laws do not protect their interests and where there is a lack of strong organisations to assist them in their struggle to gain control over their music and their living conditions.

This CD is part of a project which aims at doing something about this situation. The Tanzanian musicians' organisation Chamudata collaborates with the Norwegian aid-organisation Strømme Foundation, NORAD, the record company Kirkeligt Kulturverksted and NRK P2, one of the radio channels of the Norwegian Broadcasting Corporation, to build a basis for the development of musicians' rights in Tanzania. NORAD, the Norwegian agency for International-al development, is the main financial contributor to the project.

Through the efforts of Chamudata and its Norwegian partners, we hope to establish a situation where Tanzanian copyright laws will ensure that the musicians, composers and songwriters of the country get access to the income that their work generates. We hope to help Chamudata to become an organisation which will support and encourage Tanzanian musicians to create qual-ity music, and to promote this music both inside and outside the country.

To achieve this, there is also an urgent need to do something about the availability of instru-ments, musical education and recording facilities in Tanzania. The Tanzanian-Norwegian col-laboration project has already started working with all these problems. The sale of this CD is one of the sources of income which will enable us to do this work. [1]

It is interesting that *taarab* is now enjoying the attention of *Chamudata*. Until very recently this blended style was left on its own and generally downrated in national cultural politics presumably because of its ideological overtones and connection to the Omani Arabs.[2]

Concluding discussion

All of this then leaves us with the discussion on how to assess a product like Tran-zania.[3] I do not intend to judge out of an aesthetical parameter, rather I would like to address the issue from a more theoretical point of view.

First of all, it seems strange that a project dedicated to fighting for copyright issues, has at least five of the tracks on the record with no credit for the Tanzanian musicians and composers, although Swahili words and *taarab* melodies are clearly used and heard. It can of course be related to the fact that within the TRIPS' agree-ment and copyright system, there is no acceptance of collective rights, and accord-ingly orally transmitted songs and dances cannot be anything but 'traditional', which in copyright language means that the arranger gets the profit. But *taarab* is not in that respect a traditional music and there most definitely would be an author for the songs.

Is it then a fruitful cultural encounter or are the powers within the project still too asymmetrical?

Is the cultural-political goodwill—positive and helpful as it is truly intended— still neglecting the Tanzanian rights and interests? Is it really playing with identi-ties—or is it just playing?

And finally, can the merger of techno and *taarab* be seen as a further develop-ment of *taarab*? Is it another positive and rewarding addition to the world of in flux and an open-minded music culture? Or is it just another techno producer's wish and longing for new sources of material?

---

1. Quoted from the booklet to *Tranzania*.
2. Due to internal political tensions between African and Arab citizens in Tanzania and Zanzibar after Indepen-dence the issue of race has influenced cultural life in varying degrees. Kirkegaard 1996.
3. I do not intend to judge out of an aesthetical parameter. I do however find the product somewhat boring and with regret I have to state that I like more local forms of *taarab* better.

The concept cross-over is in my view highly relevant for a product like *Tranzania*, and it invokes Veit Erlmann's thoughts on World Music which in spite of the outspoken commitment to diversity nevertheless rests on a more fundamental 'sameness' precisely because of its strong linkages with the music business. [1]

I believe, however, that by now the juxtaposition of different musical elements in the particular *cross-over* called World Music has been taken so far, that we are now facing fission rather than fusion and creolisation.[2] While I consider the features of fusion and creolisation to be related to the processes of dynamic modernisation, I find that the period or process of fission is characterised by its petrifugal powers by which everything bristles, and where the piece only materialises in the ears of the particular listener, who interprets and thereby 'makes sense' of the randomly mixed elements. Thus in a renewed search for authenticity—so prominent in the search for new sounds in both techno and World Music—the artists present more or less undigested songs, melodies or rhythms, and with the technological possibilities of sampling, copying and manipulation, musical works are created, which audibly and structurally represent the fragmentation so typical of the postmodern life.

In this interpretation we are therefore beyond concepts like 'revival' and 'invention' of World Musical features—and deeply rooted in the particular rootlessness, which characterises societies today. This does not deny that we can still find strong revival movements in other contexts [3] I do share Clifford's evaluation of the role of the new culture, when he says that he does not think, "that postmodernism is yet a cultural dominant, even in the 'First World'".[4] This understanding, accordingly includes a recognition of the fact that several musical forms live and continue living within a dynamic process of modernisation in their local context, while at the same time these same forms obtain an imaginary meaning in the global space. Many musics can work on both levels—i.e. both as a local marker with internal identity bonds and a global imaginative sound to be used even superficially as flavours to a transcultural audience. When looking at the music in the latter role, I very much share Veit Erlmann's critical position to World Music mentioned earlier in this chapter.[5]

How does it look seen from the point of view of the musicians in Tanzania? As I said at the beginning I have not had the opportunity to ask the particular musicians involved in the "Tranzania" project. But I have met with many other *taarab* musicians who are more or less in the same situation. They all try to make the best of the situation and as it is a popular music they go where the money and the jobs are. But it is necessary to understand that the rules of the game for the World Music business affect the local musicians and at the same time represent a means to become famous and make a living. In the last event it provides the only chance for Third World musicians to get a foothold in the commercial music business. I find this effort legitimate—even if it is sometimes "bad" for the music.

Until now *taarab* has kept is strength at the local level. Finances are continuously a problem and musicians generally earn very little from their music. If *cross-over* products like *Tranzania* can help draw attention to copyright issues and provide some kind of economic awareness, this is of course welcome.

But as I hope to have demonstrated in this paper there are no easy shortcuts. And the struggle over identities in music is still a highly controversial issue.

---

1. Erlmann 1993, p. 7.
2. Hannerz 1995.
3. For descriptions of these new trends consult Kirshenblatt-Gimblett 1995 and Tamara E. Livingston 1999.
4. Clifford 1992, p. 32.
5. Erlmann 1996.

Discography

Acid Queen featuring Sisi Kwa Sisi and Egyptian Musical Club, 1998, *Tranzania*, Kirkeligt Kulturverksted, FXCD 203.

Kirsten Bråten Berg with Solo Cissokho, Kouame Sereba, Bjørgulv Straume, 1999, *Från Setesdal to Senegal*, Six Degrees Records 657036 1014-2.

References

Anderson, Benedict, 1996, *Imagined Communities: Reflections on the origin and spread of nationalism*. London: Verso.

Clifford, James, 1992, "Traveling Cultures", in Grossberg, Lawrence, Cary Nelson and Paula A. Treichler (eds), *Cultural Studies*. London: Routledge.

Collins, John, 1985, *African Pop Roots, the Inside Rhythms of Africa*. Berkshire: Foulsham & Co. Ltd.

Erlmann, Veit, 1993, "The Politics and Aesthetics of Transnational Musics", *The World of Music*, 35(2):3–15.

—, 1996, "The Aesthetics of the Global Imagination: Reflections on World Music in the 1990s", *Public Culture*, No. 8, pp.467–87.

Fargion, Janet Topp, 1992, *Women and the Africanisation of Taarab in Zanzibar*. Unpublished Ph.D. thesis, School of Oriental and Asian Studies, London.

Feld, Steven, 1996, "Pygmy POP. A Genealogy of Schizophonic Mimesis", *Yearbook for Traditional Music*, Vol. XXVII, pp. 1–35.

Garofalo, Reebee, 1993, "Whose World, What Beat, the Transnational Music Industry, Identity, and Cultural Imperialism", *The World of Music*, 35(2):16–32.

Hannerz, Ulf, 1992, *Cultural Complexity: Studies in the Social Organization of Meaning*. New York: Columbia Press Universal.

—, 1995, "The social organization of Creolization", in *From Post-Traditional to Post-Modern? Interpreting the Meaning of Modernity in Third World Urban Societies*, Occasional Paper No. 14. Roskilde: Roskilde University.

Kirkegaard, Annemette, 2001, "Tourism Industry and Local Music Cultures in Contemporary Zanzibar", in Baaz, Maria Eriksson and Mai Palmberg (eds), *Same and Other. Negotiating African Identity in Cultural Production*. Uppsala: Nordiska Afrikainstitutet.

—, 2000, "Universalisme, simulakrum og musiketnologi", *Musik og Forskning*, Vol. 25, pp. 104–29, 1999–2000. Copenhagen: C.A. Reitzels Boghandel A/S.

—, *Taarab Na Musiki wa densi, The popular musical culture in Zanzibar and Tanzania seen in relation to globalization and cultural change*. Unpublished Ph.D. thesis, Department of Musicology, University of Copenhagen.

Kirshenblatt-Gimblett, Barbara, 1995, "Theorizing Heritage", *Ethnomusicology*, Vol. 39, No. 3, Fall, pp. 367–80.

Livingston, Tamara E., 1999, "Music Revivals: Towards a General Theory", *Ethnomusicology*, Vol. 43, No. 1, Winter, pp. 66–85.

Malm, Krister and Roger Wallis, 1984, *Big Sounds from Small Peoples: The Music Industry in Small Countries*. London: Constable.

—, 1992, *Media Policy and Music Activity*. London: Routledge.

McLuhan, Marshall and Bruce R. Powers, 1989, *The Global Village*. Oxford: Oxford University Press.

Stokes, Martin, 1994, "Introduction: Ethnicity, Identity and Music", in Martin Stokes (ed.), *Ethnicity, Identity and Music. The musical construction of place*. Oxford and Providence: Berg.

Wallis, Roger, 2000, Lecture on "Copyright at Images of the World", Copenhagen, August 20, 2000.

WOMEX, Berlin 1999, Backstage interview with Sigbjørn Nedland, www.radio.cbc.ca/programs/global/Berlin/backstage.

Zemf, Hugo, 1996, "The/An Ethnomusicologist and the Record Business", *Yearbook for Traditional Music*, Vol. XXVII, pp. 36–56.

The Generational Factor in Ghanaian Music

Concert Parties, Highlife, Simpa, Kpanlogo, Gospel and Local Techno-Pop

John Collins

As is well recognised now, the notion that African societies were static and that the so called "Dark Continent" had no history is a colonial invention. In Ghana and other parts of British Imperial Africa this idea was particularly associated with the indirect rule period of the late 19th century when the British began to control their African colonies through traditional chiefs and emirs rather than the educated coastal African elites. The fact that there had been numerous African nations and empires with their own historical dynamics was quite ignored. They became relegated to mere tribes and static village systems that had to be guided and civilised. Thus the emphasis of the ethnographers of the period was to freeze African social systems into a timeless "ethnological present".

The comparative musicologists of the period likewise considered "authentic" African performing arts to be archaic and unchanging. This was, however, far from the truth and as professor J.H.K. Nketia discusses in the case of Ghana, there was musical syncretism going on between the Hausa, Dagomba, Akans, Ewe and Ga people through trade, war and migration long before European contact.[1]

Another form of traditional musical dynamic was generational change and conflict. For example youthful age-sets (secret initiation societies and warrior associations) could, through innovative performance, ridicule members of the older generation, question priests and even overthrow chiefs. Likewise the youth continually modified recreational drum-dance styles, which was often initially frowned upon by elders, thus acting as an identifier for each new generation.[2] The young in turn became elders and new recreational styles emerged in the next generation in much the same way as popular dance-music styles in the West mark out the waxing and waning of youthful sub-cultures.

Because recreational music and dance styles are continually open to generational modifications, it is from these, rather than the more conservative and slow-changing ritual and court performance, that so much of Ghana's acculturated or transcultured popular dance-music arose.[3] During the pre-colonial era novelty in recreational music was purely an internal African affair, being the combined result of the continuous youthful re-interpretation and re-cycling of older styles, and of the absorption of new elements from neighbouring ethnic groups contacted through proximity, trade, migration and warfare. However, during the 19th and 20th centuries novelty

---

1. Nketia 1971 and 1981.
2. In his book Folksongs of Ghana (1973) Nketia provides a sequence of neo-traditional recreational styles of the Akan of Ghana.
3. By acculturated or transculturated in this context I mean the numerous music and dance-music styles that evolved from the 19th century in the urban coastal areas of Africa as a result of the fusion of local African music and dance with that of Europe, the Americas and to a lesser extent India and the Near East.

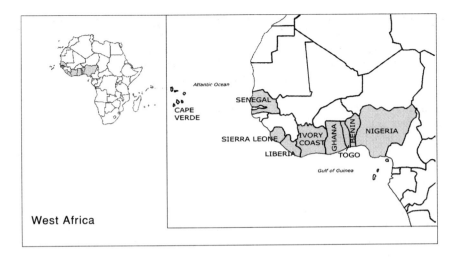

West Africa

was injected into recreational performance from external rather than internal African sources, in short from Europe and the Americas. It could be rightly claimed therefore that much of contemporary Ghanaian, and indeed African popular music, is a direct continuation of traditional but ever dynamic recreational music, albeit with elements from the West incorporated into it. In this light African popular music is just as much an Africanisation of western music as it is a westernisation of African music.

Turning now to contemporary Africa where traditional generational tension and conflict has not only been carried over into the modern context, but has actually increased for a variety of reasons. Urban migration and the formal western education of young people are particularly important, as these have resulted in a questioning of traditional and parental authority, and a turning away from the extended family towards the nuclear one. Another factor is the introduction of imported social norms such as romantic love, smoking, the drinking of alcohol,[1] and those associated with the teen-age fashions and the rebellious pop idols of western youth culture. Indeed, and as in the West, local African popular performers,[2] particularly urban ones, have become "role models" for African youth.

Naomi Ware claims this in the case of a distinct youth identity in post-war Freetown, Sierra Leone, and many other writers have commented likewise.[3] In East Africa Low refers to the clash between the older generation and young popular musicians (particularly guitarists) returning home to their villages from urban and industrial centres during the 1950s.[4] Ranger notes that the brass-band derived *beni* music 'mirrored" tensions between the young and old, especially after it had spread into the rural hinterland and became associated with self-supporting young men's societies that ignored the jurisdiction of village heads.[5] Wachira-Chiuri refers to popular songs by the Kenyan guitarist Joseph Kamaru that are about generational problems.[6] A specific Sierra Leone example referred to by Michael Banton are the

---

1. See Emmanuel Akyeampong 1996.
2. By popular performers I mean those who play transculturated urban music, dance and drama and some of the neo-traditional genres influenced by these: konkoma, simpa, kpanlogo, borborbor, akyewa, etc.
3. Ware 1978, p. 311.
4. Low 1982, p. 26.
5. Ranger 1975, pp. 165, 108–10.
6. Wachira-Chiuri 1981, p. 50.

"neo-traditional"[1] songs of Freetown's Ambas Gede voluntary association that catered for new urban migrants during the 1920s and 1930s and sometimes expressed dissatisfaction with the lethargy of the traditional leaders.[2]

As mentioned above, Western education has also enhanced generational strife in Africa, and this is sometimes linked to the acculturated music of the schools themselves. For instance, Coplan mentions that from the late 19th century mission schools in South Africa formed vernacular choirs and fife marching bands to counteract what the whites called the "revolting traditional communal dances, beer drinks and other customs inconsistent with Christianity".[3] This clash between the older "pagan" generation and the younger mission educated ones was a general feature throughout sub-Saharan Africa in colonial times. And in the post-independence era schools continue to produce music disliked by the older generation and have, as will be discussed later, been a breeding ground for youthful "pop" bands.

Just as important as the music of school children was that of school drop-outs and truants: like the "no good boys" of Ghana in the 1930s and the "street urchins" of South Africa in the 1950s who respectively created neo-traditional *konkoma* and penny-whistle *kwela* music.[4]

In West Africa, the drop-out and delinquent factor in generational conflict became more important after independence, when the dramatic expansion in the educational system resulted in an increase in the number of western educated youths unable to find employment in the modern sector. Twumasi mentions that the sudden increase in youth unemployment in Ghana during the 1950s was one of the factors that led Prime Minister Kwame Nkrumah to establish the Workers' and Farmers' Brigades.[5] These socialist type parastatal organisations also trained and hired the young and unemployed as musicians and actors for the Brigade dance bands and theatrical *concert parties* that were established from the late fifties. Chris Waterman observes that in the western Nigerian case the urban migration of large numbers of rural primary school drop-outs in the 1950s and 1960s was a factor in the dramatic rise in the number of *juju* music groups, the popular dance band genre of the Yoruba.[6] Moreover, there was a subsequent frequent fissioning of older bands and the emergence of new generations of bandleaders. Kazadi makes a similar observation concerning the Democratic Republic of Congo.[7]

To look into the subject of popular entertainment and generational conflict in English speaking West Africa and particularly Ghana in more depth, three specific areas will be examined: (1) the youthful age of many popular artists and the parental opposition that they face; (2) inter-generational strife in the content of popular song

1. By neo-traditional songs I mean music (and usually dance) performed in villages and urban neighbourhood communities for socially functional rather than solely commercial purposes—but borrowing artistic, instrumental and technical elements from both local and foreign sources. This is possible because Africa's strong living folklore allows a circular feedback relationship between popular and traditional/folkloric performance. Thus today there is a continually shifting spectrum between the 'folkloric' and 'popular' areas rather than a sharp and fixed historical distinction.
2. Banton 1957, chapter IX.
3. Coplan 1985, p. 26.
4. The reference about *konkoma* (or *konkomba*) is a personal communication from Professor A.M. Opoku 7th September 1990; it is an indigenised and 'pooman's' form of local brass band music that emerged in the Akan area of southern Ghana in the 1930s. For *kwela* see for instance Coplan, 1985, p. 157.
5. Twumasi 1975, p. 49. It should be noted that Kwame Nkrumah was Prime Minister of Ghana from 1952 (during internal self-government) right through independence (1957) and after, until 1960 when he became President of Ghana until his overthrow in 1966.
6. Waterman 1986, pp. 220, 223.
7. Kazadi (1973) says that from the 1950s and due to the rapid urbanisation many youths were left without a higher education. They were consequently forced to move into labouring jobs, the army, stealing, prostitution, soccer—and music. It can be noted that the author at this time called himself Pierre Kazadi, later using the name Kazadi wa Mukuna.

and dramatic texts; (3) examples of some specific entertainment genres that are linked to juvenile sub-cultures, fashions and delinquency.

The youthful age of performers and parental opposition

Young pioneers of Ghanaian *highlife* guitar bands and their associated *concert party* theatrical groups (local comic opera) are numerous.[1] The trailblazing *highlife* guitarist Jacob Sam (Kwame Asare) began making public appearances early, around 1910, when he sat on the shoulders of his accordionist father playing claves. Sam's nephew, the famous *highlife* guitarist Kwaa Mensah, began his musical career in the 1930s as a small boy in a drum-and-fife band. Other pioneer *concert party* performers who began their careers in their teens between the 1930s and 1950s include Bob Johnson, Bob Cole, Y.B. Bampoe ("Opia") and the famous lady impersonator and falsetto singer of E.K. Nyame's Akan Trio *concert party* and guitar band, Kwabena Okai (or Okine). The still popular Nana Ampadu of the African Brothers first went on stage with Yamoah's *concert party* during the 1960s at fifteen years old. [2]

It was also during the sixties Ghanaian pop bands appeared, which played imported rock'n roll, the twist and soul music that involved students in competitive inter-school popular music competitions or "pop chains".[3] These youths began to treat the older *highlife* dance-bands and their music as "colo"; that is colonial and old-fashioned.

The youthful nature of popular entertainment performers is also found in other areas of West Africa. Jeyifo says that Kola Ogumola's Yoruba travelling theatre group included school children, whilst those of Hubert Ogunde, Oyin Adejobi and Akin Ogumbe contained the sons and daughters of these founder-leaders.[4] Ricard says that the members of the Happy Stars *concert party* of Lomé (formed in 1965) were between seventeen and twenty-four years old. He also mentions that this group was particularly popular with school leavers and apprentices.[5] Even younger was Angelique Kidjo of the Benin Republic who began her singing career when she was a six year old member of her mother's theatre group, the first in the country.[6] Similarly Fatu Gayflor, the "Golden Voice" of Liberia began her professional neo-traditional singing career when she was eight years old; whilst the country's Daisy Moore was just five.[7]

Numerous West African dance-band musicians began their careers early. E.T. Mensah of the Tempos dance-band joined the Accra Orchestra in 1933 at fourteen and the Tempos one-time drummer, Kofi Ghanaba (Guy Warren), first began as a young boy in the late 1930s with the Accra Rhythmic Orchestra.[8] The horn player Ignace de Souza of the Republic of Benin who led the Black Santiagos dance-band

---

1. Although guitar band highlife music and the local 'concert party' popular theatre had independent origins in Ghana during the early 20th century, these two performance genres were fused together in the early 1950s (by E.K.Nyame and others) into a comic highlife opera format.
2. For Jacob Sam and Kwaa Mensah see Collins 1985a, p. 15, for Kwabena Okai see Collins 1985c and for Ampadu see Atakpo, 1992, p. 138.
3. Collins 1985a, p. 108.
4. Jeyifo 1984, p. 84, 87. Barber (1987, p. 65) refers to the 'father figure' leader of a typical Yoruba travelling theatre who is surrounded by an inner core of permanent artists and fluctuating outer rings of increasing instability. Waterman (1982, p. 67–69) has actually written a paper on the subject of band seniority which is about the problems between 'Captain' Dayo Adeyemi, the leader of an Ibadan juju-music band, and his bandsmen.
5. Ricard 1974, pp. 69–70, 178.
6. BBC interview with Kidjo on 2nd July 1992.
7. Collins 1996, pp. 238–39.
8. Collins 1986, pp. 11, 16.

in the mid-sixties began playing professionally at sixteen with the Alfa Jazz band of Cotonu.[1] The Bendel State born Nigerian *highlife* musician Victor Uwaifo played with Victor Olaiya's Lagos based dance-band as a schoolboy, as did the creator of *Afro-beat*, Fela Anikulapo-Kuti.[2] The Lagotian musician Segun Bucknor who pioneered *Afro-soul* in the late 1960s had prior to this been a schoolboy member of Roy Chicago's *highlife* dance-band.[3] Famous Nigerian *juju* music exponents of the 1950s and 1960s also began their careers early. For instance both Ebenezer Obey and I.K. Diairo began professional playing at twelve.[4] Both Waterman and Alaja-Browne talk of this Yoruba popular music genre emerging in the early 1930s from a group of "area boys" of the Saro (Sierra Leone) Olowogbowo quarter of Lagos who had been playing together from the late 1920s.[5] In eastern and southern Africa a similar youthful contribution to syncretic performance styles has been observed by Ranger, Coplan and Kubik. [6]

In Ghana popular performers are generally held in low esteem as they are thought of as drunkards and womanisers. Because the *highlife* guitar was associated with palm wine (a local alcohol) bars this instrument was particularly frowned upon. The charge of womanising is a result of the itinerant life-style of many bandsmen who were constantly 'trekking' (i.e. touring) away from home. Due to this low status there has often been strong opposition from parents, relatives and teachers to their youngsters becoming professional stage performers. Y.B. Bampoe (mentioned above) was beaten by his uncle for forming the schoolboy Yanky Trio in 1946. Jacob Sam's accordion playing father considered all guitarist as "ruffians",[7] whilst Emmanuel Akyeampong mentions the case of elders of the town of Bekwai Ashanti trying to de-stool a young chief in 1920 for playing guitar.[8]

Bame says that I.K. Yeboah's Abuakwa Trio concert group of the 1950s actually collapsed due to parental problems.[9] Another case is the previously mentioned Kwabena Okai (Okine), whose uncle tried to lever him away from the "useless profession" of music.[10]

The parental resistance that young Ghanaian popular entertainers have encountered is also found elsewhere in West Africa. Let us take a few specific cases. The Yoruba comic actor and popular theatre leader Moses Olaiya or "Baba Sala" began his professional stage career as an instrumentalist with the Empire Hotel Dance Orchestra of Lagos, which his father, says Lakoju, "did not take kindly to".[11] The father of the popular Nigerian *highlife* musician Victor Uwaifo even wanted to smash his son's first guitar.[12] The Krio elite of Sierra Leone, says Ware, "strongly discouraged their children from associating with or becoming popular musicians".[13]

---

1. Collins 1985a, p. 57.
2. Collins 1996, chapters 37 and 38.
3. Collins 1985a, pp. 77, 116.
4. Collins 1985a, p. 33 and Waterman 1986, p. 254.
5. Waterman 1990, p. 64 and Alaja-Browne 1987, p. 1.
6. A seminal influence on Beni music was, according to Ranger (1975, p. 10), the brass band music of the children of freed slaves taught to them at Christian missions like Freretown in Kenya. Likewise, Coplan (1985, p. 267) notes that makwaya music had its origin in the South Africans attending mission schools. In the post-war era, Kubik (1981, pp. 87–88) stresses the importance of urban and wage earning youth for Kenyan popular dance music.
7. Collins 1996, p. 3.
8. Akyeampong 1996, p. 62. The young Omanhene (state chief) was accused of "cadging drinks, intoxification, wearing western clothes and holding a guitar in his hands".
9. Bame 1985, p. 20.
10. Collins 1985a.
11. Lakoju 1984, p. 36.
12. Collins 1986, p. 202.
13. Ware 1978, p. 313.

The Ghanaian/Togolese percussionist Kofi Ayevor told me that his father, who wanted him to become a doctor, forced Kofi to walk twenty miles to see top Ghanaian *highlife* bands.[1] Likewise the father of the well-known Senegalese musician Youssou N'Dour at one point forbade him to sing publicly,[2] whilst the parents of Côte d'Ivoire's Alpha Blondy were so incensed by their son's interest in reggae music, his growing of rastafarian dreadlocks and his refusal to become a teacher, that they had him placed under psychiatric care for two years.[3]

The Nigerian musician Prince Nico Mbarga actually released a *highlife* song on record with his Rokafil Jazz in 1977 on the topic of parental opposition. This *highlife*, sung in pidgin English and called *Music Line* is the story of Nicholas himself. The song begins with a father warning his son against going into the music business as he will never be able to save enough money to settle down and get married. However, it ends on a happy note, with the son replying that he has become so successful in the "music line" that he can afford a large car and even several wives.[4]

Generational strife in popular entertainment texts

The theme of the young's lack of respect for their elders occurs in many of the plays of Ghanaian *concert parties* of the post-war period and we can take some examples from the Jaguar Jokers (or J.J.'s) group formed by Mr. Y.B. Bampoe in 1954. Their play *A Day Will Come* involves a young woman Asabea who follows the flashy Tommy Fire to drinking bars and is not concerned about her sick mother. In *Go Back to The Land* another young woman called Sapona ignores her father's advice and is lured to the big city. In the J.J.'s play *Awisia Yi Wo Ani* it is the obedient orphan Kofi Antobam, rather than his spoilt and disrespectful half brother King Sam, who is successful in life. In the closing moral of this play general counsel to the audience is given by their father, Mr. Johnson, who sings a *highlife* song, which includes the following line: ..."to the children I say this, young people should respect their elders, they shouldn't steal or go to beer bars".[5]

Other *concert parties* also dramatise the clash of generations. Indeed it is a facet of two of the oldest *concert party* characters, the moralising and once top-hatted "gentleman" and the mischievous comic "Bob" who is often a house-boy. The theme of the young versus the old occurs in the play *Think Twice* by the Golden Stars group which is about a "boy about town" duping an illiterate old farmer.[6] In this play the old farmer is sometimes made fun of for his poor English, which brings us to the point that it is not only the young who are criticised in concert plays, but also the old.

In the Jaguar Jokers *Awisia Yi Wo Ani*, for instance, the clownish house-boy, Opia, (Mr. Bampoe) pokes fun at his employer, Mr. Johnson's, crotchety old ways which audiences find hilarious. In their television play *Ewo Bibiara* the old gentleman, Mr. Johnson, actually has a fight with another old man, which Opia characteristically encourages.

With both Togolese and Nigerian popular theatre, contrasting old and young stereotypes can be found. The Happy Stars of Lomé had its "playboys" and "girls"

---

1. Collins 1985b, p. 41.
2. Bender 1991, p. 37.
3. Graham 1988, p. 124 and Collins, 1996, p. 172.
4. The record was released on the Rogers All Star label number 8.
5. For a transcribed translation of this 1970s play, which means Orphan *Don't Glance Enviously* see Barber, Collins and Ricard, 1997.
6. Bame, 1985.

dressed in the latest fashions, as well as a "gentleman" and old men leaning on canes.[1] Karin Barber mentions that the characters of Yoruba popular plays include "sly cynical houseboys" and illiterate old parents making comic misinterpretations of modern ways,[2] whilst Ulli Beier says that Kola Ogunmola's Yoruba dramas typically contain a "strong-headed child who is punished for his disobedience".[3]

Highlife songs also sometimes dwell on the generational topic, as with Mr. Johnson's closing moral in the play *Awisia Yi Wo Ani* referred to above. Another example from the Jaguar Jokers is Kwaw Tawia's song in their play *Onipa Hia Mmoa* in which this drunkard accuses his mother of being a witch whom he has to protect himself from by putting "medicine" in his hair.[4]

A very popular song of the early 1970s that also condemned the old was the Big Beats Afro-beat type of *highlife* entitled *Kyenkyemna Osi Akwan* which compares the old to a vine or "broken thing" that crosses and blocks the path of the youth who want to get on in life.[5] I once witnessed a case of this song actually being used in a dispute between the youth and elders of a village. It occurred at Pokuase in June 1972 when the Jaguar Jokers *concert party* wanted to perform and thus defy the traditional one-month ban on drumming preceding the annual Ga Homowa harvest-festival. This annoyed the traditionalist elders. The youngsters of the village who wanted the show to go on called them "kyenkyemna".

Some *highlife* lyrics also reflect the worries that the older generation has in understanding the ways of the young. An example by the Black Beats dance band is their mid-1950s' record *Tsutsu Blema Beneke* which translates from Ga as "the old days were not like this". This song was an adaption of an old Ga *highlife* song that laments on how things are changing, and how young lovers are behaving differently, by showing their affection too openly.[6]

Youth cultures, juvenile delinquency and generational conflict

To examine the role of youthful and even delinquent sub-cultures in generational friction I will examine two areas. Firstly, there is the influence of imported "pop" music on Ghana and other English speaking West African countries that began in the sixties with rock music and soul and continues up to today with the current fad for reggae and rap. Secondly, I will take the examples of two Ghanaian neo-traditional forms of music that have emerged as a result of the impact of both western and local popular music on traditional recreational drum-dance genres.

The sixties and seventies generation of English-speaking West Africa adopted many of the youthful "pop" fashions, heroes and heroines from abroad, and consequently treated the older generation as *colo* or out-of-date. A fashion in vogue in the mid-sixties was Italian clothes and pointed shoes and a hero in Ghana during that period was the macho 'Jack Toronto', possibly modelled on a cowboy character of Italian "spaghetti westerns". To be called by this name was a form of praise amongst youths from the late sixties. Other terms of acclaim that became current in the coun-

1. Ricard 1974, p. 179.
2. Barber 1990, p. 20.
3. Beier 1954, p. 33.
4. For a transcribed translation of this 1970s play, which means 'Man Needs Help', see Collins 1994, chapter 2.
5. This band spent some time in Nigeria where they were influenced by the Afro-beat music of Fela Anikulapo-Kuti that fuses *highlife* with soul and jazz. The late Lord Linden, the keyboard player for the Big Beats told me on 8th August 1992 about the details of this song released in 1971. Professor A.M. Opoku of the University of Ghana subsequently explained to me that the word 'kyenkyemna' meaning 'tattered' may be related to the Twi word 'kyenkyen', a local cloth made from the beaten bark of a tree that is of an inferior quality to cotton.
6. Senofone label FAO 1318 and released in 1953/4.

try were borrowed from the rock music of the "hippie" and "flower power" generation and from African-American soul and "motown" music that projected a message of black pride. These were "psychedelic", "Santana man" (i.e. Carlos Santana), "soul brother", "Afro" and "Peace Corp"; the latter stemming from the motorbike riding American Peace Corp volunteers, a number of whom before the Nixon era were males wearing beards and long hair.

Linked to the imported pop culture was the emergence of a new generation of local bands in Anglophone West Africa that played psychedelic rock, Latin-rock and soul—as well as the Africanised offshoots, Afro-rock and Afro-beat. There were bands from Sierra Leone, such as the Heartbeats and Kabassa, Smith's Dimension from Liberia and the Soul Assembly, BLO, Mono-Mono and Ofege from Nigeria. Indeed the Kalakuta house of the Nigerian Afro-beat pioneer Fela Anikulapo-Kuti became a refuge for dropouts and delinquents during the 1970s and 1980s and his militant songs became a rallying cry for Nigerian downtrodden "sufferheads". Contemporary bands in Ghana at the time included the Psychedelic Aliens, Cosmic Boom, the Aliens, El Pollos, Pagadeja, Fourth Dimension and Hedzolleh (Freedom). Some of these featured in the local Ghanaian film *Doing Their Thing* that exactly captures the fashions and ambience of the times and is about a father who puts obstacles in the way of his daughter becoming a pop musician.

Since the early 1980s other imported popular musical influences have become popular in Africa including Jamaican reggae and African-American "disco" type *soul-funk* music, followed more recently by *hip-hop* and *rap* and *ragga*. Although Jamaican reggae made its first appearance in West Africa during the 1970s, from the 1980s local versions of it, often sung in vernacular languages, were developed by Miatta Fahnbulleh in Liberia, Alpha Blondy, Jah Tiken Fakoly and Tangara Speed Ghada of the Côte d'Ivoire, Kwadwo Antwi, Felix Bell and Rocky Dawuni of Ghana and Evi Edna Ogholi-Ogosi, Majek Fashek and Ras Kimono of Nigeria. It was during this time that some local youths, much to the annoyance of the older generation, began to grow dreadlocks, become anti-authoritarian and embrace rastafarian ideas. Alpha Blondy not only grew dreadlocks but publicly disagreed with the politics of ex-President Bédié; so much so that one of his reggae songs called "Guerre Civile" was repeatedly played on the radio on the day of General Guei's military coup in 1999.[1]

It was also from the 1980s that western *techno-pop* with its synthesisers and quanticised electronic drumbeats became popular with African youth. It began in the early 1980s with "disco" and was followed in the nineties by house-music, rap and rag. These subsequently spawned a host of local variants such as South African "bubble-gum" and *kwaito* music, Zim-rap from Zimbabwe and the highly satirical *zouglou* music (and associated *mapouka* dance) of the Côte d'Ivoire that was created by school students in the early 1990s utilising both live and electronic drums.[2] In Ghana electronic drums became the basis of the current *Burgher-highlife* and *hip-life* that will be discussed later.

Before turning specifically to the present day pop culture of Ghana I will first turn to neo-traditional genres that are also pertinent to modern generational identity. One example, mentioned earlier, was *konkoma*, which was created by "ruffians"

---

1. Fellows 2000, pp. 43–45.
2. Zouglou became more political in the late 1990s when the students became radicalised by their opposition to the corrupt civilian regime of President Bédié. Since the 1999 army coup of General (now President) Robert Guei *zouglou* bands like those of Soum Bill, Magic System and the Les Salopards have been endorsed by the Ministry of Culture (Fellows, ibid).

and "school drop-outs". Two other Ghanaian examples will be discussed here; namely the *simpa* recreational drum-dance music of northern Ghana and the *kpanlogo* of the southern Ga people.

Simpa evolved in the Dagbon traditional area during the 1930s when local recreational music became acculturated with imported western and southern Ghanaian performance styles, including the music of *gome* music groups, *concert parties* and *highlife* bands, When I stayed in the Dagomba capital of Yendi in 1974 there were two rival *simpa* groups called "Wait and See" and the "Real Unity Stars". They consisted of a group of young male percussionists and female singers and dancers, all aged between ten and sixteen years old. Besides local Dagomba songs and highlifes, they also played their own renditions of *Congo jazz (soukous)*, *soul* music and the *twist*.

I was told that *simpa* music had always been associated with the young and frowned upon by the older people, as since its inception *simpa* gatherings have been considered as improper places for young boys and girls to meet. This generational stress became compounded in the post-colonial era by the fact that these two competing performing groups in Yendi each supported one of two sides of a political division in the town (and indeed Dagbon in general) based on a longstanding dispute over the chiefly succession. In 1969 this became so serious that there was major violence in Yendi and a six-month ban was imposed by the police on what they believed was inflammatory *simpa* music throughout the traditional area.[1]

Chernoff mentions a newer acculturated recreational percussion genre that swept through Dagbon in the 1970s called *atikatika* which is played by children between the ages of five years old and the early teens. These children are known for singing witty songs related to the chieftaincy dispute just mentioned and criticising local figures like school head-masters and prominent businessmen. As a result *atikatika* groups have been periodically banned by the local and national authorities.[2]

Neo-traditional *kpanlogo* is a southern acculturated music that in its early days became the focus of youthful Ga identity and protest. It was created around 1962 by Otoo Lincoln and some other Ga youth from the fishermen's Bukom area of Accra who were both influenced by local music and imported pop and belonged to the local Black Eagles rock'n roll dance club. They merged the old Ga *kolomashie* dance with elements of western "pop" and *oge* (a Liberian seaman's percussion music popular with Gas from the 1950s). Otoo Lincoln coined the resulting style *Kpanlogo*, from a character in a traditional Ga folk story.

Because of the exaggerated pelvic movements of the *kpanlogo* dance, borrowed from rock'n roll's "Elvis the Pelvis" and Chubby Checker's "twist", the older generation (including executives of the National Arts Council) initially opposed this new-fangled traditional genre, claiming the dance was sexually suggestive. As a result of the ensuing quarrel between the Ga youths and some older members of the Accra public a display was organised in 1965 for them by fifty *kpanlogo* groups. It was held at Black Star Square in Accra where President Nkrumah, and other members of his Convention People's Party (CPP) government, who were present as arbitrators, endorsed this percussion-backed dance-music as genuine "cultural" music.[3] It subsequently began to be featured in performances run by government organisations such as the Ghana Arts Council and the Dance Ensemble of the School of Performing Arts at the University of Ghana.

---

1. Collins 1985a, chapter 5.
2. Chernoff 1979, p. 212–13.
3. Collins 1992, chapter 4.

Nevertheless, I was told by the Ga musician Jones Attuquayefio[1] that for a while, even after this official blessing, *kpanlogo* performers were arrested by the police, their drums seized, with some of the musicians being caned and put in the cells for a few days. One reason for this harassment was that early *kpanlogo* (and indeed rock'n roll) were popular with the fashionably dressed young "Tokyo Joes" who were the Ga supporters and "action troops" of Dr. Busia's anti-C.P.P. United Party. These rough political activists who came from the Bukom area used *kpanlogo* rhythms to accompany their anti-Nkrumah songs.

Another factor contributing to this harassment of *kpanlogo* groups may have been the fact that the content of the short dance-dramas that are often part of a *kpanlogo* session, are sometimes anti-establishment. An example I saw in 1975 was an open-air performance by Frank Lane's group of James Town.[2] Their Ga play was about a government health inspector catching and summoning some street sellers for not putting netting over their foodstuffs as protection from flies. They begged the official to let them off and got him so drunk that he began dancing the *kpanlogo*. While he was doing this the culprits ran away and when the inspector realised he had been tricked he tore up the summons and dramatically threw the pieces in the air.

The association between acculturated entertainment and fashion conscious and often admired juvenile delinquents, such as Ghana's "Tokyo Joes", has been observed in other parts of West Africa and indeed Africa. Alaja-Browne says that although the competing groups of Lagos "area boys" who created *juju* music in the 1930s were of "low status coupled with deviant behaviour", they were also respected and feared for their courage in championing their districts. [3]

Turning now specifically to Ghana where, as mentioned earlier, it was from the early 1980s that disco music with its electronic drum beat became fashionable. This electronic variant of *highlife* was created by Ghanaians living in Hamburg, Germany at that time.[4] Their discofied "burgher *highlife*" subsequently became popular with the youth at home.[5] The burgher-*highlife* fashion was followed in the late 1990s with vernacular versions of *hip-hop*, *ragga* and *rap* that is now known as *hip-life* (*hip-hop* plus *highlife*) and is accompanied by the imported dress and hairstyles of American *rap* artists.[6]

It should be pointed out, however, that this move towards local *techno-pop* is not just a question of changing fashions but is partly a result of economic, political and technological factors which have mitigated against the large live-format popular bands, such as *highlife* dance bands, guitar bands and their associated *concert parties*. These restraints include almost three years of night curfew during the early 1980s, heavy taxes on musical instruments, the "invasion" of cheap-to-manage "spinners" (mobile discos) on the club dance-floors and the rise of local television and video productions. One interesting result of this is that live format *highlife* is now found mainly in the numerous new Ghanaian churches that are not taxed and that often use dance bands for worship and outreach purposes.

---

1. A member of my 1970s Bokoor band, information on 30th May 1979.
2. It was performed near the Palladium Cinema, James Town on the evening of November 19th 1975.
3. Alaja-Browne, undated, pp.4–5, 23. Similarly South Africa had its *tsotsi* gangs of the 1950s that patronised local penny-whistle *kwela* music and the Congo Democratic Republic had its *sapeurs* youth cult of the 1970s and 1980s whose musical champion was Papa Wemba. (See Coplan 1985, pp. 162–64, 270–71, Stapleton and May 1987 and Nkolo 1990, p. 29.)
4. George Darko and his German based band Cantata started the trend in 1983.
5. *Burgher* became a general term during the 1980s for any person who had lived abroad in Germany or elsewhere and came back sporting new fashions. It replaced the earlier expression 'Been To' (i.e. abroad).
6. Some current hip-life bands and artists include Nana King, Reggie Rockstone, Daasebre, Lord Kenya Akatakyie, Tic Tac, Ex Doe, Chicago, Lifeline Family and the Native Funk Lords.

Photo: A friend of the band.

The author with the Local Dimension Highlife Band around 1997/98. The band is based at the University of Ghana at Legon.

Other reasons for the recent growth in Ghana of mainly protestant spiritual, charismatic and pentecostal churches should also be noted.[1] These include the disappointments of the materialistic promises of independence and the economic collapse of Ghana in the 1970s, which has resulted in a general trend towards spirituality. The modern churches (especially the protestant and "born again" ones) also provide a more individualistic approach to religion than do traditional ancestor/religious cults and therefore reflect the overall rise in the individualistic ethos that has evolved in the modern sector of Ghana.[2] Then there is the ability of the churches to combat witchcraft accusations which have increased remarkably over the last hundred years or so due to the stresses and strains of class stratification and the break-up of the extended family; for the traditional belief that excessive individual wealth and power results from witchcraft and sorcery has been exacerbated in the modern urban capitalist context—and new ways of combating these anxieties and paranoias are proliferating.[3] The African separatist churches, for instance, regularly cast out devils, use dramatic healings/exorcisms and popular *gospel highlife* dance-music sessions that act as a pyschological catharsis for their congregations.

One consequence of the rise of *gospel highlife* is that since the mid-1980s an enormous number of women singers have entered the popular music (albeit sacred) sector. Indeed, women now dominate in the field of gospel singing and have, through the church, found a space previously denied them in popular dance music.[4]

In spite of the rise of *gospel highlife*, *burgher-highlife* and the more recent *hip-life* have become the dominant commercial secular music of the urban youth in the big Ghanaian cities. This local *techno-pop* presents a sharp break with the *highlife* music of the older generation in two ways. Firstly, unlike the older varieties of *high-life* that dwell on a range of topics that includes love, witchcraft, socio-political com-

1. In Ghana in 1955 there were seventeen African separatist churches (see Acquah 1958), and by 1991 there were almost 800 (National Commission on Culture's Religious Affairs Department figures).
2. For instance the rise of the nuclear family and romantic love (cf. family arranged marriages), the privatisation of culture (i.e. copyright) and the rise of democracy and the rule of law based on individual rather than collective clan rights and responsibilities.
3. There were traditional anti-witchcraft cults in southern Ghana, but these were banned by the British in the late 19th century. They were replaced by imported anti-witchcraft cults like Blekete and Tigari from northern Ghana during the 1930s and 1940s. Since the 1970s their exorcising function has been increasingly taken over by the spiritual and later pentacostal churches (see Field 1960 and Collins 1997).
4. Some current big names include Mary Ghansah Ansong, the Tagoe Sisters, Stella Dugan, Ester Nyamekye, Suzzy and Matt, Diana Akiwumi, Cyndy Thompson and the Daughters of Glorious Jesus.

mentary, the orphan state, money "palava"[1] and the problem of death,[2] the lyrics of the new styles of *highlife* dwell almost exclusively on romantic love and sometimes sexual innuendo.[3] In the case of hip-life there is a definite "macho" flavour to the lyrics and practically all local rap singers are men. Indeed in Ghana at the moment there is a distinct gender split in the two main new forms of popular dance-music; namely hip-life and local gospel. Whereas hip-life is dominated by young men who aggressively chant (i.e. *rap*) and lip-synch over imported computerised beats, young Ghanaian women are prominent in the melodic *highlife* singing in the live context of a church service.

A second generational difference between older *highlife* and today's *techno-pop* is that *burgher highlife* and *hip-life* use drum-machines and synthesisers that distance them from the live performance of previous generations. In fact, members of the older generation often complain that the present brand of electronic *highlife* is not *highlife* at all and that its use of computerised instruments and electronic gadgets is cheap and imitative of western *techno-pop*. For the youth, however, it is the very artificiality of the music that gives it its distinctive up-to-date stamp.[4] Furthermore, a young musician can nowadays become a "superstar" without actually having to manage a full band for performances and recordings. This, like the romantic love theme in contemporary lyrics reflects a further move away from traditional norms and towards an individualistic ethos by urban Ghanaian youth.

So a controversy rages in Ghana about the new *techno-pop* styles of the present-day youth. The older generation and some music critics claim it is not *highlife*, that its pre-programmed rhythms are simply imported, its synthesisers put drummers and horn players out of work, its lip-synching videos cannot substitute for live perform-ance, it does not attract foreign tourists in search of "authenticity", and its artifici-ality makes it an un-exportable product for the lucrative World Music market. For instance King Bruce bemoans the demise of live Ghanaian *highlife* music and men-tions the case of a gospel song he recorded when he was manager of the Elephant Walk recording studio in Accra in the early 1990s that was rejected in the United States because it employed a "drumulator" machine.[5] Likewise the journalist Baba Abdullai of the *Ghana Weekly Spectator* suggests that the reason why Malian and Senegalese pop bands, but not Ghanaian ones, are invited to international World Music festivals is that Ghanaian popular music is weak on percussion and heavy on digital sounds.[6]

In spite of these statements, current Ghanaian *techno-pop* styles such as, *burgher-highlife* and *hip-life* have some positive features. They are sung in vernacular lan-guages and thus from a linguistic point of view serve a positive cultural function of putting the local languages into new contexts. Likewise Ghana's young *techno-pop* artists become familiar through music with high technology. Moreover, the use of

1. West African pidgin English expression for a heated quarrel or argument.
2. For themes in the lyrics of *highlifes* up to the 1970s see Brempong 1984, Yankah 1984, Van der Geest and Asante-Darko 1982 and Agovi 1987.
3. Examples of some recent songs that have been banned by some FM radio stations include Daddy Lumba's *Aben Wo Ha* [It is Cooked], Rex Omar's *Abiba Wadonkoto Ye Me Fe* [Abiba's Beautiful Movements Sweet Me] and Tic Tac's *Philomena Kpitenge* that deals with a rash that can affect the genitals. Ex Doe and Chicago are causing a newspaper controversy in Ghana for introducing offensive, sexually explicit and misogynist themes of the African-American *gangsta-rap* variety.
4. I noticed this artificial trend from my own Accra Bokoor Recording Studio work from the late 1980s when musicians insisted that I equalise the high 'tweeter' drum-machine sound so it cut through the lyrics. I did this reluctantly as I thought it upset the overall aural balance, but was told by the young musicians that without this gimmick their music would not sell on the Ghanaian market.
5. Collins 1996, p. 275.
6. *Ghana Weekly Spectator* July 13, 1996, p. 4. For other negative comments by Ghanaian music journalists on the mediocracy and un-Ghanaianness of current local techno-pop see my World Bank report (2000).

cheap to produce digital multi-track recordings and video performances means that music making has become somewhat "democratised". It is now possible for many young people, who would not have otherwise entered the music profession, to have a go and find a voice. Finally and as pointed out before, it is the very artificiality of the music that helps draw the generational line in Ghana at the moment.

Where the next line will be drawn is anyone's guess. In the West the extreme *techno-pop* fads of the seventies were followed by quite different trends; such as the acoustic sounds of "unplugged" artists, "live band circuits", a proliferation of retro-styles and the growing interest in ethnic and "roots" music, including the World Music phenomenon. The World Music market (that includes African music) emerged as a distinct marketing category in the early/mid-eighties and according to the International Herald Tribune[1] (February 3, 2000) now constitutes 14 per cent (i.e. 5 billion dollars) of global music sales. In the United States it is the fastest growing segment of the record market and has been expanding at 40 per cent a year since 1995.

In Ghana the next generation could likewise evolve a musical movement that draws more heavily on tradition and the "classical" *highlife* tradition. This however might not only be determined by the internal music market and musical aesthetics but might be a response to the internationalisation of African music (i.e. "World Music") and the demand by foreign fans for music that has a live feel and utilises African dance rhythms. Ironically, this western search for "rootsy" music is part of a new type of anti-technology romanticism sweeping through the youth of industrial nations saturated with over-produced and hi-tech music: exactly the sophisticated sounds that the modern youth of Ghana want. However, Ghanaian musicians and music producers should be sophisticated enough to recognise and commercially exploit these two different psychological needs and markets, that is the internal Ghanaian ultra-modern techno fad and the external western romanticised "back-to-roots" one. Ironically therefore, it may be the aim of succeeding in the foreign World Music market that can draw some young Ghanaians to exploring and developing their own indigenous popular music resources.

Whatever happens, whether it is a further move in a *techno-music* direction, a re-discovery and re-creation of older forms of local music, or both directions simultaneously—the "law" of generational musical transformation explored in this paper, and which has been occurring in Ghana since time immemorial, tells us that there will be change.

References

Agovi, Kofi B., 1987, *The Political Relevance of Ghanaian Highlife since 1957*. Paper presented at the 4th International Conference of the International Association for the Study of Popular Music.

Acquah, Ione, 1958, *Accra Survey*. London: University of London Press.

Akyeampong, Emmanuel, 1996, *Drink Power and Cultural Change*. Oxford: James Currey.

Alaja-Browne, Afolabi (Undated), *The Origin and Early History of Juju Music in Lagos*. Unpublished manuscript.

—, 1987, *From 'Ere E Faaji Ti O Pariwo' to 'Ere E Faaji Alariwo': A Diachronic Study of Change in Juju Music*. Paper read at the Fourth International Conference of IASPM

---

1. International Herald Tribune, February 3, 2000. The 2000 figures are from Gerald Seligman of EMI's World Music Section.

(International Association for the Study of Popular Music) held in Accra, Ghana 12–19 August.

Atakpo, Barbara and Kwabena Fosu-Mensah, 1992, "Highlife Maestro Comes to Town", *West Africa Magazine*, 27 January–2 February, p. 138.

Bame, K.N., 1985, *Come to Laugh: African Traditional Theatre in Ghana*. New York: Lilian Barber Press Inc.

Banton, Michael, 1957, *West African City: A Study of Tribal Life in Freetown*. London: Oxford University Press.

Barber, Karin, 1987, "Popular Arts in Africa", *African Studies Review*, Vol. 30, No. 3, September, pp. 1–78.

—, circa 1990, *Ethnicity and Nationality in Yoruba Popular Theatre*. Centre for West African Studies, University of Birmingham (unpublished manuscript in author's possession).

Barber, Karin, John Collins and Alain Ricard, 1997, *West African Popular Theatre*. Bloomington, Indiana: University of Indiana Press.

Beier, Ulli, 1954, "Yoruba Folk Opera", *African Music*, Vol. 1, No. 1, pp. 32–34.

Bender, Wolfgang, 1991, *Sweet Mother, Modern African Music*. Chicago: University of Chicago Press.

Brempong, Owusu, 1984, *Akan Highlife in Ghana: Songs of Cultural Transition*. Ph.D. thesis, Indiana University.

Chernoff, John Miller, 1979, *African Rhythms and African Sensibilities*. Chicago: University of Chicago Press.

Collins, E.J., 1985a, *Music Makers of West Africa*. Washington, DC: Three Continents Press.

—, 1985b, *African Pop Roots*. London: Foulshams and Co.

—, 1985c, "Kwabena Okai: The Death of a Musical Giant", *New African*, London, August.

—, 1986, *E.T. Mensah the King of Highlife*. London: Off The Record Press, republished in 1996 in Accra: Anansesem Press.

—, 1992, *West African Pop Roots*. Philadelphia: Temple University Press.

—, 1994, *The Ghanaian Concert Party: African Popular Entertainment at the Crossroads*. Ph.D. dissertation, SUNY Buffalo.

—, 1996, *Highlife Time*. Accra: Anansesem Press.

—, 1997, *Gospel Highlife: Ghana's New Response to Urban Anxiety*. Paper read at the International Conference on Music and Healing organised by the International Centre for African Music and Dance, University of Ghana, Legon, 3–4 September. Forthcoming in Glendora Magazine, Lagos.

—, 2000, *Paper on the African Music Industry*. For the June 20th 2000 Workshop of the World Bank on Developing the Music Industry in Africa. Available from the Policy Science Center, 127 Wall St. Room 314, BOX 208215, New Haven, CT.06529-8215. (www.worldbank.org/research/trade/africa_music2.htm

Coplan, David, 1985, *In Township Tonight: South Africa's Black City Music and Theatre*. Johannesburg: Ravan Press.

Field, Margaret, 1960, *Search for Security: An Ethno-Psychiatric Study of Rural Ghana*. London: Faber and Faber.

Fellows, Catherine, 2000, "Songs of Freedom", *The Focus on Africa Magazine*, BBC, London, July–Sept., pp. 43–45.

Ghana Weekly Spectator, July 13, 1996, p. 4.

Graham, Ronnie, 1988, *Stern's Guide to Contemporary African Music*. London: Zwan/Off the Record Press.

Jeyifo, Biodun, 1984, *The Yoruba Popular Travelling Theatre of Nigeria*. Lagos: Nigeria Magazine.

Kazadi, Pierre,1973, "Trends in 19th and 20th Century Music in Zaire Congo", in von Robert Gunther (ed.), *Musikulturen Asiens Afrikas und Oceaniens*, No. 9, pp. 267–88. Regensburg: Gustav Bosse Verlag.

Kubik, Gerhard, 1981, "Neo-Traditional Popular Music in East Africa since 1945", in Middleton, Richard and David Horn (eds), *Popular Music*. Cambridge: Cambridge University Press.

Lakoju, Tunde,1984, "Popular (Travelling) Theatre in Nigeria: The Example of Moses Olaiya Adejumo (alias Baba Sala)", in *Nigerian Magazine*, published by the Federal Ministry of Information, Social Development, Youth, Sports and Culture, pp. 35–46.

Low, John, 1982, "A History of Kenyan Guitar Music 1945–80", *African Music*, Grahamstown, Vol. 6, No. 2, pp. 17–36.

Nketia, J.H.K., 1971, "History and Organisation of Music in West Africa", chapter 1 in Wachsmann, K. (ed.), *Essays on Music and History in West Africa*. Evanston, Illinois: Northwestern University Press.

—, 1973, *Folksongs of Ghana*. Accra: Ghana University Press.

—, 1981, "On the Historicity of Music in West Africa", *African Cultures*, pp. 48–57. Bayreuth: Bayreuth University Papers.

Nkolo, Jean-Victor, 1990, *Take Cover Magazine*, UK, Vol. 1, No.1, Summer, pp. 29–31.

Ranger, T.O., 1975, *Dance and Society in Eastern Africa 1890–1970*. London: Heinemann.

Ricard, Alain, 1974, "The Concert Party as a Genre: The Happy Stars of Lomé", *Research in African Literatures*, Vol. 5, No. 2, pp. 165–79.

Stapleton, Christopher & Christopher May, 1987, *African All Stars*. London: Quartet Books.

Twumasi, Patrick A., 1975, *Medical Systems in Ghana: A Study of Medical Sociology*. Tema, Ghana: Ghana Publishing Corporation.

Van Der Geest, Sjaak, and Nimrod K. Asante-Darko, 1982, "The Political Meaning of Highlife Songs in Ghana", *American Studies Review*, Vol. XXV, No 1.

Wachira-Chiuri, B.A., 1981, "Popular Gramophone Music: A Survey of Joseph Kamaru", *Mzalendo*, Kenya, Vol. 2, August, pp. 43–57.

Ware, Naomi, 1978, "Popular Music and African Identity in Freetown Sierra Leone", in Nettl, Bruno (ed.), *Eight Urban Musical Cultures: Tradition and Change*, pp. 196–319. Urbana: University of Illinois Press.

Waterman, Christopher, 1982, "'I'm the Leader Not the Boss': Social Identity and Popular Music in Ibadan Nigeria", *Ethnomusicology*, January, pp. 59–71.

—, 1986, *Jùjú: The Historical Development, Socio-Economic Organisation and Communicative Functions of West African Popular Music*. Ph.D. thesis, Department of Anthropology, University of Illinois.

—,1990, *Jùjú: A Social History and Ethnography of an African Popular Music*. Chicago: University of Chicago Press.

Yankah, Kwesi, 1984, "The Akan Highlife Song: A Medium for Cultural Reflection or Deflection?", *Research in African Literatures*, Vol. 15. No. 4, pp. 568–82, Winter. University of Texas Press

"The Air of the City Makes Free"

Urban Music from the 1950s to the 1990sin Senegal
Variété, Jazz, Mbalax, Rap

Ndiouga Adrien Benga

In the post-war years in Senegal, the young urban elite played a crucial role in promoting musical and cultural production. The colonial power was not concerned with controlling the modern music bands but rather concentrated on promoting cultural centres. Contrary to what happened in the British West African colonies and Congo the young urban music bands in Senegal posed no threat to the colonial power. Until the mid-sixties, the instruments, repertoires, lyrics, and costumes featuring in Senegalese urban music had little to do with indigenous cultural values. The nationalist movement was not able to win over the young urban musicians to put music at their service. The young bands from Dakar and Saint-Louis, the two biggest cities in Senegal, absorbed much from French culture, but they remained open *a to the* United States (jazz) and Caribbean (Afro-Cuban music). One can interpret *a posteriori* the success of these two music genres as a reappropriation of African culture.

The young musicians did not identify themselves as mouthpieces for an indigenous African culture nor for a triumphant colonial one. They demonstrated their ability to take advantage of the opportunities in the cities and they created a creole, urban identity.

Late colonialism: From peaceful relationship to *anomie*? (1946–ca. 1960)

There was no dominant music form in the period after the Second World War until independence in 1960. It was naturally, but not exclusively, coloured by the reigning French colonial rule.

The French colonial administration had already in the late 1800s drawn up a set of rules aimed at supervising movements and practices of urban populations in Senegal. By a law from June 30th 1881,[1] clubs were authorized. On June 4th 1937 a decree was promulgated on "processions, demonstrations, crowds and other manifestations in public spaces". Books, newspapers and films were censored by law. But interestingly there was no censorship of music. For research this means that although the history of music has left many traces in collective memory, there is a scarcity of archive material in the colonial files.[2]

All over French West Africa there was a close connection between musical production and colonial patronage. In the mid-fifties, only a few bands could afford to

---

1. ANS 21G 65 (17): Textes et principes relatifs aux mouvements, attroupements, manifestations et cortèges (1848–1881).
2. No information is available about music bands (composition, localisation, contents of their production etc.) at the National Archives of Senegal (that is, the police files, which contain considerable information on the censored art forms). I have found but a little material in the series 21G (Police et Sûreté).

pay for instruments of their own, and thus be free from colonial dependence on means for their music making. In Senegal, there was *La Jeunesse Rufisquoise*, whose members were the first music teachers in the country. There were other independent musicians who were educated at the *Conservatoire de Dakar*,[1] there was the *Saint-Louisien Jazz* and the *Amical Jazz* in Saint-Louis, two music bands at Ziguinchor, but hardly any in the rest of the country. *La Jeunesse Rufisquoise* had wind instruments (clarinet, tenor saxophone, alto-sax, trumpet, accordion) and string instruments (3 banjos, 2 violins) and a full set of drums.

The rule was that bands received subventions from the colonial administration. In Dakar, the municipality band *Lyre Africaine*,[2] specialized in French *variété* shows, and was generously funded by the municipal authority. The mayor of Dakar, Alfred Goux, even granted space to the band for its rehearsals in the basement of the Sandaga market. In other parts of French West Africa a similar specially favoured position was held by the brass band *Mission Catholique de Ouagadougou* in Upper Volta (now Burkina Faso) and by *Civil Servants Band* at Forecariah in French Guinea.[3] Within the limited means provided for this sector, the colonial administration provided the means for young African musicians to improve themselves by basic courses in music, instruction and practice in instruments, loans to acquire equipment for music etc. The groups were encouraged to arrange dance parties with entrance fees to make them financially self-sufficient.

This support to music bands was intended to make them collaborate with the colonial administration, and accept its power and domination. They were expected to take part in the spectacular dramatisation and praise of the glorious achievements of the metropolitan power. But if some groups did contribute to making urban masses assimilate the colonial doctrine, others rejected the *consommation somptuaire*[4] [extravagant consumption] accompanying the modernisation model that the colonial power advocated. They tried to develop their own symbols for a new identity that remained aloof both from colonial order and from African rural cultures.

The career of Omar Ndiaye, nicknamed Baraud, leader of the international music band, *Les Déménageurs*[5] (founded in 1951), is a case in point.[6] This talented saxophonist, who was born in 1927 and died in 2001 started with jazz music in 1942 inspired by US servicemen who were then stationed in Dakar after French West Africa had joined the Allied Forces. US soldiers' bands performed at Place Protêt.

Baraud's first performances were replays of famous classics like *Now's the Time, Parker's Mood, On the Moon*.[7] He paid for his own education at the Dakar Conservatory, where he studied at the same time as Mady Konate, another famous musician in the fifties. Inspired by Amsata Niang who was from Saint-Louis and leader of the *Senegalese Jazzmen*,[8] he founded the *Star Jazz* in 1949, a name that was later taken over by Pape Samba Diop nicknamed Mba in Saint-Louis in 1962. With his band, *Les Déménageurs*, Baraud set out on a grand tour in the late 1950s throughout West Africa (French Sudan, Ivory Coast, Guinea, Togo, Dahomey,

---

1. *Trait d'Union*, newsletter of French West African cultural centres, No. 1, December 1953–January 1954, pp. 45–46.
2. Lamine Ndiaye, lead; Bira Gueye, drummist and alto-sax player; Grand Diop, tenor-sax; Charles Diop, vocals.
3. *Trait d'Union*, op. cit.
4. Duvignaud 1973, p. 106.
5. This denomination reveals the adaptability of the bands and various repertoires to various audiences: tango, jazz, *highlife, merengue, gumbe*.
6. Interview May 27, 1997.
7. He admired Charlie Parker, Dizzy Gillespie, Billie Holiday.
8. Oumar Ndiaye reported that Amsata Niang was a specialist in performing on the saxophone. No one knew where he could have learnt it; he had never left Senegal.

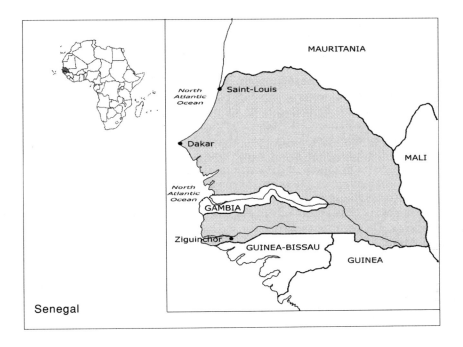

Senegal

Upper Volta, Sierra Leone, Gold Coast) and Central Africa (Cameroon, Congo Belgian, Congo Brazzaville).

The emergence of musical bands capable of converting their talent into cash gave an opportunity for musicians to live on music and escape from wage earning and its binding obligations. Music became increasingly a profession, especially among those who played jazz. In Saint-Louis, some civil servants resigned and joined the music trade: Amsata Niang (Treasury), Doudou Sy (Education), Oumar Ndiaye (employee of the Mauritanian Government). After a period of transition as part time musicians, they chose to play music full time, which if they made it could anyway be more profitable than their civil servant careers. For band members in *Les Déménageurs* in the late fifties, the monthly pay was between 90.000F CFA[1] for a maracas player and 197.000F CFA for the band leader (here Omar Ndiaye). As a civil servant, Oumar Ndiaye had earned a monthly salary of 9.000F CFA. The bands playing at dance parties charged between 40.000 and 50.000F CFA for each performance.

Music in Senegal was not a subversive weapon which could endanger colonial power. It did not try to challenge the cultural or political hegemony of the colonial administration. This was in contrast to what happened in the Congolese capitals,[2] where such artists as Essous, Kasongo, Kabassele, Adou Elenga became spokespersons for change which could sway opinion. In Dakar, on the other hand, the music scene was seen as a space for fun and play, and not an arena for expressing political views.

Only in the late fifties did Congolese music, which was influenced by the Latin American music so popular throughout French West Africa, gain ground, and first

---

1. The French franc, CFA, was used in French West Africa both during colonialism and after independence.
2. See Gondola 1992, pp. 463–87; 1997, pp. 51–81; 1999, pp. 87–111.

in Dahomey and Togo.[1] The Africanisation of cultural music came only later in this region.

Most of the urban music was dominated by young black Senegalese musicians living in Dakar. But there was also a strong French community who from time to time invited bands from the metropolis. The French ran the nightclubs where provincial identities were clearly asserted (Breton, Corsican clubs), and which only Europeans could afford to frequent. In addition a few *évolués* could attend these exclusive places where racial, social and financial discrimination prevailed. The most popular *variété* shows came from abroad (with *tango*, *waltz* etc.).

None of the Senegalese music bands was rooted in indigenous music culture. Thus developed a pronounced demarcation between indigenous music on the one hand and urban music on the other. This was so despite the fact that there existed indigenous urban music.[2]

Playing music was an urban elitist activity performed exclusively with western instruments. The performers were born and had grown up in colonial cities in West Africa. Music was played for entertainment, not to help in the emergence of political awareness. The old practices of politics in the cities of *Quatre Communes* (Saint-Louis, Dakar, Goreé, Rufisque) actually instituted citizenship for the Africans; the battle for citizenship thus was not on the agenda. For example, the city of Saint-Louis had a black mayor at the time of the French Revolution and a representative in the French National Assembly in 1848.

At first sight, it seemed that the political pattern suited the musicians in all respects. This is a mistaken view. As professionals, musical bands demonstrated their utter rejection of established rules and were escaping from the constraints and obligations of wage earning. The acceptance of the assimilationist colonial project was only a pretence. What really mattered for them were the opportunities offered by town-life to be free from colonial patronage. Insidiously there started to appear some aspects of individualization. Playing and composing music was the expression of urbanity. Music bands worked for their own success and were first professionals, and claimed that status.

The rise of *mbalax*: between "praise music" and cross-music (ca. 1960–)

From independence to the early 1980s, Senghor's ideology of *Négritude* prevailed in Senegal and particularly in the capital Dakar. It was aimed helping Africans to be aware of their culture and assume their own identity.[3] This excitement for cultural identity also affected the artists. Senghor defined the priorities and the artistic sectors to be assisted. Urban music was not an exception. Music bands had to uphold national languages through relevant compositions and adaptations. Another objective was to create an authentic local music as was being done in Zaïre and Guinea.[4] In the early seventies, the *Bureau Sénégalais des Droits d'Auteurs* (B.S.D.A.) and the

---

1. Collins 1977, pp. 54–55.
2. *Gumbe* and *assiko* are found in Ghana as early the First World War under the denominations *gombe* (name of drums) and *ashiko*. See Collins 1977. The Senegalese give to these two styles an origin from Gorée Island. In Bassaland (South of Cameroon), *asiko* is a dance rhythm that is obtained by knocking on a empty bottle with a metal stick. In Gorée Island (Senegal), the *assiko* beat is produced from a wooden square instrument covered with goat skin. The various tunes depend on the size of the instruments. In order, we have bass, counter bass, middle bass, *tintin* and *rouling*. To complete the set, the "tchatcha" produces a rattle sound. Songs are rehearsed in chorus. One of the famous songs is entitled *Rosa*. While people sing, someone dances with an unsteady step.
3. Senghor 1964.
4. Bender 1991, pp. 40–41.

Institut National des Arts du Sénégal (I.N.A.S.) and a board for subventions were set up.

But the efforts to mix traditional instruments (*kora, balafon, tama, sabar*) with modern ones (like piano) were not appreciated by the audience. As a case in point, the records released by *Wato Sita* and *UCAS Band* of Sedhiou, despite their efforts in music research, had little success while the audience still hummed popular hits like *Adama Ndiaye* or admired salsa music, jerk, be-bop, reggae, soul and pop music. *Wato Sita* was formed in 1970 by Ousmane Sow Huchard (who was named after Soleya Mama as an artist) and Andre Lo. *Wato Sita* band was a research workshop whose aim was to collect national repertoires in making a tour throughout the country (Casamance, Sénégal Oriental, Sine-Saloum). In doing so, it marked a break with the prevailing *yeye style*. The city dwellers resented the authoritarian drift of the state in their leisure space. This behaviour can be identified in dancing. The foreign musical styles were danced in a way that astonished more than one visitor, for instance the "three steps" of Cuban music. Young men in fancy dress hardly shook their bodies for a moving hit such as *Seny* by *Baobab*. In the sixties and seventies, rock and jerk festivals were being organized in Dakar[1] and the capital welcomed big bands and famous singers: Tino Rossi, Gilbert Bécaud, Claude François, Françoise Hardy, Johnny Halliday, James Brown, B.B. King, Jackson Five, Orquesta Typica Ideal etc.

Around 1950 *mbalax* appeared on the scene as solo percussion, which gave rhythm to Wolof dances on the streets of Dakar. The *Mbalax* style became popular in the 1950s with singers such as Mada Seck or Bouna Mbass Gueye. In the 1960s bands such as Star Band and Boabab tried to modernise the beat. However, despite the support of president Senghor. *Mbalax* remained marginal on the music scene, overshadowed by salsa, rock, soul, pop, and reggae.

Mbalax, an accompanying tempo, is performed with local hand drums: *nder* or *sabar* with trebble sound, *goron-yege* used by the solists, *mbeungue mbeungue*, equivalent to bass and *ndeund*, the instrument of the drum-major.

Among the heirs in the sixties were Lama Bouna Mbass Gueye, Vieux Sing Faye, Mame Less Thioune, and above all Doudou Ndiaye Rose, who composed a great number of beats.[2] Music bands such as *Star Band* formed in 1960 by Ibra Kassé[3] and *Baobab Gouy Gui* with Thione Seck, Médoune Diallo, Rudy Gomis in the seventies fused *sabar* in variety shows (Afro-Cuban, *rumba* from Congo-Zaïre, Guinean music).

During the World Festival of Black Arts held at Dakar in April 1966 that the use of Wolof language was blended with western music. The Festival hymn was performed by a famous saxophone player, Bira Gueye and sung by Mada Thiam.

---

1. The 1967 Festival of Rock and Jerk was held at the Theatre de Verdure where most of the bands from Dakar competed, according to the Dakar press: *Teenagers* (average age 10 years old!), *Butterflies, Black Devils, Dreamers, Konings, New Phenicians, Teddy Boys, Merry Makers, Beats, Chats Sauvages, Golden Accords of Rufisque*. It was sponsored by *Salut les Copains-Europe 1, Dakar Matin, Daniel Sorano Theatre Company* and *Air Afrique* and was presided over by French singer Johnny Halliday and won by the *Merry Makers*, a band from Dakar under the lead of Andre Lo. The best bands took part in this competition (first prize award amounting to 10,000F CFA). The festival was prior to the Youth National Week awarded 25,000F CFA as first prize for orchestration. The latest novelties of Paris and Dakar music shops were presented during the festival (*Dakar Matin*, March 24–25, 1967:3).
2. Born in 1930 in Dakar, Doudou Ndiaye Rose acquired a thorough knowledge of traditions and modernized the national repertoire as a drum-major.
3. Ibra Kasse is a musician and manager of *Miami*. It was in this bar-dancing that big bands were merged: *Guinea Jazz Band* and *Tropical Jazz* that gave birth to *Star Band* where most Senegalese singers started their career (Pape Seck, Balla Sidibé, Médoune Diallo, Rudy Gomis, Youssou Ndour).

Until the mid-seventies, most of the musical production was under the influence of Afro-Cuban style (*El Manisero, El Vagabonde* by *Star Band*). Each music band evolved under its own inspiration: *Star Jazz* from Saint-Louis adopted jazz from New-Orleans, *Dakar University Sextet* (founded in 1964 by Ousmane Sow Huchard and Dreyfus brothers from Guinea) was enriched by European inspiration.[1]

After 1968, *Mbalax* started to be modernized with orchestras such as *Xalam I* (Mbaye Fall, Cheikh Tidiane Tall, Charlie Dieng, Lucky Thiam, Gana Diongue etc.), the *Sahel*,[2] *Ouza* (Ousmane Diallo) and his *Ouzettes*. As early as in the seventies, *Xalam II* experimented with a new style based on the *mbalax* beat in which it was blended with other rhythms such as jazz, rock, rhythm and blues. Their records *Mbaye Sasu, Yumbeye* and later *Ade* and *Doley* were to be disseminated throughout the world. The *Number One*, formed in 1976 from a split of *Star Band* considerably improved its compositions and lyrics backed by a chorus of high quality (Pape Seck, Maguette Ndiaye, Doudou Sow, Mar Seck, Pape Djiby Ba).

Mbalax music developed through a combination of the praise music tradition (with strong reference to Muridism and traditional values, above all those of the Wolof, the main Senegalese ethnic group)[3] and opening up to styles from abroad.[4] The next generations would be under the influence of Super Diamono, Toure Kunda, Youssou Ndour, Ismaël Lo, Baba Maal, Thione Seck Ballago in the eighties. The end of the 1980s is marked by *zouk-mbalax, rock-mbalax, rap-mbalax*.

The beginning of the 1980s saw a tremendous upsurge of *mbalax*, which was no doubt linked to the popularity both at home and abroad of groups such as Xalam and Toure Kunda and artists such as Youssou Ndour and Ismael Lo. This popularity was a result of a conscious effort to find a place for this music in the arena of world music. The rising role of *mbalax* evolved in competition with music styles from abroad.

Youssou Ndour takes a special place in the Senegales universe of music. He has some 150 interpretations to his name, 70 of them his own compositions. "You" started in the theatre, first *Sine Dramatic*, then *Diamono*. After a time with the *Star Band* he founded *L'Etoile de Dakar* in 1976, which then was reformed into *Super Etoile*. His themes are taken from everyday life and African realities. He has received the Golden Record twice, in 1994 for *Seven Seconds* and in 1997 for *Anime*, and has invested the prize money in music, the food industry, fashion and the press. He is one of the millionaires in Senegalese society. In January 2001 he created a foundation, Youth Network for Development, which takes care of all non-commercial as-

---

1. Interview with Ousmane Sow Huchard March 13, 1999. *Dakar University Sextet* competed with *Super Star* of Dexter Johnson and *Star Band* of Ibra Kasse. It was the representative of the Cape Verdean bands to the Youth National Week in Senegal in 1967. See *Dakar Matin*, March 15, 1967. (The Cap-Vert region on the mainland was administratively part of Senegal, and is not to be confused with the Cape Verde islands under Portuguese rule.)
2. *The Sahel* (Pape Djiby Ba, Mbaye Fall, Seydina Wade, Idy Diop) released its first 33 rpm record in 1975, entitled *Bamba* in remembrance of the *murid* Muslim brotherhood founder.
3. Representative of this tendency were *Ouza et ses Ouzettes* in *Lat Dior* and *Weet or Nguewel* of Dakar in *Xaadim*.
4. Representative of those seeking inspiration from abroad are, among others, Idrissa Diop "Idy" (Dakar, 1949), drum player in the famous *Sahel* band in the seventies. He is increasingly looking for his own way and has refused to be confined into a local music trend. His multiple musical choices are in opposition to show-biz rules.
   Cheikh Tidiane Tall, (Dakar, 1946–), drummer and pianist, is interested in the blending of jazz music with instruments from throughout the world (*tama* or talking drum from Senegal, *m'vett* from Cameroon).
   Seydina Insa Wade (Dakar, 1948–), is a professional. He took part in the Dakar Festival of Arts in 1966 and introduced a new and controversial style in Senegal, the *folk*, that was performed in Wolof idioms and based on string instruments. His songs are backings on popular music (*Xandju*). He was the lead vocal of *Sahel* band in the seventies; then of *Xalam II* in the eighties. He also has a solo career (*Libaas*). Recently he has been accompanied by the French violin player Hélène Billard (*Wal Fadjri*, February 1, 1999:12).

pects of his activities, above all the provision of basic social services for young people.

Rap your Senegal: Urgent and urban words of a youth recomposing the nationalist memory (1988–)

The *hip-hop* movement started in Dakar in 1988, and its rise was related to the contested elections in February and the closing of the university.[1] Its background was the deterioration of the economy ever since the early 1970s. The demographic development of the cities had been spectacular, especially in Dakar, where 75 per cent of the people were under 30 years of age. Among these there were many who, without education, could not see how they could enter into the society of modernity.

Dakar had seen many periods with outbursts of uncontrolled violence, partly in reaction to the crisis of the political transition, partly in reaction to an erosion of political culture during times of economic crisis. In February 1988, in the midst of strikes, demonstrations and riots students and marginalised youth assembled in demonstrations against the symbols of power: buildings, government and public authority vehicles, buses, telephone boxes etc. One can interpret this as a counterattempt to redefine public space on the part of the suffering youth. Music assumes an important role in this redefinition.

There are today (in 2002) 3,000 rap groups in Senegal of which 2,500 are found in Dakar. In Senegal, the *hip hop* movement took ten years to free itself from American and French patterns. The *Senegalese Touch* lies in the specific use of idioms that are drawn from "the cultural soup" of the suburbs. The young rappers use French, Arabic, English, Wolof and other local languages to transform the words, and create a new lexicon which destabilises the conventional literary order.[2] On this basis their unique and spontaneous way of expression is formed somewhere between modern poetry and oral tradition (*tassou*).

Rap is above all a flow of loose words regardless of standard norms, whose main characteristic is the defiant attitude of the young towards political, economic, social and cultural institutions. The main features of this art are improvisation, rhythm and slogans. The measure of success is the efficiency of the message and its impact on the audience.

The historic fabric of rap is woven from cities and bears their characteristics. Today as more than ever, the main authors are the young because music is the mode of expressing their very identity. In a changing world where they are unemployed and deprived of wage earning opportunities, the young find in musical creation the possibility to inscribe themselves more positively in society. The young refuse to be oppressed and stifled. In order to be heard, the young appropriate a new way of protest that originated in the United States, namely in New York: rap. This new form of art is known as *hip hop*, a slang word meaning "to challenge oneself through words, paint and action". Rap is a manifest preaching of political messages on the daily urban hardships. It embodies the shout of city dwellers that are condemned to silence. The culture of the ghetto finds an echo where anxiety focuses on the same problems: unemployment, precariousness, violence, inequity of education, school failure, AIDS and drugs. Rap music enables the outcasts to communicate and claim their rights as well as to voice youth despair.

---

1. Diouf 1992, pp. 41–54.
2. As one example of the literary inventions, let us mention *dolécratie*, which emanates from Wolof *dolé*, "firce", and stands for exercising power through force.

One of Dakar's rap groups
with Iba, K.T., and Bibson.

What do these musical practices represent, particularly when young people are uniting in their common desire for *posse*, a word signifying 'close' to a rap group and
working for the success and the achievements of its projects.

Rap is deeply rooted in the same origins as those of the preacher. From the tale
teller to the praise singer of modern times, a kinship can be found in that this is a
kind of "oral literature" which takes place in "urban poetry". There is a rapport
between social message and awareness, between deeds and words. Most of rap is
deeply rooted in social reality. It illuminates the opposition between popular areas
and the state. Through its own techniques, rap reveals a peculiar strength in being
defiant to the "system". It appears as a mediator, that is to say, the one that rises
above or solves conflicts by first identifying the fields of conflict, the legal practices,
the state, media, as causes and consequences. It aims to restore dignity to those who
are socially marginalized.

The rapper is not interested in politics but his role is eminently political. In some
circumstances, rap represents the only vehicle for voicing the social claims of people
that are subject to exclusion and economic crisis. Through an increasing awareness,
it comes to question politics and challenges authorities.

Some tensions in the Senegalese rap movement

The female presence in the rap movement is not significant. In the United States,
France as well as in Senegal, little space is left to women, as witnessed by the small
number of female rap bands. Female rappers are confined to secondary roles as
members of the chorus or as dancers. Some personalities are emerging, however:
Sister Joyce (Ndeye Fatou Niang) *Pee Froiss* ex-chorist; *Sister Kaya* with a funk
style; *Sister Yaki* (Rokhaya Sow, 21 years old), and *Lady Chiki* from *Tim Ti Mol*;
Sister Mia (Ndeye Ami Ndiaye, 18 years old) from *Gëstu Bi*; *Sister Keisha* (Absa
Dème) from *Domou Djoloff*, who composed *La Banlieue Attack* with famous titles
such as *Silence* in which Keisha defends female rappers and *Lambi Golo* that de-

nounces rap bands waging war. Until now the rivalries of rap bands have not reached the fierce tension we find in New York or on the Pacific Coast (Los Angeles).

The first female rap band *Saf Sapali* formed in 1997 from Guediawaye suburbs did not last long. There is still in Dakar another female group from Grand-Yoff suburbs composed of three girls (Mina, Myriam, Oumy), *Alif*. The group is looking for its way in the universe of rap; its album, *Viktim*, was released in November 1998. The male dominant *hip hop* is an image of what is going on on the street where women are considered as saints or inferior people.

So far in Senegal, rap production has not been censored. The emergence of private radio stations since 1994 (*Sud Fm, Walf Fm, Dakar Fm, 7 Fm, Nostalgie*) encouraged the promotion of rap music. Potential sources of conflict arise from the rapper's mood but also the understanding that journalists and press agencies have of the movement. For instance, *Rap 'Adio*, a *hardcore* band from Medina accuses the press of being contemptuous. One can note that the major radio stations put their choice on clean and harmless rap played by *Positive Black Soul* (PBS) rather than *Wa BMG 44*[1] whose beat is overheated. Because of its revolting content, hardcore rap has, by and large, not been diffused on radio stations.

Like in many other rap movements one can find in Senegal a tension between underground rap and market-oriented rap. In ten years this has risen to become both an artistic and financial issue.[2] Rap music can make a big profit, partly due to sampling of old songs and rhythms. The same phenomenon is found in French rap which is divided into the *cool* (MC Solaar, Menelik, Alliance Ethnik, Les Sages Poètes de la Rue etc.) and the *wicked* (Suprême NTM, Ministère AMER, Démocrates D etc.). The productions of the latter are often censored or sued in court.[3]

Likewise we find two major trends in Senegalese rap—light rap versus rebellious. Some bands such as *PBS*, *Sunu Flavor*, *Jant Bi* work on a *soft* beat and complex sounds. The *Positive Black Soul* story starts in 1989. Didier Awadi (born in 1969) and Amadou Barry *Deug E Tee* (born in 1971) participated in a dance championship that gathered together young people from rival districts (*Syndicate* from Amitié II and *King MC* from Liberté VI). After enduring hard times, *PBS* met the French-Chadan rapper *MC Solaar* who enabled them to penetrate the European rap world with albums produced by the Island Records label. *PBS* is the head of the Senegalese rap movement and wants to be positive: "No racism, nor appeal to violence. *PBS* embodies positivity. We want to deliver messages since we are aware of hardships in which Senegalese are living".[4] They have released albums such as *Bagne Bagne Beug, Boul Falé, Salam, Dow Thiow, Revolution 2000*. Their productions denounce the hypocrisy of politics and the evils of society. *Daara J* (Lord Alaji Man, Faada Freddy, Ndongo D.) has got a style bordering on *hardcore* and *cool*.

Other groups such as *Da Brains, Wa BMG 44, Rap'Adio* play *hardcore rap*, less commercial and more defiant of the "system". As Rap'Adios says:

> Change after change, the rappers' discourse becomes softer and *hip hop* is no longer playing its role. Some are doing rap for business while others are doing everything except rap. As far as we are concerned, we reject this compromising attitude and set up as the champions of authentic rap which denounce injustice and speak for the voiceless.[5]

---

1. In this band we have *D.J. Oz* and rappers such as Nigga Lyrical Ceddo, Moctar le Cagoulard, Omar Ben Xatab and Babacar. The groups *Tous ensemble pour mieux réfléchir* (Together to Better Reflect) and *Wa BMG 44* have produced a tribute the Senegalese artillery soldiers who were fired in 1944 at Thiaroye, not far from Dakar. *Wa BMG 44* is a band from the underground and is opposed to sampling.
2. One of the first market-oriented rap bands was *Sunu Flavor*, whose members before they separated, were each leading a solo career. Other bands such as *PBS* do advertising for *Topic* paper business.
3. *Prose Combat*, No. 3, 1998.
4. *Dakar Soir*, No. 9, August 1997.

Rap'Adio is a group of young people (Iba, K.T. and Bibson) who wear cowls during their performance. The main features of this band lie in their aggressive pitch and harsh lyrics, in which the language is direct (see their albums *Ku Weet Xam Sa Bop* (One knows only oneself in solitude) and *Soldarumbe* (Streetsoldiers). *Rap'Adio* is a supporter of the Underground Cartel, a group of posse which declares that they are

> ... working to collect funds in order to help young Senegalese people to cope with necessities. The State does nothing to improve the conditions of living of poor classes. Its only purpose is to maintain this status for ever. It's high time to put an end to this situation.[1]

Conclusion

Cities and music are closely linked. In cities the realities are fragmented and in constant movement. One can observe various aesthetic and musical realities that are often spontaneous. In this essay we have reflected on how the everyday changes in the city since the colonial era have changed our vision, first by making possible the rise of a class of professional musicians, then by linking to oral culture in the cities through *mbalax*, and then through the importing and reforming of *rap*. Rap music has developed its own identity based on cross-sounds and idioms. In their oral expression, rappers object to the idiom prescribed by the first president, Leopold Senghor, by breaking syntax and meddling with grammar. Their songs are urban life scenes, contemporary tales that report social facts, raising problems, and calling for responses. This is where we stand today.

Foreign and local press

Dakar Matin

Dakar Soir

L'Info 7

Prose Combat

Wal Fadjri

References

Bender, Wolfgang, 1991, *Sweet Mother. Modern African Music.* Chicago: Chicago University Press.

Collins, Edward John, 1977, "Post-War Popular Band Music in West Africa", *African Arts* (London), Vol. X, No. 3, pp. 53–60.

Coplan, David, 1997, *In Township Tonight. Musique et théâtre dans les villes noires d'Afrique du Sud.* Paris: Karthala.

Diallo, Nafissatou, 1975, *De Tilène au Plateau. Une enfance dakaroise.* Dakar: NEA.

Diouf, Mamadou, 1992, "Fresques murales et écriture de l'histoire. Le Set-setal à Dakar", *Politique Africaine* (Paris), No. 46, pp. 41–54.

Duvignaud, Jacques, 1973, *Fêtes et Civilisations.* Genève. Weber.

Gondola, Didier, 1992, "Ata Ndele ... et l'indépendance vint: musique, jeunes et contestation politique dans les capitales congolaises", in D'Almeida Topor, Coquery-Vidrovitch, Goerg and Guitart (eds), *Les Jeunes en Afrique. La politique et la ville.* Paris: L'Harmattan.

---

5. *Rap'Adio*, interview in *L'Info 7*, October 17–18, 1998:3.
1. *L'Info 7*, op. cit.

—, 1997, "O Rio ma! Musique et guerre des sexes à Kinshasa, 1930–1990", *Revue Française d'Histoire d-Outre-Mer* (RFHOM) (Paris), tome 84, No. 314, pp. 51–81.

—, 1999, "Bisengo ya la joie. Fêtes, sociabilités et pouvoir dans les capitales congolaises", in Goerg (ed.), *Les trajectoires de la fête en Afrique noire urbaine*. Paris: Karthala.

Martin, Phyllis, 1996, *Leisure and Society in Colonial Brazzaville*. Cambridge: Cambridge University Press.

Ranger, Terence, 1975, *Dance and Society in Eastern Africa, 1890–1970. The Beni Ngoma*. Los Angeles: University of California Press.

Senghor, Leopold Sedar, 1964, *Liberté I. Négritude et Humanisme*. Paris: Seuil.

Waterman, Chris, 1990, *Jùjú. A Social History and Ethnography of an African Popular Music*. Chicago: Chicago University Press.

Sources

ANS (Archives Nationales du Sénégal), 21G 65 (17): *textes et principes relatifs aux mouvements, attoupements, manifestations et cortèges* (1848–1881).

Trait d'union, newsletter of French West Africa cultural centres, No. 1, December 1953–January 1954:45–46.

Ousmane Sow Huchard, leader of *Dakar Université Sextet* and after, *Wato Sita*. Interview, March 13, 1999 in Dakar, Senegal.

Oumar Ndiaye nicknamed Baraud (1927–2001), jazz saxophonist, founding member of *Dakar Star Jazz* (1949) and *Déménageurs* (1951). Interviews May 27 and October 30, 1997 in Dakar, Senegal.

Playing It "Loud and Straight"

Reggae, Zouglou, Mapouka and Youth Insubordination in Côte d'Ivoire

Simon Akindes

In hysterical, violent, and emotional scenes that took people by surprise, the Ivorian youth mourned the death of their idol Roger Fulgence Kassy, (RFK) from January 26 to January 29, 1989. For more than ten years RFK, as he was called, had hosted television shows such as *Tremplin, Première Chance, Nandjelet, Podium,* and *the RFK show* which had spellbound a large audience of teenagers and youngsters across the country. His shows provided young and promising artists, especially musicians with a golden opportunity to be known, and eventually, to find a producer. His effrontery in a society that valued obedience and submissiveness to elders and authority, his non-conformist "American" looks (blue jeans, tee-shirts, sneakers), his informal language and his identification with the youth who had lost their illusions about the official discourse and promises for the future shot him to stardom.

The youth reaction to his death through an aids-related ailment revealed three connected phenomena: the growing importance of television as a social phenomenon, the role of television-mediated music in youth culture, and the urgent need for the youth to "breathe" and express themselves.[1] Through the reappropriation of *reggae*, the re-invention of *zouglou* and the explosion of *mapouka* and new forms of local expression, popular music gradually became a voice for the voiceless and a mouth for the speechless, especially at a time when the myth of the "Ivorian miracle" was quickly crumbling.

RFK jumpstarted the career of many musicians, the most famous of whom was the reggae star Alpha Blondy, whose first release *Jah Glory* (1982) with its hit *Brigadier Sabari* was an instant success. The "RFK generation",[2] as they were later called, immediately embraced it, identifying with Blondy's unconventional, and sometimes anti-conformist manners, his critique of police abuses, and his Rastafarian mystique which re-ignited Bob Marley's legend.

The "RFK generation" used music, especially *reggae* and *zouglou,* in political conscientization and mobilization at key turning points of contemporary Ivorian political history:

- Firstly, it helped in the 1990 movement for the return to multiparty politics. From February to April 1990, students and other youth organizations, protesting their own living conditions, took to the streets to demand political freedom. Driven to the wall, Houphouët-Boigny had to reinstate multiparty politics, a constitutional provision he had ignored in practice since 1957. But the opposi-

---

1. Cf. Bailly 1995, pp. 26–28 who also says that the violent reaction expressed their anguish for the future, and showed that young people were capable of organizing themselves spontaneously.
2. Bailly 1995, p. 26.

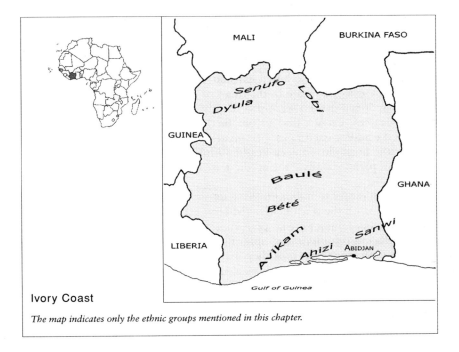

Ivory Coast

The map indicates only the ethnic groups mentioned in this chapter.

tion was still weak, and on October 28, 1990, Houphouët-Boigny was re-elected president.[1]

– Secondly, it contributed to the political demands that, in 1999, led to the overthrow of Henri Konan Bédié, the political heir and successor to Félix Houphouët-Boigny who died in 1993 after thirty-three years of authoritarian, conservative and pro-French presidency. As the president of the National Assembly, Bédié then became president of the country until the next election. Then, after multiparty elections in 1995, he was elected the country's president on Houphouët's party (Parti Démocratique de Côte d'Ivoire, PDCI) ticket. The coup in 1999 by Robert Gueï, ended the rule of the Parti Démocratique de Côte d'Ivoire (PDCI) and its wealthy elite.

– Thirdly, *reggae* and *zouglou* musicians turned against Gueï when he ran for the presidency on October 22, 2000 and prevented elections from being fairly organized.

Ivorian youth

The Ivorian youth are not a homogeneous and cohesive group that has acquired the political consciousness, organizational skills and vision needed to orchestrate fundamental changes. Many ethnic and partisan schisms have undermined their ranks. Organized in factions, students have killed each other in demonstrations. Many of those born in rich families belonging to the *bourgeoisie d'affaires*[2] [the political bourgeoisie] of Houphouët-Boigny are studying, living and working in Europe and

---

1. Bailly 1995, p. 24.
2. Amin 1967.

North America. For a long time the youth in general were mystified by the official discourse of peace and dialogue wrapped in a nationalistic sentiment that Côte d'Ivoire, unlike other African countries, had "taken off".

Zouglou and *reggae* musicians who, for the most part belong to dominated groups or classes, sing their bitterness and their frustrations with a system that promised them a bright future in the times of the so-called "Ivorian miracle" and suddenly abandoned them. Like Alpha Blondy, many are school dropouts, or when they have degrees, cannot find a job. In the track *Galère Nationale* [National Misery] on the audiocassette *Les Titrologues* (2000), the band Les Garagistes complain that "the unemployed pack neighbourhoods like refugees in their own country" and that, paradoxically, "the neediest are the farmers who are the pillars of the economy".

On their audiocassette *Les jumeaux s'amusent* released in 2001, the twin brothers Les Jumeaux, on the track *Galère* [Misery] ask God when the suffering will end and why so many families are so poor that they cannot feed themselves. *Ivoiriens grouilleurs* [Resourceful Ivorians] notes the changes occurring among young Ivorians who now accept menial jobs they used to shun—stevedores in harbours, yam pounders in restaurants, street shoeblacks. Now men compete against women for jobs they used to turn away from. On his 2001 maxi audiocassette *Peuple sacrifié* [Forsaken people] and in his title track of the same name, Fadal Day also gives the listeners a litany of the ills afflicting the youth: unemployment, growing pauperization, political manipulations, etc. According to him, the people are the hostages of politicians, laws are passed to serve the interests of the ruling class, and state institutions—army, supreme court, state media, national assembly [parliament], presidency—are their captives. The recurring dichotomy of we/they or us/them is not clearly spelled out in any song, but they/them often refers to the ruling bourgeoisie and its clientele, the rich, those who "live in mansions" and can "fly overseas as soon as trouble arises".

Themes such as political corruption of the political system are common. In 1999, Tiken Jah Fakoly released the CD *Mangercratie,* a word he coined and defined as "the power that allows all to eat in equality". In this song, he advises politicians to stop fooling and manipulating the Ivorian people because they "now understand it all".

He accuses politicians of starting a fire, activating it, and later, of pretending to extinguish it. The same metaphor is used by Fadal Day who affirms that "one does not extinguish a fire with a straw." Unlike Fela Anikulapo Kuti, the Nigerian musician who created Afrobeat and used to cite financial scandals and corrupt leaders openly in his songs, Ivorian musicians focus on morality and righteousness. For example, when Meiway, known for his *Zoblazo* series of CDs, released *Gbouniac*, a rap-styled track to denounce the upper classes who profit from poor people's hard labor, he carefully avoided mentioning names. He openly said that he was likely to be censored. On occasion, Alpha Blondy was bolder. On his CD *Elohim*, he defends journalists, particularly Norbert Zongo who was assassinated in Burkina Faso. When he was asked if he was not afraid, he stated that everything was in the hands of God.

Although a form of romanticism prevails in their treatment of the poor and the unemployed, a few tracks do criticize some aspects of their behavior. For instance, *Bilan 1: Pauvreté* by Espoir 2000 reproaches impoverished men for making their situation worse by having too many children, by drinking, by marrying more women, or by gambling in the French lottery.

Alpha Blondy

The music scene is gendered. Women are hardly present at all in socially committed genres such as *reggae* and *zouglou*. Female stars such as Chantal Taiba, Monique Séka, Joëlle Séka, Nayanka Bell, Aicha Koné, etc. tend to sing romantic compositions. Other women artists have, on occasion, deplored men's irresponsible behavior in their relationships with women.

Alienation typifies relationships between men and women in urban areas, and this is reflected in music. The malaise has many dimensions. First, the economic boom of the 1960s and 1970s gave rise to new social relationships in which materialistic values prevailed. Poor youngsters resented well-to-do men seducing their girlfriends, and the girls themselves for being lured by money. For instance, *Premier Gaou*, the continent-wide Ivorian success by Magic System, recounts the story of a young man who lost his girl friend as soon as he went broke. When he became a successful singer, she wanted to resume the relationship, but he refused arguing that "he who is fooled twice is a real fool." Such relatively common lyrics both reflect old machismo traditions and the corruption of social life and personal relationships.

National identity: Peculiarities, fractures and fissures

Côte d'Ivoire is made up of more than sixty ethnic groups with diverse social structures and particular political histories. They were brought together under an undemocratic, centralized, French colonial power that had militaristic/disciplinary tendencies. France forced its language, social and religious institutions on the country, and used divide-and-rule tactics to play ethnic and social groups against each other. The destruction of local economies and their subordination to French imperial needs have engineered a set of dislocations and dysfunctions handed down at independence in 1960.

Until the early 1990s, a ruling Baulé elite controlled the politics and resources of Côte d'Ivoire. The Baulé are the largest component of the Akan group in Côte d'Ivoire and they account for about 23 percent of the total Ivorian population. The first president, Félix Houphouët-Boigny, a Baulé himself, adroitly designed a political system that served a small class of landowners and industrialists, mostly from the Baulé subgroup. The one-party system and the economic boom known as the "Ivorian miracle" of the first twenty years, the official discourse of peace, dialogue, and stability as conditions for progress, as well as a combination of violent repression and political patronage[1] made it possible to establish a definition of national identity which served to safeguard the hegemony of the ruling Baulé elite.

Other critical issues contributed to the official configuration of the notion of national identity. These conflicts had often been quenched and explained as the result of alleged plots, manipulation of youth organizations, high unemployment and dropout rates, North/South divide, the emergence of social classes. The musicians dealing with the identity crisis took up many such issues, and found in Nouchi (Ivorian French, see below) the suitable language for their dissent.

Bloody conflicts

In his track *Conflit à l'Ouest* [Conflict in the West] released in early December 1999 on his album Jahsso (House of God) Fadal Day mentioned the conflict which has historically opposed the Bété and the Baulé. The Guéré and the Baulé also clashed in the late 1990s. The song implores them not to fight and not to listen to politicians.

The hostility between the Baulé and Bété predates independence. In 1959, Victor Biaka Boda, a Bété charismatic leader of the PDCI and an internal rival of Houphouët, a Baulé, was mysteriously assassinated.[2] The conflict between the Bété and the central government continued, and flared up in 1970 when Ivorian and French troops massacred entire Bété villages around the town of Gagnoa in the Midwestern region of Côte d'Ivoire. About 4,000 people were killed[3]. This area had become the stronghold of the opposition to the rule of Houphouët-Boigny and his PDCI party.

The massacre was the culmination of a ruthless hunt for Jean-Christophe Kragbé Gnagbé, a young leader who created a party and wanted to run for election according to the law of the Constitution. Kragbé Gnagbé disappeared, but his name which is obliterated in public discourse has reappeared in songs, for instance in *Les Martyrs* by Jah Tiken Fakoly, a reggae star.

Another conflict originated in a power struggle between Houphouët and the Agni King of the Sanwi region in the southwestern part of the country. In 1843, the Sanwi kingdom had signed a treaty with the French that made it a protectorate. Because they had come into contact with the French long before the ruling Baulé and employed the latter in their plantations, the Agni king had developed a superiority complex towards the Baulé. The Sanwi argued that the protectorate status gave them the right to be or not to be part of Côte d'Ivoire. They attempted to secede from Côte d'Ivoire after it joined the French Community in 1958, but the secessionist movement was brutally quelled in the late 1960s and caused 2,500 deaths.[4] Houphouët also alleged other plots in order to torture and eliminate his opponents. The case of Ernest Boka, who died in Assabou prison, is referred to in Tiken Jah Fakoly's *Les Martyrs*.

Such scars remain in the collective memory of people who can go to extremes when vengeance becomes the major or only form of dealing with the past as was the

---

1. See Fauré 1989; Diarra 1997.
2. Samba Diarra (1997, p. 34) believes the French plotted his murder, mistaking him for Houphouët.
3. Diarra 1997, p. 219.
4. Diarra 1997, pp. 48–54.

case in Algeria, former Yugoslavia, Burundi or Rwanda. They sometimes constitute demarcating lines for self-definition and subject positioning. Ivorian urban popular music has resuscitated the conflicts, not to generate more strife but rather to remember as a necessity for collective memory, and to forgive.

The North/South divide

After Houphouët's death in 1993, a rift emerged between the "Muslim" North and the "Christian" South.[1] The conflict crystallized around the struggle for succession. There were two candidates. On the one hand, there was Bédié, the President of the National Assembly (Parliament) and a Catholic Baulé Southerner. On the other hand, there was Allassane Dramane Ouattara (Ouattara), the Prime Minister and a Muslim Dyula Northerner, who had been the Prime Minister for three years, but who was now the leader of the Rassemblement Des Républicains (RDR), a party created by dissidents of the PDCI in September 1994. Northern ethnic groups—mainly the Sēnufos, Lobi and Dyula—felt that they had not had enough influence and power in the political process for 33 years, were deprived of the spoils of the rentier economy, and had seen few development projects implemented in their regions.[2] They also complained of state contempt towards Islam—the largest religion. In reality, Christianity, and especially Catholicism had, since colonial times, been the "natural ally of political power"[3] and was the quasi-official religion of the state.

Northerners thought Ouattara could bring about a regional power balance in the ruling class, until then primarily composed of *planteurs* (plantation owners), the political class, the *bourgeoisie d'affaires*, and industrialists from the larger Akan group. The Akan account for about 42 per cent of the total population of the country and can be found especially in the southeastern regions, although many have settled in other regions of Côte d'Ivoire as plantation owners. Aside from the Baulé majority, the Akan include the Agni, the Aburé, the Abidji, Ahizi, Appollo and others. They also extend to Ghana where they include the Asante.

Disparities between the North and the South exist in many West African countries. They result from colonial neglect of non-coastal or mineral-poor areas. Missionaries and *colons* established their schools and administrative offices in the South, near the coast. Therefore, the educated elite—mainly Southerners—developed a complex of superiority vis-à-vis the Northerners, who had actually adopted Islam centuries before Christian penetration. After independence, the Southerners who inherited power from European colonizers, not only refused to address the internal inequalities engendered by the *colons*, but they deepened them. As a consequence, the state became another hegemonic institution rewarding only those affiliated with it ethnically, regionally, and through class, or those docile towards it.

In 1996, Alpha Blondy started chastising the PDCI leadership who accused him of being an ethnicist because he disapproved of the witch-hunt taking place against Northerners and opposition leaders. In *Guerre Civile* [Civil War], he warns that one ethnic group's monopoly of power can lead to a civil war, even if such control were achieved through elections—an allusion to Bédié's rule.[4]

---

1. In fact, the religious lines are not so clear-cut. Many people in the South are Christians and many Christians also inhabit the North. In addition, a large number of Muslims and Christians have in common the practice of African religions. To learn more about the North/South conflict, see Tiémoko, 1995, pp. 143–50.
2. Tiémoko 1995.
3. Akindès December 2000.
4. Earlier, Alpha Blondy had openly supported Houphouët-Boigny in his tracks *Multipartisme, Jah Houphouët, Les chiens aboient* released on the CD *Masada* in 1992.

The class factor

In *Cabri Mort* [Dead Goat] Serges Kassy illustrated the class divide in terms of "we" to refer to the poor, and "they" to designate the rich:

> A dead goat does not fear a knife
> Yeah, a dead goat does not fear a knife
>
> They say they are our gods, never mind them,
> They say they are our masters, never mind them,
> They think they have built this world, never mind them.
>
> Just because they ride Mercedeses
> Just because they ride Nissan Patrols
> Just because they have Swiss bank accounts
> Just because they are wealthy
>
> But what do we care!
> We don't give a rap!
> What do we care!
> We eat, we drink, we sleep, and we don't give a rap![1]

Poverty and inequalities have increased since the late 1980s and have sharpened class divisions.[2] The number of unemployed and urban poor is on the rise, and the informal sector has expanded.

In Côte d'Ivoire, ethnicity and social class interface with state control to engender exclusions. Therefore, patterns of cultural consumption, though divergent, crisscross from one group or class to the other. *Zouglou*, *reggae* and *mapouka* are consumed by people of all classes, despite the tendency for the educated upper middle-class elite not to embrace them.

The slow revenge of "Ivorian French"

Under Houphouët-Boigny's rule, many artists sang his praises for career safety, out of prudence, or for presidential monetary gifts "generously" distributed in a culture of corruption and obedience. None of them went publicly against the grain.

The democratic movement ushered in a more critical and rebellious line. This has strengthened the use of "Ivorian French", or Nouchi. It is a language, developed as a medium of communication among illiterate labourers, house servants, shop attendants, and other low-rank workers with little or no formal education, and people originating from Burkina Faso. Currently, it has grown into an urban language nationwide that does not abide by the rules of French grammar, and it incorporates words, sentence structures, images, and forms of expression from local languages. More and more popular songs, plays and comedies, written by literate and illiterate artists alike, use Nouchi for its spontaneity and to reach larger audiences. The whole process, in a sense, could be interpreted as revenge on that idea of high culture, which attaches a primary importance to French ways of thinking and doing things.

---

1. The translation of this and other quoted songs is by the author. The original in French or "Ivorian" French: "Cabri mort n'a pas peur de couteau/Cabri mort n'a pas peur de couteau, yeah!//Laissez-les, ils disent qu'ils sont nos dieux/Laissez-les, ils disent qu'ils sont nos maîtres/Laissez-les, ils disent qu'ils ont construit ce monde/ /Cabri mort n'a pas peur de couteau/Cabri mort n'a pas peur de couteau, yeah!//Parce qu'ils roulent en Mercedes/Parce qu'ils roulent en Patrol/Parce qu'ils ont des comptes en Suisse/Parce qu'ils sont riches/Mais nous on s'en fout/Mais nous on s'en yangne/Mais nous on s'en fout/On mange , on boit, on dort, on s'en yangne." Kassy Audiocasette *Cabri Mort* 1992.
2. Sindzingre 2000, pp. 24–37; Akindès June 2000, pp. 128–35.

Nouchi has been pejoratively called *Français de Moussa* [Moussa's French]. "Moussa" was used to designate the uneducated Burkinabe laborer because it is a common name among Muslim Northerners in general. *Français de Moussa* pejoratively meant "the type of French spoken by uneducated Burkinabe".

Ivorian culture, ethnicity and *Ivoirité*

Throughout their rule, the PDCI had proclaimed their desire to consciously create an "Ivorian culture," and a new "Ivorian man." When Bédié succeeded Houphouët in 1993, he gave the same ideal a new twist by promoting the "Ivorian cultural personality." He termed it Ivoirité [Ivorianness] and conceptualized it as being a hybrid culture, made of foreign positive influences and national cultural values. As a journalist of the government-owned daily expounded, the notion of *Ivoirité*:

> ... is shaped by tradition and modernity. Culture must be promoted in the sense of *Ivoirité* whose objective is to create a new Ivorian citizen who has a very sharp national consciousness, i.e. who is proud of being Ivorian at all times, everywhere, on every occasion and in every undertaking.[1]

In this arbitrary PDCI conceptualization of Ivorian culture, folklore, traditional dances, rituals, ceremonies, are promoted, but only as long as they sustain the structure of power and economic relations. The notion of *Ivoirité* was given a more intellectual orientation when scholars, officially gathered in a research group meant to promote President Bédié's actions and ideas and known as CURDIPHE, published an official document about the meaning of Ivoirité.[2] This document was largely regarded as an ethnonationalist manifesto for the Akan group and against Northerners.

The idea that music should reinforce local values, contribute to nation-building around a new Ivorian person, with roots in the past and embracing modernity, already existed in music, even in the times of RFK. Many were eager to see the emergence of an Ivorian music based on local traditions, and rivaling *soukouss* from the Congos and *makossa* from Cameroon, the best selling and most popular musical genres in Central, West and East Africa in the 1980s. Côte d'Ivoire, as an economic success in the region, needed the music that would fit its reputation and satisfy the nationalistic ego. This artificial project did not bear fruit. After the late 1980s, Ivorian music spontaneously came into existence with new sounds.

As in many African countries, the political elite in Côte d'Ivoire has refused to take into account the identities and differences that make up their society and has undemocratically attempted to create a nation-state without a critical reappraisal and reformation of the foundations of pre-colonial political systems and of the colonial state. The effort to create a national identity by all means necessary is a continuation of the colonial project, which posited the nation-state as the only form of modern political organization. Furthermore, it negates the fact that identities are created and reshaped within relations of power and domination, while it attempts to melt everybody into a hypothetical, problematic and one-dimensional national identity. The post-colonial discourse, which is expressed in the new music, has a different dimension. Giroux describes it as

---

1. Man Jusu 1996, p. 12.
2. Dozon First Quarter 2000, and June 2000, offer insightful analyses of the Ivoirité concept, its political purposes and the intellectual framework in which it was developed.

Photo: Bugs Steffen

Tiken Jah Fakoly

... a space in which to retheorize, locate, and address the possibilities for a new politics based on the construction of new identities, zones of cultural difference, and forms of ethical address that allow cultural workers and educators alike to transform the languages, social practices, and histories that are part of the colonial inheritance. This position offers a new hope for expanding both the practice of cultural work and the liberating possibilities of crossing borders that open up new political and pedagogical possibilities.[1]

This is exactly what the Ivorian youth has been doing since 1990—opening up spaces for themselves and for the voiceless, the powerless, and legitimately occupying a non-subaltern position in a new political dispensation as African rappers in France and the United States are also trying to do.[2]

The concept of Ivoirité almost split the country in the late 1990s and has been a recurrent theme in all styles of Ivorian music. In *Le descendant* [The descendant], a track released on the album *Mangercratie* (1999), Tiken Jah Fakoly, the reggae musician from the Northern town of Odienné, traces his origins seven or eight generations back, to a time when present day Côte d'Ivoire did not exist. Other reggae musicians such as Ismaël Isaac, Issa Sanogo, Hamed Farras have referred to it. Many *zouglou/logobi* bands (Espoir 2000, Petit Yodé et l'Enfant Siro, Fitini, etc.) have treated the theme with the humor that characterises the genre.

On his CD *Nationalité* [Nationality], Tiken Jah Fakoly traces the migration paths of various ethnic groups, and identifies the period when they settled in the present territory of Côte d'Ivoire. Being himself a Dyula from the northern town of Odienné, and from a group generally accused of being recent foreign immigrants, he responded to the historical distortions that give some Ivorians of Akan descent the right to believe that they are more Ivorian than others.

In a track entitled *Plus Jamais Ça* [Never That Again] Tiken Jah Fakoly, nicknamed "the history professor" complains that "when it [the folly] all begins and when you change sides, you immediately become Liberian or Ghanaian or they simply call you Burkinabe". He refers to political opponents who are prevented from exercising their citizens' rights because of alleged "foreign" origins. He forcefully indicates that "he does not know where he is going", but knows "where he comes

---

1. Giroux 1992, p. 28.
2. Warne 1997.

from". While recognizing that within the same ethnic group people have different lineages, he admits that at the level of the country, people have different origins (Mali, Guinea, Ghana, Burkina). Even Ismaël Isaac, a reggae singer who has often avoided political controversy, criticizes the expensive residence permits foreigners are obliged to carry in his track *Carte de Séjour* [Residence Permit].

The tracks questioning official "Ivoirité" discourse with its different attributes: "centuries-old", "100 percent", "full-blooded", "authentic", "questionable Ivorians" etc., signal a national identity crisis, where musicians express both the anguish and the options open to them. Most of their tracks advocate peace and harmony, and stress unity, responsibility and stability rather than physical resistance, rebellion and confrontation.

Relocalising reggae

In 1980, Bob Marley was invited to perform in Zimbabwe at its Independence Day celebration. In South Africa, the liberation struggle was intensifying. Marley had often sung of African unity and rebellion against *Babylon*, a term used by Rastafarians for Western European and North American capitalism.

The Ivorian youth, stifled by an authoritarian government echoed the liberation message of reggae. When, in 1982, Alpha Blondy released *Jah Glory* his first album, he immediately became a national star, and gave reggae both a new "home" and a new life. Alpha Blondy created his own mystique around symbols of Rastafarianism: dreadlocks, marijuana, red, green and gold, walking stick, the Bible (even though he was Muslim). He sang exclusively in Dyula, French and English about Jah (God for the Rastafarians), peace, love, brotherhood, and hope for the oppressed, which are reggae favorite themes.

In terms of musical style, Alpha Blondy and most other Ivorian reggae artists have remained close to "roots reggae", which is described by Hebdige:

> The first thing you hear when listening to reggae is the jagged, 'chikka-chikka' guitar rhythm (sometimes called the chicken-scratch) which seems to cut against the hypnotic, grumbling bass.[1]

Depending on the artists, the bass can be more or less punctuated and heavy, or as with Marley, the melodies can be fluid and smooth. Drumming, as one of its core elements, has been largely influenced by Rastafarian drumming, a style close to West African traditions. Ivorian musicians have taken very few liberties regarding spirit and form, although their tempo is often a little faster.

Ivorian reggae played a mobilizing role in the return to multiparty politics in 1990 under Houphouët-Boigny, and in the December 1999 coup that toppled Bédié and put an end to the rule of the PDCI and its wealthy elite. In 1990, Serges Kassy, a young reggae musician close to the Front Populaire Ivoirien (FPI) and the illegal student movement Fédération Estudiantine et Scolaire de Côte d'Ivoire (FESCI), released *C'est pas daniblo* [This is no boasting]. It mentioned an unnamed individual who always boasted that he had everything under control, but who was now "was barking like a dog that had seen something dangerous/ominous," or, "like a fish", which "had jumped out of the river because its bed was too hot". Everybody knew he was alluding to Houphouët, and metaphorically implied that he could no longer stop the popular movement for democracy. Serges Kassy openly supported the street

---

1. Hebdige 1990, p. 45.

demonstrations. Such an audacious form of commitment marked the beginning of a new role for Ivorian popular music.

In 1999, Fadal Day's track *Kpêkpêro nous a bri* [The little guy robbed us] from his audiocassette *Jahsso* foretold the fall of Bédié's government, which came about through a bloodless coup by young military officers only a few weeks after the release of the album. Its chorus reads:

> Because everyone said no to your yes, and yes to your no
> Because everyone said yes, yes to your isolated no
> We here, God willing, God willing, we will bring you down
>
> Not through violence, but in love, in brotherhood, and through dialogue
> You can impose anything on a people, but you cannot buy a people's love.[1]

In the same track Fadal Day asks his listeners a question central to the understanding of citizenry in a democratic society. He disagrees that young men should be called upon to defend the country while they are not given the rights to vote and participate in decision-making. Fadal poses here a crucial question: If the youth are part of the nation, if it is their nation, do they not therefore have a right to participate in every decision-making process? He is essentially indicating that the youth's social consciousness is rising, and that they will not continue to obey and serve a government that fools them.

In 2000, Alpha Blondy released *Elohim*, an eclectic CD, mixing up rock and rhythm and blues, but still dominated by reggae. The track *Dictature* [Dictatorship] explicitly criticizes Ivorian politics, without naming it.[2] Alpha Blondy warns:[3]

> Divide and rule
> Divide to better dupe us
> Divide and rule
> Divide to better rob us ...
>
> Xenophobic totalitarianism
> Will breed adversity
> With its corollary of widespread anger
> All of the cruelty of the city

The Bédié government banned these tracks by Fadal Day and Alpha Blondy. When the government was overthrown on December 24, 1999, these reggae songs were aired on many radio stations, especially on Radio Nostalgie, the station from which Gueï made his broadcast to the nation, just after the coup. Later, soldiers met with some artists and visited Alpha Blondy in his house thanking the singers for their role in raising people's consciousness. Before the coup, Radio Nostalgie aired some of the banned tracks in defiance of the PDCI and its government, which made many speculate that musicians may have played a role in preparing the coup.[4]

---

1. Fadal Day, *Jahsso* 1999. Original in Ivorian French (Nouchi): Parce que tout le monde a dit non, non à ton oui/Parce que tout le monde a dit oui, oui à ton non/Mais nous-là, Inch'Allah, Inch'Allah, on va te dépo/Pas dans la violence, mais dans l'amour, dans la fraternité, et par le dialogue/On peut imposer tout à un peuple, mais on ne peut pas acheter l'amour du peuple /
2. Before the release of the CD, tracks were aired for promotional purposes. The tracks of the CD were already known to the public and to the government. In an interview given to the magazine *Top Visages*, the week before the coup, he explained why the album was made and released at that particular time. Cf. Camara 1999; Bagnon, 1999.
3. Alpha Blondy 2000, CD *Elohim*. French original: "Diviser pour régner /Diviser pour mieux nous entuber /Diviser pour régner /Diviser pour mieux nous arnaquer /Le totalitarisme xénophobe mènera à l'adversité/Avec son corollaire de colère généralisée /Toutes les atrocités dans la cité."
4. Fellows 2000.

Since most Ivorian reggae musicians, with the exception of a few such as Serges Kassy, are from the North and often sing in Dyula, one may be tempted to think that reggae has become the music of Dyula youth. In reality, other explanations make more sense. First, most reggae musicians try to emulate Alpha Blondy who, as a pioneer, was from the North and became a model for urban youth, and the history of reggae in Côte d'Ivoire cannot be dissociated from his mark and personality. Second, many of the singers have had the experience of Abidjan popular neighborhoods where the most widely used languages are Dyula and Nouchi. Reggae, and later rap, continue to be used for political critique. When Meiway, the famous Ivorian singer sings about political corruption as in *Le gbouniac* and *Le choix du peuple*, he uses reggae and rap.

At this juncture, one can note that the music of the African Diaspora in the Americas (calypso, rhythm and Blues, Jazz, Afro-Cuban rhythms, samba, zouk, etc.) has always resonated well in Côte d'Ivoire, and in Africa in general, partly because of big corporations' ability to market, distribute and sell it, but more importantly, because Africans, African Americans (including the Caribbeans and South Americans) share similar cultural patterns and values, and common experiences of colonialism, racial discrimination and other forms of exclusion and marginalization. Because of the nature of its lyrics and its resistance character, reggae's appeal has always had a strong impact on identity formation and political consciousness. This appeal also exists among the African Diaspora in Europe and the Americas. For instance, in Brazil, Olodum, the popular *bloco afro*—carnival performing group—from Salvador, Brazil, created a black movement whose band fuses reggae, samba and other African rhythms to create samba-reggae, an original percussive sound famous in Brazil. Olodum's lyrics emphasize the necessity for Brazilians to take pride in African identity and to resist political oppression. As Tenaille points out:

> While other imported musical genres—Cuban, rhythm and blues, rock, jazz, and possibly *chanson française*—have had important stylistic and orchestral influences, reggae had an impact in another area, that of identity.[1]

Since the early 1980s, the same messages are also conveyed through rap which has become a medium for protest for the youth across Africa.[2] As was the case with Fela Anikulapo Kuti of Nigeria, Alpha Blondy and many others, African artists rediscover their continent and a new sense of identity through their contacts with the descendants of former slaves. Such (re)connections often occur spontaneously at the grassroots level as very few official exchange programs exist. Nevertheless, music flows are often one-directional, from North America and Europe to Africa. For example, while hundreds of rap bands hive off the African continent, the average North American has no clue that rap bands exist in Africa and has no knowledge of other African genres, except for those which filter through the carryall category of World Music.

Zouglou: From the Abidjan campus to the African stage

Zouglou, drawn from the Baulé expression *O ti lê Zouglou* which means "dumped together like trash" designates both an urban musical genre and its accompanying dance created in the early 1990s in the midst of students' protests for political freedom. A few university students living in Yopougon, a popular neighborhood of

---

1. Tenaille 2000, p. 175.
2. See Servant 2001; Aby November 5, 1997; Cannon 1997, pp. 150–68.

Abidjan, used to get together to provide "ambiance" or "animation" for social events, using traditional percussive styles, especially the Bété sound of *alloucou*. Their groups soon grew into bands that put their frustration and anger, but also their *joie de vivre*, into a more elaborate form soon known as *zouglou*. *Zouglou* also borrowed from Congolese guitar riffs, and ways of talking and "shouting".[1]

This musical experiment had a triple function. It told the nation what the students' life was all about, it exposed the corruption of politics and everyday life (love, personal and family relationships, etc.), and it helped the youth cope with the future. *Zouglou* quickly positioned itself as the music of the disillusioned youth and the unemployed who could now tell overtly, honestly and in a straightforward manner, their stories and those of their villages and communities: pauperization, lack of political freedom, elitist nature of education, high failure and dropout rates, corruption, burden of traditional family structures.

In a particularly interesting *zouglou* track *Sans papiers* [Undocumented aliens], the artists Les Salopards travel quickly from pre-colonial times to a recent forced repatriation incident of Malians from France. They sing that although "black people did not kill Jesus they still have all the problems of this world", and deplore that in the French language, the adjective "noir", [black] is used to designate everything that is bad. They continue asserting that in pre-colonial times, "our ancestors had a good life and no problems", before the arrival of the intruders "one morning at 6 a.m. to disturb us". However, they remark that "they [the ancestors] were so stupid", and "would give away the whole village in exchange for a mirror". The lyrics continue:

> ... blacks were taken into slavery to build their country. Today, they [the whites] say that we disturb them, and they have created all kinds of obstacles to prevent us from going to their country.[2]

Then they point to the unequal conditions of travel, and go on to recount the incident of Malians who were deported back home and who, on their arrival, beat the French police officers who had escorted them. Other tracks, in *zouglou* and other genres, mention how life is hard in France where racism still exists. Colonization and its effects are still present in everyday life. Popular music, in its current form and content, is part of the process of mental decolonization still taking place.

The dance of *zouglou* echoes the percussive style of the genre in that the gestures, moves and steps are fast and jerky. They metaphorically represent the rebellious nature of the genre itself and the "unclean, garbage-like" living conditions of the urban poor and students.

Another characteristic of *zouglou* is its language. Most bands use a mix of Nouchi (see above) and local languages, which gives the genre an anti-conformist and close-to-the-common-person appeal. It took *zouglou* about a decade to accomplish what *polihet*, *lekiné*, *zaouli*, *ziglibity* and other musical genres had unsuccessfully tried to achieve, that is to create a musical genre based on local rhythms the Ivorian youth would identify with, and sell it internationally. *Zouglou*'s glorious hour came when Magic System's audiocassette *Premier Gaou* swept the African continent in 2000.

Nevertheless, not everyone approved of the genre with its open social and political criticism, and its crude and sometimes insolent language. Abissiri, who had earlier claimed that reggae gave a deadly blow to the identity quest of Ivorian music

---

1. Throughout the 1980s, Congolese music, and to a lesser extent *makossa*, have had a tremendous influence on Ivorian popular music. Abidjan was always hosting concerts by major Congolese musicians and singers, many of whom had lived there.
2. Les Salopards 1998, *Génération sacrifiée*.

asserting the latter should be pure and authentic,[1] now blasted that *zouglou* was a suspect genre which did not deserve to be called music, and should not be exported because of its use of vulgar local expressions. In his opinion, *zouglou*, a musical genre without any "real musical baggage" promotes drinking, sexual promiscuity, misogyny, does not use correct French, and as a consequence does not elevate.[2] Such attacks, directed at different times and places at reggae, rap and hip hop, often reflect the ambivalence of such genres and why large segments of the upper classes do not accept them.

Zouglou did establish itself without being forced onto the nation, and even Abissiri notes its popularity. He wonders why the Ivorian people lack a taste for poetical lyrics and love perversity. He writes that exposing the ills of the society is laudable and noble, but cannot be an excuse for vulgar language. Abissiri is stuck here in a mode of governing and discourse that encouraged various forms of paternalism and implied that one should beg for one's rights and wait for leaders' or elders' magnanimity. The youth had rejected such practices. As Espoir 2000, another famous *zouglou* band warn in their track *Bilan 2: Abidjan*:

> Instead of jobs, we have layoffs
> Stop training us, or else we shall show our muscle
> Watch out, because when there is a fight,
> We know its beginning but we do not know its end...
> We were full of hope, the millennium changed
> We trusted God, now we trust you
> Allow us to eat, at least bones
> Look below, we are dying[3]

To compose a *zouglou* piece, all that was needed was a synthesizer or a drum machine, local drums, a few other instruments, a good storyteller/singer, and a story relevant to people's lives. Abissiri's only satisfaction was that the youth turned to *zouglou* in displeasure with the multiplicity of foreign rhythms—*highlife, makossa, rock'n roll, soukouss, ndombolo*—that the cosmopolitan Côte d'Ivoire had experienced at different times.[4] Yet the appeal of *zouglou* locally and internationally derives from what Abissiri disliked: the crudeness and humour in the language, its social critique stance, and its upbeat percussive rhythms.[5]

Mapouka: A controversial music and dance

Mapouka designates both a traditional rhythm and a dance style that originate in the southwestern coastal region of Côte d'Ivoire, among the Ahizi, Alladian and Avikam ethnic groups. It is based on strong, steady and fast percussive rhythms. It hit the musical and dance scene in 1997, and, after a televised show by the band *Génération Mot à Mot*, it was banned from national television by Bédié's government for being sexually perverted, lewd and obscene.[6] The ban remained in effect

---

1. Abissiri 22 July 1997.
2. Abissiri 15 October 1997.
3. Espoir 2000, audiocassette *Le Bilan*. Original words: "A la place des emplois, c'est que des licenciements Arrêtez de nous former, sinon on sera muscle/Faites très attention, parce que palabre qui est là/On sait quand ça commence , on ne sait pas quand ça finit .../On a trop espéré, les millénaires ont changé/On a compté sur Dieu, aujourd'hui on compte sur vous/Laissez-nous manger, même si c'est les os/Regardez en bas, on est en train de mourir."
4. Abissiri 22 July 1997.
5. Writing about the success of *Zouglou* music in Cameroon, Sibatcheu notes that the Cameroonian audiences love Ivorian music because it recounts, with humour, everyday life scenes one experiences in any African city. Cf. Sibatcheu, 2001.
6. Onishi 2000, section 1, page 4, column 3.

until the new president after the 1999 coup, Robert Gueï, lifted it in December 1999, to the pleasure of many, especially young Ivorians. Onishi describes its success and its controversy as follows:

> Banned from Ivorian television—chased away by officials in neighboring countries like Togo, Niger, Burkina Faso and Benin—*mapouka* spread nevertheless along the West African coast, from Dakar to Kinshasa, in the last couple of years. The dance—which focuses on, though is not limited to, the surprisingly difficult act of wiggling one's buttocks without moving one's hips—also became an endless source of discussions and newspaper ruminations on culture, sex, women and men, especially here in Côte d'Ivoire.[1]

There have been extreme shows of *mapouka* in night clubs, and videotapes with women almost naked dancing *mapouka* are sold at home and abroad as pornographic materials. However, in its original form, *mapouka* is a dance whose integrity villagers and bands try to maintain. For example, in September 1999, Nigui-Saff K-Dance won the award for the best traditional music at Kora '99, the annual African Music awards ceremony in South Africa.

Mapouka is part of what it means to be Ivorian; it is part of the heritage of the country, even if it shocks. The controversy about it exemplifies the prevailing class, generational and religious tensions, and their moral underpinnings. Dances such as Senegalese *ventilateur*, or Congolese *ndombolo* or its Cameroonian version *zingué* (banned with *mapouka* from Cameroonian television) have caused controversies. However, they have not had as much intensity as *mapouka* with its various dimensions. *Mapouka* could be interpreted as the reaffirmation of local aesthetics that does not show preference for slim women. With the Euro-American beauty pageant globalizing the planet, the concept of a beautiful woman—skinny, blonde, proportionately balanced—is being standardized and promoted across nations. Côte d'Ivoire has its own "Ivorian" woman beauty contest called *Awoulaba* which started in the early 1980s, and despite the problematic nature of attempting to define what an "Ivorian" woman should look like, the *Awoulaba* contest provides an alternative. With *mapouka*, women reclaim the ownership of their bodies that they do not want to see regulated from outside, by males or by a dominant group.

Mapouka is also a reaffirmation of the functionality of traditional dancing for which shaking one's hips and bottom is neither immoral nor vulgar, as people with puritan Christian values would claim. The lyrics of *mapouka* tracks are in Nouchi too, but are not socially or politically as charged as *zouglou* and *reggae*. However, the controversy that surrounds it is part of the democratization of public life.

Zouglou and *mapouka* make an extensive use of percussive instruments. With the exception of reggae, they make use of synthesizers and basic instruments like a lead guitar, a bass guitar. They use little piano and, occasionally, wind instruments. This reflects the nature of the Ivorian musical culture. Since independence, very few resources have been devoted to the promotion of music in schools or to musical training. The infrastructure is lacking, and, consequently, it is rather complicated for musicians to find the resources and producers they need. When they overcome those obstacles, despite their urgent need to "exist" "talk" and be creative, there is an absolute survival need to live off their art. Unfortunately, they do not fully benefit from their work because copyrights can hardly be enforced, and because of malpractices by record companies such as reporting to the artist fewer CDs than were actually sold.[2]

1. Onishi 2000, ibid.
2. Sangaré 2000.

Concluding remarks

Zouglou and *reggae* have the potential, like rap—a diasporic style extensively practiced in Côte d'Ivoire—of making the youth, the poor and the voiceless visible and heard. For a long time, the urban youth were muted and prevented from discovering, expressing and forging their own identity because of social traditions of respect for age, combined with a culture of silence, acquiescence and obedience cultivated by the French administration, local kingdoms and chiefdoms, as well as repressive political structures institutionalized after independence. They were unable to engage a public dialogue with their own people, especially the urban and rural poor. As both the genres and the lyrics exemplify, youth identity has no clear shape and contour. It is a confluence of colonial, neocolonial, and diasporic identities that merge with residual traditions and power relations. Through the adoption/relocalization of reggae and other diasporic forms such as Zouk, the re-invention of *zouglou*, the new directions of *mapouka* and other local rhythms and dances, the uninhibited use/mix of Nouchi, local languages and French, the use of hip hop and rap and Afro-Cuban sounds, the urban youth are forging ahead with an identity more composite than before.

By using local humor and indigenous ways of telling stories, Ivorian popular music has embarked upon rewriting the people's history of the country in all its dimensions and in accessible language. The youth, still divided and thrown into disarray by their difficulties and frustrations have moved away from griot-like subservience, obedience, and indifference to agency, claiming their rightful place in the never-ending movement of identity construction, of carving out new ways of being and struggle, and of making history.

Discography

Alpha Blondy, 1992, *Masada* [CD]. Paris, France: Pathé Marconi.

Alpha Blondy, 1998, *Yitzak Rabin* [CD]. Abidjan, Côte d'Ivoire: Alpha Productions.

Alpha Blondy, 2000, *Elohim* [CD]. Abidjan, Côte d'Ivoire: Alpha Productions.

Compilations: Ivoir' Compil, 2000, *Le meilleur de la musique ivoirienne: Spécial an 2000.* [CD], Vol. 4. Paris, France: Production Ivoir'.

Espoir 2000, 2000, *Le Bilan: 2* [Audiocassette]. Abidjan, Côte d'Ivoire: Jat Music.

Fadal Day, 2001, *Peuple sacrifié* [Audiocassette]. Abidjan, Côte d'Ivoire: Jat Music.

Fadal Day, December 1999, *Jahsso* [Audiocassette]. Abidjan, Côte d'Ivoire: Jat Music.

Fitini, 2001, *TouT MignoN* [Audiocassette]. Direct Digital Recording.

Hamed Farras, 2001, *Transition* [Audiocassette]. Abidjan, Côte d'Ivoire: Jat Music.

Ismaël Isaac, 2001), *Black system* [Audiocassette]. Paris, France: Syllart Productions.

Issa Sanogo, 2000, *Gbangban Acte 2 d'avril* [Audiocassette]. Abidjan, Côte d'Ivoire: Showbiz.

Les Garagistes, 2000, *Titrologues* [Audiocassette]. Abidjan, Côte d'Ivoire: Showbiz.

Les hits du Mapouka, 2000, (Compilations, CD) Paris: David Monsoh and Kid Touré.

Les Jumeaux, 2001, *Les jumeaux s'amusent* [Audiocassette]. Abidjan, Côte d'Ivoire: Showbiz.

Les Salopards, 1998, *Génération sacrifiée* [CD]. Paris: Sonodisc.

Magic System, 2000, *Premier Gaou* [Audiocassette]. Abidjan, Côte d'Ivoire: Showbiz.

Magic System, 2001, *Poisson d'avril* [Audiocassette]. Abidjan, Côte d'Ivoire: Showbiz.

Meiway and Zo Gang International, 2000, *Le Procès* [CD]. Paris, France: JPS Productions.

Petit Yodé et l'Enfant Siro, 2000, *Victoire* [Audiocassette]. Abidjan, Côte d'Ivoire: Jat Music.

Serges Kassy, 1992, *Cabri Mort* [Audiocassette]. Abidjan, Côte d'Ivoire: KAS Production.

Soum Bill, 2000, *Zambakro* [Audiocassette]. Abidjan, Côte d'Ivoire: Showbiz.

Tiken Jah Fakoly, 1998, *Le Caméléon* [CD]. Abidjan, Côte d'Ivoire: Jat Music.

Tiken Jah Fakoly, 1999, *Mangercratie* [Audiocassette]. Abidjan, Côte d'Ivoire: Jat Music.

Tiken Jah Fakoly, 1999, *Cours d'histoire* [CD]. Abidjan, CI: Globe, Vouma.

Yang System, 2001, *Multisystem* [Audiocassette]. Abidjan, Côte d'Ivoire: Showbiz.

References

Abissiri, Fofana, 1997, July 22, "Musique ivoirienne: La quête identitaire", *Ivoir'soir* (Abidjan), 2537. Available at www.africaonline.co.ci/AfricaOnline/infos/ivs/2537NUI1.HTM [August 17, 2000].

—, 1997, October 15, "Musique *zouglou*: Bacchus, Eros et plus rien!", *Ivoir'soir* (Abidjan), 2596. Available at www.africaonline.co.ci/AfricaOnline/infos/ivs/2537NUI1.HTM [August 17, 2000].

Aby, Serge, 1997, November 5, "Rap en Côte d'Ivoire: Les poètes de la rue", *Ivoir'soir* (Abidjan), 2612.

Akindès, Francis, June 2000, "Inégalités socials et régulation politique en Côte d'Ivoire: La paupérisation en Côte d'Ivoire est-elle réversible?", *Politique Africaine*, 78 (Côte d'Ivoire: La tentation ethno-nationaliste), pp. 126–41. Paris: Karthala.

—, December 2000, "A travers les origines et les incertitudes des mutations politiques récentes en Côte d'Ivoire: le sens de l'histoire. Des origines des crises politiques récentes au sens de l'histoire en Côte d'Ivoire". Available at http:// perso.wanadoo.fr/forum.de.delphes/Forum_de_Delphes_56.html [July 24, 2001].

Amin, Samir, 1967, *Le développement du capitalisme en Côte d'Ivoire*. Paris: Editions de Minuit.

Bagnon, Francis, 1999, September 6, "Nigui Saff K-Dance et Axel Govinda, lauréats", *Le Jour* (Abidjan), 1375.

Bailly, Diégou, 1995, *La restauration du multipartisme en Côte d'Ivoire ou la double mort d'Houphouët-Boigny*. Paris: l'Harmattan.

Camara, Mam, 1999, "Alpha Blondy: Peur de personne", *Top Visages*, 313, 16–22 December.

Cannon, Steve, 1997, "Paname city rapping: B-boys in the banlieue and beyond", in Hargreaves, A. and M. McKinney (eds), *Post-colonial cultures in France*, pp. 150–68. London, New York: Routledge.

Diarra, Samba, 1997, *Les faux-complots d'Houphouët-Boigny-Boigny*. Paris: Karthala.

Dozon, Jean-Pierre, First Quarter 2000, "La Côte d'Ivoire au péril de l'ivoirité: Genèse d'un coup d'etat", *Afrique Contemporaine* (Paris), No. 193, pp. 13–22.

—, June 2000, "La Côte d'Ivoire entre démocratie, nationalisme et ethnonationalisme", *Politique Africaine*, No. 78 (Côte d'Ivoire: La tentation ethno-nationaliste), pp. 45–62. Paris: Karthala.

Fauré, Yves-André, 1989, "Côte d'Ivoire: Analysing the crisis", in Donal B. Cruise O'Brien, John Dunn and Richard Rathborne (eds), *Contemporary West African States*, pp. 59–74. Cambridge: Cambridge University Press.

Fellows, Catherine, 2000, "Ivory Coast: Songs and Soldiers (Rhythms of the Continent)", *BBC World Service* (London). Available at http://www.bbc.co.uk/worldservice/africa/features/rhytms/ivorycoast.shtml [September 30, 2001].

Giroux, Henry, 1992, *Border crossing: Cultural workers and the politics of education*. New York: Routledge.

—, 1994, "Doing cultural studies: Youth and the challenge of pedagogy", *Harvard Educational Review*, Vol. 64(3), pp. 278–308.

Hebdige, Dick, 1990, *Cut 'n' Mix: Culture, Identity and Caribbean music*. London, New York: Comedia.

Man Jusu, Kinimo Kanga, 1996, January 31, "Identité culturelle: La tête de l'éléphant d'Afrique", *Fraternité-Matin* (Abidjan), p. 12.

Onishi, Norimitsu, May 28, 2000, "Dance has Africans shaking behinds, and heads", *New York Times* (New York), section 1, page 4, column 3.

Sangaré, Y. and Ben Doumbia, Aboubacar, 9–15 December 1999, Interview with Alpha Blondy "Je suis infidèle et jaloux", *Top Visages* (Abidjan), 033, p. 8.

Sangaré, Yacouba, 2000, "Le marché de la musique n'est pas encore mûr en Afrique: Entretien avec Jean-Alain Texier (Directeur de Jat Music en Côte d'Ivoire)", *Africultures* (Abidjan), 29, pp. 30–34.

Servant, Jean-Christophe (Emery, Ed. Trans.), January 2001, "Rap: Africa talks back", Le *Monde Diplomatique* (Paris), (English subscription electronic version) pp. 1–4.

Sibatcheu, Marlyse, 2001, "Magic System, Espoir 2000: Les victories de la musique ivoirienne", *Le messager* (a weekly electronic publication of the GMM Group. Available at http://www.wagne.net/messager/messager/archi/eco108d.html [September 14, 2001].)

Sindzingre, Alice, First Quarter 2000, "Le contexte économique et social du changement politique en Côte d'Ivoire", *Afrique Contemporaine* (Paris), 193, pp. 24–37.

Tenaille, Frank, 2000, *Le swing du caméléon: Musiques et chansons africaines 1950–2000.* Paris: Actes Sud.

Tiémoko, Coulibaly, June 1995, "Démocratie et surrenchères identitaires en Côte d'Ivoire", *Politique Africaine*, 58, pp.143–50. Paris: Khartala.

Warne, Chris, 1997, "The impact of world music in France", in Hargreaves, A. and M. McKinney (eds), *Post-colonial cultures in France*, pp. 133–49, London, New York: Routledge.

Sounds of the "Third Way" – Zulu Maskanda, South African Popular Traditional Music

David B. Coplan

> It is in the production of audiences that the political and
> social reality of art can be found.
>
> (*John Fiske*, Television Culture)

Many of you will have already remarked the word "traditional" in my title and perhaps prepared yourself for yet more spilled ink and discourse in the quest to define
this rare, possibly mythical concept of musical style. Indeed, Katheryn Olsen's paper
for the conference *Playing with Identities in African Music* on Zulu *maskanda* guitar
styles focuses centrally on the variable, shifting constructions of this term.[1] But as it
is not my purpose here to interrogate the notion of tradition, let me rather cut this
problematic mercifully short. I shall not be concerned with the sounds of southern
Africa that evoke most ineffably its cultural geography: the demonstrably indigenous, audibly other-than-Western music of imagined communities of custom that
ethnomusicologists might deem *truly* traditional. Yes, players of acoustic percussion,
string, and wind instruments made of materials animal and vegetable can still be
found if one has the endurance and four-wheel drive vehicle required to seek them
out. People who sing in the old pre-hymnodic way, with scales unadjusted to Western harmonic intervals, are yet more common in rural areas. I propose rather to give
up the ghost of alien organological and tonal categories and simply use "traditional"
to mean what Black African people in my corner of the world, Johannesburg, mean
by it. Their conception, à la Chris Waterman's Yoruba slogan, "Our tradition is a
very modern tradition",[2] is that musical tradition is quite adequately maintained and
signified through continuities of genre, verbal idioms of experience, polyvocalities of
tone, tune, and texture, of hue and cry. Indeed Joseph Nhlapo has convincingly
argued in a recent thesis that *maskanda* guitar need not be termed "neo-traditional"[3]
as I had done,[4] but simply "traditional". Electric guitars, basses and keyboards,
penta- and hexatonic scales, and staggered linear melodic polyphonies; shiny drum
kits thumping out rhythms of centuries-old stamping dances; leopard tails, antelope
skin or string skirts with sneakers and spandex underwear, miraculously balanced
beaded headdresses and Kangol caps worn backwards, rhythmically bouncing, nude
(insouciant rather than provocative) breasts, antiphonal lead vocalists and a chorus
of back-up singers, synchronized hip swinging and stealthy Afro-Christian step-
dancing: all are part of Zulu traditional popular music. Tellingly, references to rural

---

1. Olsen 2000.
2. Waterman 1982.
3. Coplan 1985, p. 268.
4. Nhlapo 2000, pp. 29–30.

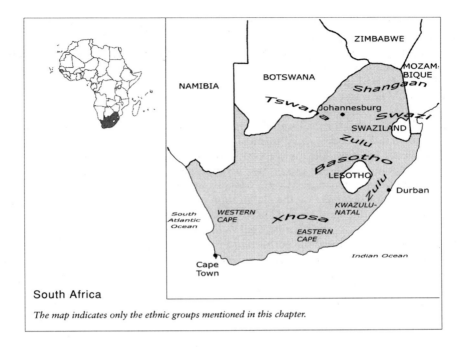

South Africa

The map indicates only the ethnic groups mentioned in this chapter.

districts of origin are encoded in scales and other stylistic features of *maskanda* traditional guitar playing, which has its roots in the percussive polyphonies of the *ugubu* and *umakweyana* gourd bows.

Ezodumo ("It shall sound"), the state broadcaster's (SABC) single live-performance music television offering explicitly devoted to "traditional" music, features bands of rural-born labour migrants whose only acoustic instruments are the guitar, the German button concertina, and piano accordion. The gourd or mouth-resonated monochords, hand-beaten wooden drums, and reed and animal horn aerophones of pre-industrial Africa are almost never heard on the broadcast media, although they are still played in rural communities. Significantly for our discussion, when such instruments do appear on an urban stage it is as syncretic elements in the eclectic ensemble music of serious African jazz composer/performers. These include Johannesburg's Sipho Mabuse, who employs a lesiba (mouth-resonated monochord) player from Lesotho, and Cape Town's Pops Mohammad, who himself plays Khoi (pre-Bantu herders) stringed instruments in an explicit attempt to musically reconstitute his self-avowed Khoi ("Hottentot") aboriginal origins. "Traditional" hence means the popular music of African urban labour migrants and dispossessed peasants. Go into any music chain-store outlet in the formerly "white", now broadly middle-class suburbs and one will not find any shelf, bin or CD labelled "traditional". Black people with rural or small-town roots do not buy at these outlets, even when they reside or work in those areas. They buy their music from inner-city cassette stalls, street-corner pirates, or at the general supply stores where they buy the primus stoves, portable stereos, and other items that comprise their mobile material culture.

So has it been since the early 1960s, when *apartheid* legal structures intended to keep rural and small town migrants from urbanizing permanently either in residence or culture began to have practical effect. Among the expressions of this enforcement of what the white government called "influx control" in popular culture was the emergence of a new, more rural-derived indigenous style of music known as *mqhashiyo* (bouncy), 'simanje-manje (the now-now thing) or *mbaqanga* (everyday corn-meal porridge). Important exponents of the style included Simon Nkabinde, known as Mahlathini, and his female backing vocalists the Mahotella Queens, as well as Zulu lead guitar virtuosos such as John "Phuzhushukela" Bhengu whose music would now be called *maskanda* (Afrikaans: "*musikant*"). The term *mbaqanga* is interesting in this connection, as it had been in wide circulation since at least the mid-1950s as a label for the local style of African jazz band music that appropriated well-known folk melodies and phrasing from a variety of African language corpuses. The audience for *mbaqanga* was mostly working-class urban African jazz enthusiasts, for whom these home grown jazz arrangements of folk material were a staple form of musical sustenance. Miriam Makeba and Hugh Masakela both built their early international careers on the elaboration of *mbaqanga*. When the leopard-skin bedecked Mahlathini and his Zulu head-dressed, beaded beauties were subsequently awarded this term, it was because *apartheid* had cleared the near-suburban black neighborhoods and closed the performance spaces that had nurtured African jazz in the city. *Mbaqanga* was now held to identify the musical daily bread of uprooted African proletarians who were not allowed to put down roots in the city but could not sustain themselves in the country.

In those days, more than thirty years ago, Mahlathini and the Queens did not perform in Johannesburg's elegant theatres and halls or on the prestigious stages of Europe and North America, as they did during their revival in the 1990s. Nor could they, under the terms of the Separate Amenities Act, use the venues local African jazz orchestras such as the Harlem Swingsters had once used. They rather put on musical variety shows at segregated black cinemas in the inner cities or in the dingy, ramshackle halls in the new municipal African townships such as Soweto in Johannesburg or KwaMashu in Durban. And unforgettable shows they were. Antiphonal Zulu vocals backed up by an electric guitar band and dancing to a souped-up 8/8 township beat. Multiple costume changes displaying the range of contemporary African elegance from Zulu fringe-skirts and loin-skins to Bermuda shorts, sneakers, and baseball caps, to svelte evening gowns and flashy suits. Comedy skits and comical dance turns provided variation and relief amidst the musical items, but were often outdone by a resident contortionist. Most intriguing, to an outsider anyway, was not the display of a re-invented performative traditionality, but its deliberate burlesque in the acrobatic turns and mugging of the animal-skin costumed male dancers. In the cities and industrial hostels, at least, the self-parodic and crowd-pleasing antics of the *icomic* ("comic") dance routines showed that it is indeed part of African tradition, mercifully, not always to take itself so seriously.

During the late 1970s, divisions between urban and determinedly urbanizing workers on the one side, and doggedly rural-rooted labour migrants on the other, hardened. This was due in part to outbreaks of violence between migrant hostel residents and township communities during the Soweto Uprising of 1976–1977 that were both a cause and a result of this rural-urban opposition. Public performances of *mbaqanga* declined as labour migrants sought a lower social profile, and audiences drifted away from Mahlathini and his imitators towards the more urbanized African language vocal and instrumental styles of groups like the Soul Brothers. It would take overseas interest and concert tours in the 1990s, not local revival, to bring back Mahlathini from obscurity. Mahlathini was assisted in this of course by Joseph Shabalala and Ladysmith Black Mambazo, a traditional choral ensemble that adjusted Zulu male polyphonic vocalization to four-part Western harmony in the old *isicatamiya* style.[1] Rich and in a way famous at least locally by the mid-1970s, Ladysmith Black Mambazo were placed on the world stage through their collaboration with American popular balladeer Paul Simon in the mid-1980s and went on, like Mahlathini, to enjoy international success in "world music" in their own right.

Mahlathini's return from obscurity was likewise accompanied by a host of other ensembles, playing what I am calling "popular traditional" music, that had retained all along their rural, small-town, and urban migrant working-class African language audiences. These groups included not so much the semi-urban *mbaqanga* performers as the more rural indigenous styles such as Zulu guitar *maskanda*, Basotho accordion and drum band[2] vocalists straight from the mines and mine shantytown taverns, and village bands from every corner of the country singing in Xhosa, Pedi, Shangaan, Tswana, and Swazi. The provision of socially and sexually segregated housing in migrant workers' hostels in urban and mining communities helped to maintain and more importantly develop popular traditional ensembles in the cities. The main vehicles for what was not simply a revival of popular traditional music but indeed a creative movement closer to indigenous rural-based musical styles than those popular in the 1960s and 1970s, were the regular programming on African language radio, and on television, *Ezodumo*. Begun under the old SATV (South African Television) segregated channel system that featured African language programming on channels 2 (Zulu/Xhosa/Swazi) and 4 (Tswana/North and South Sotho), the program has survived every structural re-organization of the past decade to root itself firmly for the past few years, not on SABC 2 (South African Broadcasting Corporation), the staid, what's-good-for you, "family viewing" channel, but in prime time on SABC TV1, the channel for the young and frisky. Despite the disdain of many citified viewers, *Ezodumo* has consistently maintained some of the highest ratings of any regular program on SATV, and the commercial staff cannot cope with the demand from sponsors to purchase advertising time on the show.

Ezodumo is the principal public cultural space in which traditional amplified bands from virtually every Black African (other racial groups do not perform on this program) language group both perform and play with both their own and other cultural identities while attempting to establish themselves as musical professionals and also very clearly having a damn good time. Peculiarly, traditional bands rarely if ever give live performances in the urban black townships as they did in the bad old *haut-apartheid* period of the 1970s, nor do they any longer seem to tour the small town community halls in groaning old buses as they did then. A few of the best-selling groups, such as that of *maskanda* composer Phuz'hukemisi and *maskanda*-gospel group Pure Gold do tour around the country, backed by their recording companies. Until early 2001, *Ezodumo* was compered in Zulu by producer Bhodloza Nzimande (who also hosts a *maskanda* music program on Zulu radio) and in Sesotho by Thuso Motaung, a preacher and agony uncle on Sunday mornings on Sesotho radio.

The other seven African macro-languages are somewhat neglected, although the Ndebele band of lead guitarist and grandmother Nothembi Mkhwebane and the Tsonga guitar band of Thomas Chauke, who have achieved national fame and popularity through *Ezodumo*, are among the perennial favorites on the show. The program presents itself as a repository of a cultural conservatism that is by no means confined to or even identified with rural origins. Indeed city people with rural or small-town origins, who constitute a major proportion of *Ezodumo*'s audience, crit-

---

1. Coplan 1985, pp. 65–73, Erlmann 1996.
2. Interestingly, these bands had no real generic or stylistic name, and informants simply referred to this music as *lipina tsa Sesotho*, Sesotho songs, but admittedly not as *'mino oa setso* "music of origin".

icized Nzimande and Motaung for pitching their presentation in the discursive style of migrant workers. The ensembles themselves are not only recruited from the workers' hostels, but are sent over by the recording companies to air their latest recordings, and there are many more requests from the companies to present their groups than available space on the program.

Some groups are composed of rural people hoping to find musical success in Johannesburg through the media, and do not care that they are not paid for their appearance. SATV provides these performers with return transport, food, and in some cases accommodation. Studio sidemen recruited to strengthen a weak ensemble for the occasion are paid perhaps 20 pounds. In line with the concept and practice the broadcast of "traditional" culture on the state media under the present government as under its white minority predecessor, the professional exposure and the prestige and notoriety "back home" (where the performers are held to properly reside) bestowed by an appearance on television is held to be sufficient reward, and perhaps this is so.

The flow of people and cultural formulations is of such duration and diversity in South Africa that urbanized but not fundamentally Westernized cultural styles are as much a background to concepts of tradition as rural indigenism. Indeed, one might well conceive of contemporary African identity practices, regardless of regional origin, as "cultures of mobility"; forms of practice not merely transported by but formulated "on the road" within the social context of multi-sited, mobile networks of kin, homeboys/girls, and reciprocal friendship. Indeed in the case of *maskanda*, the form itself begins in the late 19th century as a musical expression of self-propelling individuality, as courting songs sung "on feet" as isiZulu puts it, by young lads on amorous walkabout. When the early recording companies came searching the migrants' hostels in search of musical products for the African market in the 1930s, they found the solitary itinerant guitarists (and violinists and concertina players) competing against one another after the manner of a country stickfight. Over time the studios recognized, rightly, that the appeal of the form could be widened by backing up the individual songsmiths and guitarists with ensemble players, creating traditional bands if you will, and later when urban concerts became established cultural events, with dancers. In *maskanda* we are dealing with what is still rural traditional music, popularized and progressively transformed on the road, in the hostel, at the tavern, in township and inner-city halls, on the urban streets, in the radio and record studios.

Innovations have continued. Rural performers, observing that a folk entertainment had become a sector of the commercial music industry, now form up their own bands and try their luck with the urban media market, sometimes appearing on *Ezodumo*. The musical dominance of the lead guitarist/vocalist/composer over the performance is now sometimes shared with other popular members of the ensemble. Traditional self-praises, apostrophising the lead performer, his home district and community, now may alternate with a younger vocalist rapping on wider topical subjects in Zulu. Electric keyboard on occasion appears in the instrumental ensemble.

Conversely, some aspects of rural Zulu dance music have been strongly retained in urban performances of *maskanda*, such as the indescribably powerful and dramatic dance challenges between male dancers, accompanied by the "rolling thunder" of the great *isigubu* cow-hide drums. These challenges, so gripping to the eye and ear, rarely feature in *maskanda* band performances on *Ezodumo*. I would be tempted to the facile speculation that they evoke some perceived atavistic power of Zulu militarism that disturbs the senior producers at SATV, if I were not afraid that

I might tune into the next broadcast and see such a male dance challenge in full swing. Phuz'ukhemisi noKhetane, a leading *maskanda* composer and performer whose ensemble built a successful recording and touring career with appearances on *Ezodumo*, wrote the song *Sicela kuBhodloza*, "We request, Bhodloza" in order to demand that the *umgangela* ("stick-fighting") singing and guitar playing challenges be featured on the program, as well as on Zulu language radio:

> We give praises to Bhodloza's programme
> We dance to the music down in Durban's waves
> I am requesting Bhodloza to announce that we should resume
>   killing each other, Nzimande
> I am requesting Bhodloza to announce that we should resume killing
>   each other in song.
> We say: 'Announce that the fierce song competition should resume'.

What is certain is that SATV management has made several attempts over the years to cancel *Ezodumo* and alternatively to shift the musical content towards more characteristically urban "township" genres such as "soul-*mbaqanga*" and *kwaito*, because, like most highly-educated Africans for the past century they considered popular traditional music embarrassingly pre-modern and ethnically differentiating for their own ideological self-image.[1] Such attempts were always met with a deluge of protest from the black viewing public, who wanted *Ezodumo* left as it is. Even Sesotho presenter Thuso Motaung, who briefly departed to further his career in radio, leaving Bhodhloza Nzimande on his own, had to return by popular demand. Not to be deterred, the hormonally imbalanced modernisers at SATV 1 brought in young, jeans-clad presenters and a more music-video oriented format early in 2001.

It is not really my purpose here to delineate the musical and performative qualities of *maskanda* today. Rather I would only consider these qualities in relation to their ideological significance within the field of cultural production. First I would note the thorough embeddedness of the form in demonstrably continuous Zulu performance traditions, albeit they are indeed modern traditions. *Maskanda* musicians, in partial contrast to Zulu *mbaqanga* performers such as the late Mahlathini, have not innovated in search of a wider commercial audience but in effect insisted that their audience, now expanding but still largely confined to South Africa, come to them and to what they insouciantly remain: parochial Zulu and proud of it, were pride to be consciously required. As Nhlapo puts it, they continue "to reaffirm a specifically African cultural identity and expressive mode, despite its assimilation into a commercialized context".[2] Not that explicit entertainment values are eschewed: as Nhlapo further notes, entertainment is a fundamental expressive principle of *maskanda*, from the flair of the instrumental technique, the eloquence of the lyrics, the flamboyance of the animal skin costumes, the acrobatics of the male dancers, to the fetching rotations of the ample derrières of the female singer/dancers.[3] This quality explains why the old performances I saw at black inner-city cinemas in the 1970s, as well as the ones I enjoy today, could be so artfully serious about comedic burlesque. There is even a time-honoured term, *ukukekela*, for antic movements "played" by Zulu suitors to impress a woman with a mixture of amusement and performative prowess.

---

1. Coplan 1985, p. 118.
2. Nhlapo 2000, p. 29.
3. Nhlapo 2000, pp.12–13.

Second, *maskanda* currently enjoys a broad popularity among a range of work-ing-class African language speakers, not only the Zulu. By the same token, anyone observing the listening habits of primary African language speakers will find that many listen to stations broadcasting in other languages than their own, indeed ones that they may not even understand. Why? *Because they like some of the music styles of other language cultures*, even when they understand the lyrics imperfectly, or not at all. On *Ezodumo*, ethnic dance and dress, the more local-exotic the better, of en-sembles from all southern African language groups are popular with viewers of all backgrounds. Exposure through the broadcast media has promoted popular tradi-tional music and dance beyond ethnic boundaries and helped this category of genres to find a secure place in the commercial music industry and in urban performance settings as well as in the musical life of small regional communities. It is important to note along with Karin Barber, however, that the broadcast media float in the sea of popular culture that surrounds it: *maskanda* merely surfaces on TV and radio; these media do not create it.[1]

For the whole of the 20th century the opposition between urban and rural oper-ated as one of the central organizing metaphors in black popular culture and social interaction. Now at the dawn of the 21st, presaged by an epochal non-racial political transformation, the city and the country appear to be negotiating modes of cultural acceptance of one another. *Maskanda* and the other ethnic styles too have now be-come trans-culturally accepted, a trend contrary to the previous denigration of forms unreflexively categorized as pre-modern or pre-Christian. Lead singers and guitarists in popular traditional music have previously been male, but today perhaps the most innovative exponents of this trend in performance are female composers and performers such as singer and lead guitarist Tu Nokwe, who plays a style of tra-ditional Zulu pop-rock, and vocalist Busi Mhlongo, whose superb CD *Urban Zulu* from 1999 features an evocative, seamless blend of popular traditional musical re-sources and sophisticated styles of Afro-jazz-fusion. All this is occurring at a time when other black musical genres in South Africa, including African jazz, gospel, and the best selling and most visible form in the country, *kwaito*, are attempting to flour-ish by broadly approximating African-American models while retaining and devel-oping a local cultural stylistic character.

By final way of illustration, popular—not popular traditional[2]—music of the rest of sub-Saharan Africa, specifically artists from Congo-Kinshasa, Zimbabwe, Mozambique, and Senegal, some of whom are well-known in the Euro-North Amer-ican field called "Afro-Beat" or "World Music", have begun to find a place in South Africa's popular black dance culture and on radio. In noticeable contrast to the widespread black South African chauvinism that rejects anything and anyone from Africa to the north as inferior, prominent popular musicians such as veterans Sipho Mabuse and Brenda Fassie, and township youth icons Bongo Maffin have attempted tentative but successful collaborations with performers of *kwasa-kwasa*, as the neighboring south-central African musical styles are called. Indeed, even in the cul-turally bounded *is'camto* township argot, *kwassa* is now a local dance on its own, based on the Congolese *ndombolo* dance style, popularized in a popular song and

---

1. Barber 1997, pp. 1–12.
2. Contemporary Congolese popular music, known by various names, embodies a stylistic process of hybridiza-tion begun in the 1940s, in which African elements were layered on to a Latin American popular dance rhyth-mic foundation in rumba and merengue. Zulu *maskanda*, in contrast, represents a technological and performative modernization of what remains a style substantially indigenous in origin. Having once termed this music "neo-traditional" I am presently most comfortable with the term "popular traditional" for *maskanda*, one that cannot be accurately applied to Congolese *kwasa-kwasa* or its most recent label, *ndombolo*.

music video by Abashante lead singer Iyaya, a standard-bearer of unapologetic African female sexual self-assertion. As we shall see, all these are but performative signs of larger ideological movements in South African public culture.

* * *

At the World Economic Forum in Davos and also the G8 Economic Summit[1] held earlier in 2000, South African President Thabo Mbeki successfully popularized the notion of a "Third Way" by which marginalized economies outside Euro-North American or East Asian spheres of economic dominance might construct more locally relevant pathways to stability and prosperity; that is, to competitive economic modernism. Known or unknown to rhetorical enthusiasts such as US President Bill Clinton, who repeated the "Third Way" catch phrase in his addresses to the G8, the notion derives from the local concept of "African Renaissance" with which Mbeki has replaced the earlier, more ethnically pluralist Mandela representation of South Africa as a "Rainbow Nation". A substantial literature has already begun to accumulate on the subject[2] and local print and broadcast journalism has picked up strongly on the idea. For our purposes we might only note that the concept attempts explicitly to resolve, or find the way forward from, a set of evident contradictions in the social character of the country and subcontinent. These include a call for the revival of Black Africa's "past glory" in a world where traditional monarchs are enjoined to reign and not rule; the engagement of the marginalized black masses in a nationalist project from which there is little real prospect they will personally benefit; and the promotion and empowerment of distinctly "African" modes of managing modernity and globalisation against the backdrop, with admitted exceptions and contrary positive indications, of over thirty years of regional failure, conflict, and decline.

Past glory? Unless people want the present Zulu king, mild-mannered, cultivated voluptuary Goodwill Zwelethini, to re-invent himself as Shaka, or to model the region's republics after the functioning absolutism of Mswati III in Swaziland, it is difficult to know precisely what glory should be revived. Difficult, but on further reflection, not impossible: the point being made is that pre-colonial African state-builders did create highly organized polities within the historical circumstances and technological resources of the time and place, leaving a legacy in which their descendants might justifiably take some pride. But what is actually to be saved from that independent era? The answer is forms of social relatedness, their moral and spiritual foundations, and their associated cultural practices. Further, presently available but obscure and often denigrated African contributions to the knowledge base of improved human futures are well worth valorisation and serious study. Transforming "African Renaissance" from an exercise in political ideology into a vehicle for the mobilisation of mass nationalist commitment? If indeed the Rainbow Nation offered nothing more by way of economic advancement to the majority of dispossessed black people than the rueful sight of a small number of their more fortunate brethren and sistren enjoying economic privilege, then the African Renaissance might still serve as an ideological weapon in the struggle to extend benefits and opportunities more broadly. If in the end this is but a suggestion that if the poor are hungry, let them eat rhetoric, then at the very least distinctively African cultural practices—the

---

1. G8 is the group of eight of the main industrialised democracies, i.e. Britain, Canada, France, Germany, Italy, Japan, Russia and the United States.
2. Mbeki et al. 1998.

only materials from which many can still construct a positive social self-image and experiential narrative—are publicly validated. Participating successfully in modernity? By now it should be clear to Africans and non-Africans alike that this can be facilitated only by integrating rather than opposing ideologies and practices of tradition and modernity. Otherwise the silenced past, as in the case of the European renaissance, inevitably exacts a terrible revenge.

As to the embedding of Western empirical knowledge into an African epistemological and social context, this is not as unproven or far-fetched an idea as its detractors assume. In the late 19th century in South Africa's eastern Orange Free State region, African peasant farmers combined European agricultural plough technology and methods with the economies of the African family and communal system of labour deployment and exchange. The result was a level of productivity that threatened to drive the far less efficient white family farmers out of business and off the land. Only overt state intervention in the form of racial land expropriation, legal discrimination, and economic dispossession prevented this from occurring and preserved white supremacy in South African agriculture.[1] More to the point, in post-apartheid South Africa today one of the industries in which this marriage of Western technology and organisation and African social and cultural materials and resources has the greatest potential is popular music. In the field of cultural production, African artists in every medium and genre, including popular music of course, continue to demonstrate that, against the self-serving, crooked odds of Western prejudice, they can access and demonstrate the generative diversity and power of the sub-continent's creative resources, and if allowed, compete on even terms.

Professionally, however, the well of African musical tradition has not slaked the musicians' thirst for livelihood and recognition. From the very outset in the 1920s and 1930s, the South African recording industry has used the concept of traditional music to legally inscribe the industry category "trad." as a compositional credit on African recordings. Until 1964, the "trad." label kept African compositions in the public domain, made the composers anonymous, and obviated royalties or copyright protection.[2] For the next 25 years, apartheid helped keep these ideas and practices in place despite ameliorative legal remedies and new institutions such as the SA Music Rights Organisation (SAMRO) and the SA Recording Rights Association Ltd. (SARRAL). Sipho Mngadi, keyboardist for the urban *maskanda* band Umkhonto ka Shaka, complains that the traditional/communal concept of African culture is used to deny African musicians individual recognition and even their rights as professionals in the music industry, both local and international. Historically, thanks to racism, African traditional musical resources and performers are supposed to come cheap, and the industry and the SABC still work to keep things that way. Recently, Pete Seeger said in a reply to Joseph Shabalala: "The word 'traditional', when used by a publisher [to credit a songwriter], usually means that somebody is keeping some money that should have been sent somewhere else".[3] Nor are recording companies the only ones to blame. More industry-wise urban black popular musicians often re-arrange and record the compositions of *maskanda* composers, whom they regard as amateur rural folk artists, without credit or payment.[4]

All this plays out locally with something of a contrary motion. In the one turn, music and other domains of cultural production popularly identified as African have

---

1. Keegan 1986, pp.14–19.
2. Coplan 1985, pp. 139,178.
3. *Sunday Times* 27 August, 2000, p. 15.
4. Hare Hare Myandu, interview 26 August, 2000.

been steadily acquiring increased acceptance and status. Black urbanites seldom, at least publicly, dismiss migrant workers' popular traditional music as backward, and performances of these styles in the cities attract a significant urban working-class audience. Interestingly too, the resistant strain of African political and cultural nationalism expressed in the Ethiopianist church movement at the turn of the 20th century has re-appeared in the form of the increasing cultural influence of Rastafarianism in South Africa. Once dismissed as marijuana-smoking lumpen proletarians affecting alien dress and slang, rastas have gained acceptance of their cultural style of pan-Africanist revivalism and re-woven the Ethiopianist/Garveyite thread even if as a movement and as persons they are still profoundly, even defiantly marginalized. When I visited the syncretist Afro-Christian shrines of the Basotho people in the remote caves of the eastern Free State in April, 2000, I found amidst the colorful panoply of ancestral rituals and Basotho nativist ("Zionist") Christian mysticism the unmistakable outward signs and inward spiritual influences of Jah and Rastafari.

Back in Johannesburg, the self-consciously traditional ensemble Umkhonto ka Shaka ("Spear of Shaka") is led by Rastafarian John Sithole, who performs in long dreadlocks and antelope and leopard skins. Sithole is lead singer and dancer in the group, and while keyboardist Sipho Mngadi, from Stanger (near Shaka's original headquarters) who has been in Johannesburg for 22 years, is a rasta, lead guitarist Mangisi Dhlamini is a dyed-in-the-zebra-skin traditionalist from kwaZulu who dresses like a hostel migrant and has no Rastafarian leanings. While one might expect Umkhonto ka Shaka to have fashioned a musical blend of reggae and *maskanda*, such is not the case, and even though it incorporates some urbane reflexivity, the style is securely *maskanda*. Indeed rastaman John Sithole is principal dancer, and leads the thoroughly traditional *isigubu* male drum-dance challenges, his chest-length dreadlocks flying. When not performing, Sithole dresses rasta, speaks elegant South African black English, and is usually glued to his bead-covered cell phone. Sithole lives in Soweto and runs a small agency in the Federated Union of Black Artists (FUBA) arts school in west central Johannesburg called the African Cultural Heritage Trust that rents out sound systems, books engagements and handles organisational and promotional problems for aspiring *maskanda* groups in Johannesburg.

As a teenager in rural southern Natal, Sithole acquired enough education and political consciousness to protest the cynical, manipulative contempt in which the apartheid system held Zulu culture. His natural organisational and leadership abilities were expressed in a commitment at first to Pan-Africanism, but his immersion in cultural and spiritual concerns led him then to Rastafarianism. He felt then as he does now that Rastafarianism provides the ideal non-violent and politically non-sectarian bridge between Zulu ethnic tradition, a generalized South African black nationalism, and Pan-Africanism; between the urban and the rural areas of continent, country and region. Indeed he does not view Shaka as an empire builder or Zulu national hero but as a sort of regional power for African unification; a commander who fought to bring all of South Africa's black polities into a single hierarchical structure. The partnering of Zulu cultural practice, Rastafarianism and performance suits Sithole as an urban township-based Africanist, providing an independent lifestyle that avoids proletarian wage work for "Babylon" through culture-based self-employment. Such a strategy provides as well an affirmative existential answer to the crucial question facing the students as well as the practitioners of resistance in marginalized communities: whether battles lost in economics and/or politics can be won in culture?

Such self-conscious hybridity, however, points up a potential contradiction in popular traditional musicians' play with South African black identities. *Maskanda* is very much a Zulu genre, and beyond that, many of its identifying stylistic features, such as the interspersed clan and self praises, the song texts and dance forms with their stick-fighting metaphors, references to specific ancestral lines, the short *ihlabo* melodic runs and scales on the guitar that introduce each dance song:[1] all these serve to identify the leader's origins in a specific rural district and as a display of (very) "local knowledge". Such localism can expand to represent contemporary performance tradition as a whole, as is currently the case with *umzansi*, "south", a style of male dancing from southern Natal that is today performed by just about all popular traditional Zulu dance groups. These expressions are opaque to non-Zulu people, and would seem to present difficulties for *maskanda* in serving as a performative representation of a pan-African cultural identity for black South Africans, less than a third of whom speak Zulu as their home language. Interestingly, this has not appeared as a problem. While Africans of other groups are wary of militant Zulu ethnic nationalism and the Zulu reputation for using violence as a favoured means of dispute settlement, the power of Zulu performance culture to evoke an image of a resilient, autonomous Africa is widely accepted and enjoyed by all South Africans, black, brown, and white. So the predominance of Zulu *maskanda* on *Ezodumo*, accepted as partly a function of the explicit Nguni (Zulu-Xhosa-Swazi) language programming focus of SATV1, nonetheless has a broader cultural effect. Umkhonto ka Shaka recently put on a successful performance at Johannesburg's bastion of Rastafarian dub and reggae, Tandoor club, for a crowd of black city teenagers. At the recent national Conference on the African Renaissance, Zulu performance groups were featured as representative of South Africa's overall billing in the African "stage show", fitting in neatly as well with African-American delegates' parochial preconception that South African black people all belong to the Zulu "tribe".[2]

What then finally of the vaunted African Resaissance in the domain of musical identities? If S'bu Ndebele, head of the ANC in KwaZulu-Natal, is correct in noting that "The African Renaissance has been emotional to intellectuals and intellectual to the masses",[3] how can it be turned instead into a vehicle of what Habermas called "communicative competence", ..."the ability to, in an interpreting manner, search for a consensus about the value of people and their co-existence, about the kind of life that is worth living and the nature and content of the symbolic forms which best express those values".[4] This task is particularly difficult in a society so multifariously divided, not least in its access to the dynamisms of modernity, a place of not one but many "todays" in many South Africas, as post-apartheid cultural theorist Graham Pechey notes.[5] In such a situation, the African Renaissance becomes what Sehume calls a necessary strategic essentialism, wherein the romance of the distant past, informed by an awareness of dispossession, leads to a militancy for change that privileges an African discourse.[6] This route to social power through cognitive reintegration is guided by a search for new post-apartheid black identities based in a conscious cultural moralism. The many song texts devoted to social commentary (*amaculo akhayo*) in *maskanda* explicitly link the revival of tradition, including cus-

1. Nhlapo 2000, p. 18.
2. Sehume 1999, p. 132.
3. Sehume 1999, p. 128.
4. Habermas, cited in van Niekerk 1999, p. 76.
5. Pechey 1993.
6. Sehume 1999, pp. 131–32.

tomary practices, ancestral spiritualism and the chieftaincy, with moralistic prescriptions against practices that are "killing the black nation" as one text puts it.[1]

Professor Pitika Ntuli of the African Renaissance Institute is of course quite correct to dispute the ANC's construction of the Renaissance as centrally a Third Way to nationalist modernism, since modernity simply does not accommodate indigenous epistemologies or their historical cultural frameworks. Fight tradition, even under an Africanist banner, and you will lose, observes Ntuli, who suggests that the valorisation of Africans' knowledge and modes of knowledge production is the only means to provide the majority of the people with some sense of agency and a basis for participation.[2] Echoing Ntuli, Umkhonto ka Shaka's John Sithole insists that the Renaissance only has meaning if driven by such "grass-roots" participation, and is therefore positive as a basis of identity, pride, and self-reliance, but negative as a basis for participation in neo-liberal globalization and in a modernist homogenization of Africa's cultural resources that consigns pre-capitalist practices to the dustbin of a non-history. If Mbeki's fear of the divisiveness of ethnic traditions leads him to the bland, shallow, generalized concept of African heritage contained in his "I am an African" public speeches,[3] there is of course the equal danger of constructing African identity as exclusionary out of a need to define Africa in opposition to the West and the rest, promoting the false and dangerous notion of a mono-racial continent. Whites and other "Others" in Africa may have only themselves to blame for this exclusivity, of course, since while they might be African they have certainly not Africanized. The way forward, as embodied in popular traditional music is: first, to envision a moral universe based in local cultural knowledge and practice;[4] second, for Africans to do what they do well the best they can and to be insistent in demanding full exchange value for it; and third, to play productively with identities within the established structures of creativity that constitute African traditional music.[5]

Discography

Busi Mhlongo, 1999, *Urban Zulu.*

Interview

Hare Hare Myandu. Interview August 26, 2000.

References

Barber, Karin, 1997, "Introduction", in Barber, Karin (ed.), *Readings in African Popular Culture.* Edinburgh: Edinburgh University Press for the International African Institute.

Boloka, Gideon, 1999, "African Renaissance and the Revitalization of the Public Sphere", *Critical Arts,* Vol. 13, No. 1, pp. 121–26.

Coplan, David, 1985, *In Township Tonight! South Africa's Black City Music and Theatre.* London: Longman.

Erlmann, Veit, 1996, *Nightsong: Performance, Power and Practice in South Africa.* Chicago: Chicago University Press.

---

1. Nhlapo 2000, p. 71.
2. "Repositioning the African Renaissance", public lecture delivered at the University of the Witwatersrand, 2 September, 2000.
3. Mbeki et al. 1998.
4. See Boloka 1999, p. 123.
5. See Joyner 1975, p. 262.

Joyner, Charles, 1975, "A Model for the Analysis of Folklore Performance in Historical Context", *Journal of American Folklore*, Vol. 88, No. 349, pp. 254–65.

Keegan, Tim, 1986, *Rural Transformations in Industrialising South Africa*. Johannesburg: Ravan.

Mbeki, Thabo, et al., 1998, *The African Renaissance*. Johannesburg: Konrad-Adenauer-Stiftung.

Nhlapo, Joseph, 2000, *Maskanda: A Study in Zulu Traditional Guitar Music*. Master in musicology thesis. Witwatersrand.

van Niekerk, Anton, 1999, "The African Renaissance: Lessons from a Predecessor", *Critical Arts*, Durban, Vol. 13, No. 2, pp.66–80.

Olsen, Kathryn, 2000, "Marking Time—Discourses on Identity in Contemporary Maskanda". Paper presented to the Conference, *Playing with Identities in Contemporary Music in Africa*. 19–22 October, 2000 in Åbo/Turku, Finland organised by the Sibelius Museum/the Department of Musicology and the Centre for Continuing Education at Åbo Akademi University, and the Nordic Africa Institute in Uppsala, Sweden.

Pechey, Graham, 1993, "Post Apartheid Narratives", in Barker, F., P. Hulme and M. Iversen, (eds), *Colonial Discourse/Post-Colonial Theory*, pp. 151–72. Manchester: Manchester University Press.

Sehume, Jeffrey, 1999, "Strategic Essentialism and the African Renaissance", *Critical Arts*, Durban, Vol. 13, No. 1, pp. 127–33.

Sunday Times (Johannesburg) 27 August, 2000, p. 15.

Waterman, Christopher, 1982, "'I'm a Leader, Not a Boss': Popular Music and social identity in Ibadan, Nigeria", *Ethnomusicology*, Vol. 26, No. 1, pp. 59–72.

Expressing Cape Verde

Morna, Funaná and National Identity

Mai Palmberg

Cape Verdean identity rests on three pillars, asserts Manuel Veiga of the National Institute of Cultural Research in Praia: "Mar, milho, musica—the sea, maize, and music".[1]

The past few decades have seen interesting cross-currents redefine the national music treasure in Cape Verde, and with it the musical expression of national identities. On the one hand one music form has won increasing acceptance since the 1950s and 1960s as the prime expression of the national character and national condition, crystallised in the *sodade*, a sad acceptance of unfulfilled dreams and longing. This is the *morna*, arguably the best-known Cape Verdean music internationally. On the other hand the period of independence since 1975 has seen a celebration of *pluralism*, which has meant the upgrading of music genres previously not celebrated as part of the cultural treasure, but rather seen as rough popular music localised to the isle of São Tiago. These musics, especially *funaná*, are also believed to have stronger African roots than the *morna*.

These two trends are different but not necessarily contradictory ways of expressing collective identity, similar to what Thomas Hylland Eriksen found in his studies on Mauritius. In the first trend, nationalism is seen as supra-ethnic or non-ethnic (and we may add: supra-class or non-class). Commonly embraced icons and symbols express this transcending identity. In the second trend, which can be labelled multicultural, the nation is seen as a "mosaic of cultures".[2]

Three meanings of identity

Before examining the extraordinary role of music in expressing identities in Cape Verde, let us look at the concept of 'identity'. It has at least three basic and different meanings.

- Identity is, firstly, about *the unique individuality of each person*. A bureaucratic form is encountered, for example in Sweden, in the ubiquitous "personal ID number" without which authorities or banks treat you as a nobody. In psychology discourse, 'identity' stands for the development of the self into a unique and hopefully mature personality. This sense of identity formation tops the league in library searches on the keyword 'identity'.

- The second concept of 'identity' is about *sameness, belonging to a community*. The community is often, in Benedict Anderson's term, an "imagined commu-

---

1. Manuel Veiga, interview July 17, 2000.
2. Eriksen 1993, pp. 118–20.

nity", whose members are not all in close contact, yet share a sense of belonging.[1]
Nationalism has been one of the most powerful forces in internalising identification with such much-wider-than-neighbourhood communities.

Cape Verde certainly is such an imagined community. As far as I can judge all
persons born in Cape Verde identify themselves as Cape Verdeans, despite the
fact the people live on nine fairly isolated islands. Although there is airline and
ship traffic between the islands, only a minority of those living on the islands
travel between them, and many have never been beyond their native island.

–   The third concept of 'identity' can refer to other things than persons, *to phenom-
    ena that are identified in an attempt to classify them*, in relation to both their
    uniqueness and their belonging, usually in an effort to place them in a tree of
    evolution. Carolus Linnaeus' classification of the plants of the world is such a
    classification exercise to establish identities. In both ethnography and ethnomu-
    sicology establishing typologies and classifying the study objects has in the past
    been a celebrated ambition.

At first glance the first two senses of "identity" above are contradictory and mutually exclusive—uniqueness *versus* sameness. But there is a bridge, the concept of
"cultural identity". Central to an individual's development of his/her personality is
the self-definition and often revisited definition of his/her belonging to a community.

The concept of cultural identity is contested. Stuart Hall distinguishes two ways
of talking about "cultural identity". The first position defines cultural identity in
terms of a shared culture, "a sort of collective, one true self", which provides us with
stable, unchanging and continuous frames of reference and meaning. This oneness
is an essence that can be brought to light from behind the superficial vicissitudes of
our actual history.[2] One can add that this unchanging identity is based on ideas of
purity in cultural forms.

The other way of thinking about cultural identity emphasises as equally important as "what we really are", "what history has done", "what we have become". In
this sense cultural identity is not something that already exists, transcending place,
history, and time. It undergoes constant transformation. Identities are the ways we
position ourselves within the narratives of the past. What elements of difference and
contrast are important and emphasised at different times, and in different social contexts, must by necessity vary.

In order to understand in what ways Cape Verdean popular music has become a
marker of cultural identity, let us look briefly at what kind of society Cape Verde
has been and become.

At the crossroads

From the start of its modern time habitation in the 15th century to independence in
1975 Cape Verde was under Portuguese power (apart from the years 1580–1640
when Portugal was ruled as a province of Spain). With the first settlers came the
Catholic church which soon entrenched itself. Not long after the settlers arrived
Cape Verde became a relay station at the crossroads of the slave trade. Slaves were
taken from the West African coast, particularly from the areas of present-day
Senegal, Gambia, and Guinea-Bissau. Some of the slaves were retained on the Cape

---

1. Benedict Anderson 1983.
2. Stuart Hall 1990, p. 223.

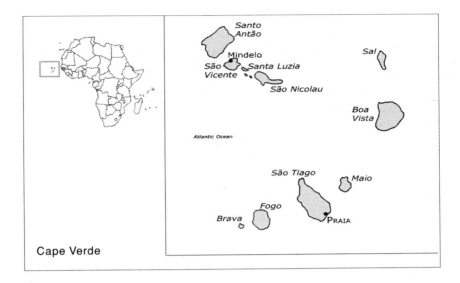

Cape Verde

Verde islands, but most captives were sold across the Atlantic after a period of "seasoning".[1]

A feudal plantation system was instituted in Cape Verde on the model of the Canaries and Madeira. Land was cleared for sugarcane and cotton, and slaves were brought in to work the fields. Some slaves were assigned to work in the salt mines of the isles of Sal or Maio, collect indigo or weave cotton (which Wolof women were considered particularly good at). African men and women were also used as domestic labourers.

Cape Verde's location at the crossroads of many shipping routes opened up for many different influences. New England whalers who began to sail these waters around 1800 recruited many Cape Verdean crewmen, some of whom settled in New England. An American consulate was opened in Praia (now the capital) on São Tiago. Shipping also formed the destiny of São Vicente's Mindelo, placed on a half-moon formation of an ancient volcanic crater. The British established a coal depot there in the 1860s, when motorships began replacing sailing ships. Mindelo became a booming and cultural city, with a middle class influenced by British social life. But depression in Europe and North America in the 1920s and 1930s meant the cruel end of Mindelo's prosperity.

Race, class and gender

The two pillars of this "slavocratic" society, the European colonisers and the slaves, soon became minorities.[2] There were never many white settlers on Cape Verde and since almost all of them were men they started taking black women as partners. The mixed population grew by leaps and bounds.

The observation that Cape Verdean society is extremely "racially" mixed is commonplace, while the fact that this process was based on extremely unequal gender relations has escaped many. One exception is the American anthropologist, Deirdre Meintel, who from her fieldwork just before independence, concludes that racial

---

1. Davidson 1989, p. 26.
2. Carreira 1972, pp. 510–11.

barriers are most visible in the customs in courtship and marriage. For a man of the upper strata the sexual debut was with a black woman, whom he would desert when it was his time to marry, whether she had a child from the liaison, whether she was pregnant or not. He would seek his marriage partner among women with light skin.[1] Whatever else might have changed after independence, single mothers, whose husbands or lovers have left the scene, are still a common phenomenon in Cape Verde.

Differences and prejudices had more to do with class than with colour, but there was a substantial overlap. Lowest on the social ladder were the descendants of slaves. Highest were those Cape Verdeans who were descended from the landowners and the colonial administrators, and the few Europeans. Before independence you could not see many black Cape Verdeans in white-collar positions of any status, says Duarte, but adds that it would be a mistake to see this as racism.[2] This is contestable, but Duarte's main point can hardly be denied: the whites or near-whites in Cape Verde, in contrast to, for example, Angola and Mozambique, were simply too few to impose a cultural supremacy.[3]

Portuguese '*patria*', African '*matria*'

How cultural identity is defined relates to power over people and their thought and knowledge. This hegemony can be questioned in a variety of passive or active forms of resistance or counter-power.

The binary concepts of European, read "civilised", and African, read "primitive", were not only found in colonial thinking but were also adopted among the literate in colonial society. In Cape Verde, the educated petit-bourgeoisie first uncritically adopted the colonial disdain for the African elements of culture, then developed an ambivalent stance from the 19th century. While Portugal for them still represented their *patria* (fatherland), and Lisbon their spiritual capital, they started to interest themselves for and partly identify with the ordinary people of Cape Verde, seeing it with its many African influences as a romantic *matria* (motherland).[4] It was from this intellectual milieu that the classical writers and composers of *morna* came. Lyrics in the Kriolu language became an outstanding feature.

African or European?

It is not the idea of unity but the notion of different cultural identities, which has coloured thinking about Cape Verdean culture. Here we meet the binary terms "developed" (West) versus "undeveloped" or "primitive" (Africa). Deirdre Meintel, in the early 1970s, found this ideological pattern prevalent in Cape Verde as synonymous with black (preto) and white (branco). She summarises:

> Virtually any cultural form believed to be of African origin constituted a sign of backwardness; at the same time, any form considered primitive was assumed to be African.[5]

She notes, for example that carrying objects on the head, walking barefoot, believing in magic, such as belief in the evil eye etc. were widely disparaged although most of these customs also could be found in rural Portugal. The belief in the evil eye, for example, was a Mediterranean custom. She concludes:

---

1. Meintel 1984, p. 93.
2. Based on interview with Dulce Almada Duarte, July 21, 2000.
3. Davidson 1989, p. 31 (based on Davidson's conversation with Dulce Duarte).
4. Interview with Dulce Almada Duarte July 21, 2000.
5. Meintel 1984, p. 104.

> The folk ethnology that ascribed them African origin expressed on the popular level the coloni-
> alist ideology whereby civilisation was synonymous with metropolitan culture.[1]

This way of structuring cultural phenomena in the world is also reflected in the way that Cape Verdean music styles have been divided into the music of the *badius* (the black rural poor), the *brancos* (whites), and the Kriolu (mixed), or into European-influenced versus African-influenced style. By and large this categorisation reflects the facts of African and European influences. But the classification is crude (what is "European music" or "African music"), it ignores the fact that cultural meetings take place in all genres, it plays down the changes over time, and sometimes mis-interprets influences to make preconceived notions fit.

Moreover, the preoccupation with origins can distract from seeing Cape Verdean musics as contributions to the world music treasure. The number one question be-comes: "From what pure forms did this bastard come?" There is a risk that one is looking for the roots but missing the flower.

Globally today cultural mixing is not denied, but often celebrated. Yet even those celebrating often use concepts that presuppose pure forms. Dulce Almada Duarte used the word "bastardisation".[2] She here turns a condescending naming into some-thing positive. "Hybridisation" is another concept, which is often employed in post-colonial discourse. Both of these terms are, however, borrowed from the world of biology and breeding, and carry with them the baggage of biological analogies that ill fit cultural discourse. They seem to imply that there are precedent pure forms, which by intercourse give rise to hybrids or bastards. Mixing is a ubiquitous feature of cultural development, and it is only necessary to stress this in order to counter static and essentialist concepts.[3]

In the following overview of the main Cape Verdean music genres I will use the conventional categories, but point to their blurred borders.[4]

"The music of the *badius* or music of African origin"

Fusion of different elements started early in Cape Verdean music. Catholic feasts to celebrate the saint for a particular island were particularly important. Some music genres hardly became part of the celebration of the saints at all, and are therefore seen as having retained a more African character. *Batuco* (or *batuque*) is the oldest Cape Verdean music form with more apparent African traits than other music forms.[5] Unlike similar types of music on the African mainland and in Brazil, there are no drums. The reason says more about Cape Verdean conditions than about cul-tural origins. There were simply neither enough trees nor animals available to the slaves and their descendants to make drums. Peter Manuel points at the polyrhythm, call-and-response singing, the percussive intensity, and the dance style in the *batu-que/finaçon*, and says they all strongly suggest African derivation.[6]

---

1. Ibid., p. 105.
2. Interview with Almada Duarte July 21, 2000.
3. Cf. Tomlinson 1999, pp. 141–49.
4. My main source is Carlos Gonçalves, musician, radio director, and author of a two-volume book on Cape Ver-dean music, "Kap-Vert Band", which in 2000 had not yet found its publisher. A short first draft was included in 1998 in *Découverte des îles du Cap-Vert*. This is supplemented by two interviews I made in July 2000 in Praia. For the facts in the music overview I only indicate Gonçalves, as a source where I believe his statements are contested.
5. Fryer 2000, pp. 95–103.
6. Manuel 1988a, p. 21.

Batuco was originally more than a song. It was a ceremony performed only by women at certain rituals, generally before and during the celebration of marriage, or at the special occasions such as the ceremonial nights of the *tabanka* (see below).

Finaçon is a solo that opens the *batuco*, accompanied by a mono-cord string instrument of an African type, the *cimboa*. In some texts *finaçon* is treated as a special music genre.[1] It is traditionally performed as a competition between two female vocalists who improvise topical verses, which cover a broad range of subjects, and are rendered in a highly rhythmic, but at most semi-melodic style.[2] The songs are often satirical, and criticise public or even private life. The song texts are almost always improvised, and the singers are elderly women.

The central part of the *batuco*, which consists of an elaboration of the rhythm, is executed by the women singing the chorus, sitting in a circle and clapping hands and beating on cushions or plastic bags filled with water between their legs. One or two women dance in the circle with a *pano bicho*[3] or shawl around their waists. *Torno* is a dance that concludes the *batuco*, with the rhythmic movement of the loins in imitation of a sexual act.

Tabanka is another music style, which historically was an elaborate symbolic ceremony. Its origin probably lies in the mutual-aid organisation born with the liberation of slaves. The *tabanka* is also the name of an organisation with a hierarchy of authority, and the paraphernalia of society beyond: court, military, hospital, prison etc. It has a king with his adviser, and a queen who commanded the children, all elected by the members. The centre of the *tabanka*, called a chapel, has a courtyard where the dances and the rituals take place. The festivities of the *tabanka* begin on the 3rd of May, and continue until July. About a hundred persons take part in the procession, representing the various groups in what must be seen as a satire of society. Some European influences are obvious, such as the use of big drums, which are carried only on one side, to mark the rhythm. Women sing in chorus, always the same traditional songs, of which the best known are "Nha Corne Tinha" and "Manito Bomba".

The third popular music genre attributed to African origins is the *funaná*, developed in rural São Tiago. Again, *funaná* earlier referred to the festive occasion rather than to the music. *Funaná* earned a reputation for being associated with rowdy parties, which sometimes ended in physical fights, even in killing. At weddings, where *funaná* was often played, a playful abduction of the fiancée could sometimes end in violent clashes between families.

Funaná used to be vocal and accompanied by only two instruments, *ferro* and *gaita*. *Ferro* is a thin iron bar scraped with a peg or a knife, which marks the rhythm, while the *gaita* is a diatonic accordion or concertina used for the melodic accompaniment.[4] The songs were often about specific events or persons.[5] The dance accompanying the *funaná* was inspired from Europe with one man and one woman holding each other.

The *funaná* probably dates from the end of the 19th century. Some suggest that Portuguese settlers had packed this popular instrument in their luggage. Others again think their import was started by the Catholic church who found the accordi-

---

1. Monteiro 1998, p. 52.
2. Manuel 1988a, p. 51.
3. The *pano bicho* is a woven cloth of a kind that was used as payment for slaves on the mainland, and has also been used as exchange currency on Cape Verde.
4. Gonçalves 1998, p. 180.
5. Sandahl 1993.

Carlos Gonçalves Photo: Mai Palmberg

ons cheaper than church organs, which could be consistent with the claim that the style was born with the importation from Portugal of accordions by a Praia firm.[1]

The musicologist Felix Monteiro thinks that *funaná* is definitely not African, and says that equivalents are found in the Brazilian *funganga* and the Portuguese *fungaga*, both popular dances among poor people.[2]

"The music of the *brancos*" or "European music"

Portuguese landowners and Jews escaping persecution, brought with them dances of high society, such as the *mazurka, polka*, and *contredanse*. On Santo Antão, considered as the most "European" island, this heritage lived on and took on a Cape Verdean character, and even gave rise to new dance styles, such as the *kola*. Here the mazurka and contradance are still danced with all the rituals from the old days, including the master of ceremonies, "marcor", who gives instructions to the dancers in French. Some writers think this dance was introduced during the 19th century through Porto Grande in São Vicente, while Gonçalves thinks it came with pirates even earlier.[3]

The violinist Travadinho has for some decades successfully popularised this music from Santo Antão, which is very much respected as an integral part of the Cape Verdean treasure.

"Kriolu music"

The concept "Kriolu music" stands for the music of the mestiços, the mixed population. Since Kriolu is also the language (in which all music is sung) the concept "Kriolu" appears in two meanings of identity: first, neutrally as the language ele-

---

1. Vladimir Monteiro says "all sources agree" that the accordions were introduced by the church. Monteiro 1998, p. 62, but see also Gonçalves 1998, p. 181.
2. Loc.cit.
3. Gonçalves 1998, p. 182–84.

ment in cultural identity, second as an essentialised and racialised notion of identity of the *mestiços*.

The *morna*, the "Kriolu music" *par excellence*, dates back only to the beginning of the 20th century. Scholars have accepted Eugenio Tavares' observation about the oldest known *morna*, a song called "Brada Maria" and sung on the isle of Boa Vista.

The undisputed creator of the modern *morna* was the poet and, composer Eugénio (1867–1930) from the island of Brava in the southwest. He and Pedro Cardoso started to write *mornas* in Kriolu, (early *mornas* were in Portuguese). The classical *mornas* were thus part of a literary movement, and this was also true of the second generation of *morna* composers and writers.

In the1930s in Mindelo, the port town of the isle of Sâo Vicente, a group of intellectuals around the review *Claridade*, most of them poets, became the first constructors of Cape Verdean cultural identity—Jorge Barbosa, Baltasar Lopes, Osvaldo Alcântara, Joâo Lopes and others. As part of this milieu, Fransisco Xavier da Cruz (1905–1958), who called himself B. Leza (from "Beleza", beauty) was the prolific leading *morna* writer and composer. He had learnt the guitar from Luis Rendall, who introduced the solo guitar as a genre its own right, inspired by Brazilian music.[1]

Morna consists of a poem that is sung in medium-tempo quadratic meter by a solo vocalist accompanied by stringed instruments such as the violin (*rabeca* in Portuguese), the guitar-like *violâo*, the 12-stringed viola, and the ukulele-like *cavaquinho*.[2] The clarinet can also be used as solo instrument. The early *mornas* were often fast, and had more humour and social critique than you find today (except in the *mornas* from Boa Vista). Today these characteristics have been taken over by the *coladeira* (see below). *Morna* was also a dance in the period 1930–1945, especially on Sâo Vicente.[3]

Vasco Martins, one of the few who has made a musicological analysis of the *morna* argues that the *morna* has definite European roots for its instrumentation. Composing a *morna* requires a polyphonic instrument, and only the *violâo* (or Portuguese guitar) could perform this function.[4]

Tavares and B. Leza gave *morna* its present classical form, with its imprint of *sodade*, related to but not identical with the Portuguese *saudade*, meaning "longing", "nostalgia", "feeling of loss", and a destiny of deprivation. Some of the best-known *mornas* by Tavares and B. Leza, are love songs, often about unattained love. Many lament the necessity to go away from the poor and arid isles, and the nostalgia about returning. Perhaps no other country's popular music contains so many references to the country as do the *mornas* (and *coladeras*) of Cape Verde. The *morna* belongs to the towns and is insolubly linked with the sea and with longing for friends, loves, and countries. In the *morna* lyric probably only the word *cretcheu* (darling, loved one) can compete with "Cabo Verde" in frequency.

In the 1950s the *coladera*, a more recent genre, had definitely arrived on the scene and was greeted as a new exciting genre.[5] *Coladeras* were sometimes created simply by changing the rhythm of the slower *mornas*.[6] While the *coladeras* often serve as social comments, the *mornas* express inner emotions. But they function as a pair, and those who sing *mornas* also sing *coladeras*. Some important *coladera*

---

1. Sandahl 1993.
2. Manuel 1988b, p. 96 and Manuel 1988a, p. 75.
3. Monteiro 1998, p. 25.
4. Martins 1989, p. 21.
5. B. Leza is reported to have already spoken in the 1930s of a musical novelty called *coladeira* by Gonçalves 1998, p. 184.
6. Loc.cit.

composers are Gregorio (Goy) Gonçalves, Frank Cavaquim and Manuel de Novas (whose real name is Manuel de Jesus Lopes).

In the "classical" era of the 1950s and the 1960s the music was performed on two different occasions: (1) at big balls played at by orchestras with wind instruments (trumpet, clarinet), strings /guitar, *cavaquinho*, banjo) and percussion (drums, maracas); (2) at serenades and cultural events, played at by smaller groups of violin or clarinet as solo, guitars, *cavaquinho* and light percussion, often with a pianist or bass player. *Conjunto de Cabo Verde* was one of the most famous bands, with singers like Titina.

Even this cursory overview should show that it is time once and for all to shelve the question whether Cape Verdean culture in general or the specific music styles are African or European. We can begin by agreeing with Manuel Ferreira that Cape Verdean culture is an amalgamation, a synthesis.[1] But we should add that all culture is the ever changing result of mixing, and that even Ferreira's words imply the prior existence of pure categories. In culture there are no parents, only old and new mixed forms.

Popular music for which people?

During colonialism the *tabanka* was prohibited several times. The Catholic church disapproved of the *bautco*, and *funaná* was looked upon with suspicion. The *morna*, however, was never banned, even though the use of the Kriolu language was often restricted and partly prohibited. Why?

There could be several reasons why the *morna* was allowed, while "the music of the *badius*" (the lower classes, descended from slaves) was persecuted. *Batuco* was repressed because of its sexually suggestive dance style. Both *batuco* and *tabanka*, with their obliquely militant texts[2] often contained abuses and spite towards the authorities. *Funaná* was seen as a symbol of resistance to colonial authority on São Tiago. The Portuguese authorities feared the drumming in these genres as a secret African language, and as a powerful means of mobilisation to protest and revolt.

The colonial tolerance of the *morna* had to do with class and cultural affinity to the Portuguese—*morna* was "musique de salon".[3] Although sung in Kriolu, in colonial times often called a "black" language, the *mornas* with their love and *sodade* lyrics did not agitate the masses. Rarely did the *mornas* contain a political message, apart from the lamentation of conditions which forced people to leave their homes to work in, for example, the plantations of São Tomé. B. Leza was the first to write *mornas* with outright political content. He wrote one against Hitler, which also is an implicit criticism of the pro-Nazi sympathies of the Portuguese, and another praising the rise of Africa against the invaders, in a song on Ethiopia during Mussolini's invasion.[4] These songs, however, did not become part of the standard repertoire.

This raises the question of the representation of the musical genres. If *morna* was a *musique de salon* of the middle class and the composers were from an elite with education, literary gifts and ability, how did it become the genre *par excellence* to express Cape Verdean national sentiments and character? Was this a case of cultural imposition by the middle classes and the petit-bourgeoisie? That is implied in asser-

1. Ferreira 1973, pp. 41–48, 71–83. His statement was a rejoinder to a thesis by the influential Brazilian sociologist Gilberto Freyre that it certainly is European.
2. Manuel 1988a, p. 21.
3. Duarte interview July 21, 2000.
4. Monteiro 1998, p. 29. The anti-Hitler song was composed during B.Leza's stay in Portugal, where he was disgusted with the pro-Hitler sympathies there.

Photo: Mai Palmberg

Cesaria Évora

tions that the *morna* is rejected by the *badius* of Sâo Tiago, and appreciated there only by the most assimilated. This could be a racialised myth.[1] More than geographic differences in the identification of the *morna* as "our" music, I found a generation gap.[2]

It is not unusual, however, that cultural forms take the road from a middle class phenomenon to becoming popularised and embraced by "ordinary people", and the opposite (as with jazz, reggae, *fado* etc.). Partly this is the result of processes whereby culture becomes accessible to the majority. In Cape Verde the role of the radio is important. One should also add that even though the *mornas* were composed by men of education, they were often performed by men and women of the people. This is certainly true of the "queen of the *morna*" Cesaria Évora.

In the beginning the *mornas* were being sung by women, such as Celibania in Sâo Vicente. "The golden age" in the 1950s and 1960s brought many female singers to the fore, like Arlinda Santos, Titina, Mité Costa, Arminda Sousa, Bia Randall, Cesaria Évora and many others. But after this the presence of women in the *morna* was reduced. Zezinha Chantre, responsible for information and propaganda in the Cape Verdean women's organisation (OMCV) took the initiative for a festival of female voices in March 1985 in Praia, and persuaded Cesaria Évora, then already a recognised star of the *morna* but whose voice had been silent for many years, to take part. This was Cesaria's come-back and the start of her career as the "cultural ambassador" of Cape Verde, now even sealed by her diplomatic passport.

---

1. A North American ethnomusicologist, Joanne Hoffman, from her field-work in Cape Verde in 2000 said she believed there were more *mornas* being composed in Sâo Tiago than elsewhere, but they were seldom recorded.
2. An idol of the young is Gil (Semedo), with his group The Perfects, whose portrait you can see on wall paintings, for example in Praia. He lives in Holland, and sings in Kriolu to a techno music. The older generation reacted vehemently to the mention of his name, saying "this is not Cape Verdean", or even "that is not music".

Enlarging the musical treasure

While the *musique de salon* of the *morna* is increasingly seen as the music of the people at large, in another movement of inclusion the music of the *badius* has to a growing extent been adopted as the music of all Cape Verdeans.[1]

Just before independence in 1975, a music movement had started on the platform going back to the roots of Cape Verdean music. In 1978 a break-through came with the group *Bulimundo* ("Shaking up the world"), who began to collect the melodies and rhythms of what came to be called *"rural funaná"*, and adapt them to electronic instruments, under the lead of musician and composer Alberto Martins, "Catchass".[2] The electrification of the *funaná* was criticised by many intellectuals but embraced by young people, and by the people of São Tiago.[3] The new *funaná* became the most favoured disco music, on all the islands. Gonçalves writes:

> The upsurge of what can be called the *funaná* electronic, gives a new impulse to music in Cape Verde, which finds itself enriched with yet another music form. It is a music form with new instrumentation, another structure and thematic, but with roots in the tradition *funaná*. In actual fact the *funaná*, in its new version, is along with the *morna* and *coladera* a genre of national music, whose compositions make up the repertoire in all bands and orchestras.[4]

There is today in Cape Verde a strong movement to revive musical traditions of all genres, including children's songs,[5] and work songs chanted by those who make *grogue* in Santo Antão.[6] Old people are being interviewed, and youth groups are formed to dig out their local music. On Santo Antão today young dance and music groups perform the local dances. In Assomada (formerly Santa Catarina) in the heart of the São Tiago island a Tabanka museum has been opened.

The seeking of roots inevitably means stressing pluralism, since all islands had their own local traditions and celebrated musicians. The revitalisation of tradition cannot, of course, be the replication of music of earlier periods. It is simply not possible to know exactly how old music genres sounded. In addition, the social contexts in which they occurred have changed enormously. For example, there are no big halls in which the large orchestras can play. *Simentera* is the only existing group, which has followed in Bulimundo's footsteps.

In the meanwhile there is an increasingly canonised idea of what classical *morna* is, sometimes given a ahistorical and timeless definition. In the Cape Verdean case this can be illustrated by Cesaria's reply to me when I ventured that *coladera* was younger than *morna*. She first said: "No, they are equally old." Then she hesitated and added: "Actually I do not know. They both existed when I grew up." And indeed, the 1950s and 1960s seem to be accepted as the classical age of the *morna* and *coladera*, the model for that tradition.

While Cape Verdeans look back, they also look abroad. Increasingly since the 1980s Cape Verdean music, particularly *morna* and *coladeira*, but lately also the new *funaná*, has boarded the World Music train. Since a few years back a big music

---

1. Duarte says that this has been possible only because this music, especially the *funaná*, is well received abroad, while Lobban speaks of a market-orientation during independence whereby the African roots are seen as having an exchange value. More likely, in my view, is the fact that conceptions about higher and lower civilisation, and higher and lower culture, are being questioned, and that the *badius* are simply more visible and have better chances to make themselves and their experiences heard.
2. Catchass tragically died in a traffic accident in 1988.
3. Gonçalves 1998, p. 181.
4. Gonçalves 1998, p. 189.
5. Celina Pereira has collected and recorded children's songs, many not used today as children watch Brazilian *telenovelas*.
6. See Monteiro 1998, pp. 80–85. *Grogue* is a grape-based strong liquor "produced in Santo Antão and drunk in Mindelo".

festival is organised at the first full moon in August in Bahia de Gaitas on the shores of São Vicente. This festival has been hailed as the only true heir to the spirit of Woodstock.

The question is what inclusion into world music means to the form and contents. What did it mean, for example, when Cesaria Évora's producer in Paris, Lusafrica's Jorge da Silva removed Bau (a musician from Bulimundo) as leader of the orchestra for Cesaria Évora's world tours to replace him with a Cuban musician? Cesaria says it means not a thing, the Cubans just have to play Cape Verdean,[1] while Bau has said that apparently they wanted to give a more Cuban sound to Cesaria's new records.[2]

Yet changes from the supposed original forms are expected and necessary if the art is to grow in new circumstances. "Authenticity" is perhaps best reserved as a reference to artistic quality, which of course to a large extent is a subjective judgement.

The Kriolu language

Through these *morna* writers the Kriolu language in Cape Verde began to become a recorded, and written language. Young girls who had gone to school in the 1950s and 1960s in the towns wrote down the words of the *mornas* in precious private notebooks.[3] Yet it is only now, at the beginning of the 21st century, that the orthography of Kriolu is being established. Experiments are starting with Kriolu as the language of instruction at the primary level of schooling

In Cape Verde today the Kriolu language is spoken by all inhabitants as their mother tongue, with somewhat different versions on the nine different islands. "Em Cabo Verde, a vida decorre em Crioulo—In Cape Verde, life runs in Kriolu", as Almada Duarte says.[4] She points out that Cape Verde is a case not of bilingualism, two languages existing parallel, but of *diglossía*, where two languages (Portuguese and Kriolu) co-exist but have quite different functions.[5]

Kriolu in Cape Verde is one of many Creole languages in the world, which often have developed in encounters between a minority of plantation owners and a majority of slaves or forced labour. They developed as a communication language for commanding labour power, but also for the communication between the slaves, who often did not share one common language. Because of this background with its connection to the slave trade, which uprooted hundreds of thousands of Africans, quite a few Creole languages are found on both sides of the Atlantic.[6]

The Creole languages take the larger part of their vocabulary from one dominating language, English, French, Spanish, or Portuguese (as is the case in Cape Verde). The grammar, however, is constructed entirely differently, with different systems for indicating time, number etc. It is not possible for a speaker of the language that has served as the main source of the Creole vocabulary to understand much of the relat-

---

1. Interview with Cesaria Évora, Uppsala May 13, 2001.
2. Lira Folk & Världsmusik (Sweden), Dec. 1999–Jan. 2000. Euclides Carvalho pointed out how the instrumentation on Cesaria's CD "Café Atlantico" broke with tradition, as sometimes the *kora*, not the guitar took the lead.
3. I was told this by an educated family in Praia in July 2000.
4. Almada Duarte 1998.
5. See also Robert K. Hall 1966, p. 131 where, with the example of Haiti, he calls it a situation of "linguistic schizophrenia".
6. Robert K. Hall differiantates between a *lingua franca*, which is any language used as medium of communication by people who have no other language in common, *pidgin* languages which have reduced grammar and vocabulary and are not native to any of its speakers; and *creole* languages which arise when a pidgin has become the native tongue of a community.

ed Creole languages. The Creole languages have almost everywhere remained vernaculars of low prestige, spoken by underprivileged groups.[1]

In Cape Verde during colonialism Portuguese was the language for encounters with the authorities, in all schools, and the language for writing. This is still so. Kriolu is still not a recognised official language, only Portuguese is. Asked why Kriolu was not accorded official status, Almada Duarte replied: "The colonised mind is very complex". When I asked whether it was practical or ideological considerations behind the language policy, she stated emphatically: "Not practical".[2]

The future of the Kriolu language is a matter of speculation, hopes and fears. Almada Duarte believes that Kriolu will in time become a recognised national language. She points to the fact that Cape Verdean emigrants returning for brief or long visits reinforce the demand for an official status of Kriolu, their mother tongue which they have retained while emigrants outside Portugal have forgotten Portuguese. José Luis Almada on the other hand points at a de-creolisation process taking place with social ascendancy, and the looking down on Kriolu by the elite. This is, he claims, a process reinforced by mass media and political leaders.

While Kriolu has been and continues to be relegated to the homes and streets it has becomes publicly celebrated through the music. For the people the use of Kriolu in the lyrics for the music became a source of pride and cultural assertion, for the ambivalent educated elite it became a demonstration of their loyalty to their *matria*. These sentiments could perhaps explain the harsh criticism of Fernando Quejas in the 1950s who had the audacity to sing *mornas* in Portuguese. He was also perhaps the first to record and introduce Cape Verdean music to Europe.[3] Only now is he beginning to receive recognition for his pioneering work. Perhaps one can interpret this acknowledgement as a move from a hegemonic to a pluralist expression of cultural identity.

Cape Verde can seem like a society of great cultural and "racial" variety. Its identity is based on difference, one of its authors and musicians said, also calling Cape Verde a "universal" society, with the concept of racism something he encountered only when going to Cuba.[4]

Cape Verde is in fact a very homogeneous society with many shared identity markers. Kriolu is an identity glue, and most Cape Verdeans are Catholics. They also share the perception of a common history, and a shared notion of a shared destiny. Cape Verdeans constitute one ethnic community.[5] The pluralism is very much a pluralism of the images in our minds. To call Cape Verde a heterogeneous society shows how difficult it is for the Western or Westernised mind to leave behind the notion of race as a significant ingredient in an essentialised notion of identity. It is as if the colour of the skin not only indicates very broadly a geographic area of origin, and also certain histories (such as that of the slaves, and segregated), but also a stable and unique set of characteristics, culture, abilities, and weaknesses, which is inherited from one generation to the next.

---

1. T. Jansson in *Nationalencyklopedin*, Vol. 11, p. 394. Few countries have developed Creole into a written language, and even fewer have given it the status of official language, such as the French-based Haitian on Hispanola.
2. Interview with Almada Duarte July 21, 2000.
3. Gonçalves 1998, p. 183.
4. Mário Lúcio Sousa at the Nordic Africa Institute September 29, 1999 in the seminar series "The authors' Africa".
5. See Anthony Smith 1991, p. 21 on the attributes of an ethnic group.

The Cape Verdean diaspora

In many ways the Cape Verdean diaspora has played a vital role in distributing the popular music from the islands. There are more Cape Verdeans in the diaspora than at home. Boston is said to be the biggest Cape Verdean city in the world, and some suburbs are dominated by Cape Verdeans. This was the earliest destination of emigrants on a large scale. In Europe the biggest number of Cape Verdeans are found in Portugal, but there are also Cape Verdean communities in Belgium, Holland, France, and Italy. The remittances from the Cape Verdean diaspora amount to about 50 per cent of the GDP, with the Cape Verdean communities in the United States leading the league.

The diaspora was also instrumental in recording and thereby preserving and spreading the popular musics of Cape Verde. As mentioned, in Lisbon in the 1950s the singer Fernando Quejas recorded songs by the classical composers of B. Leza, Eugenio Tavares, as well as the oldest *coladeras*. Some 78-rpm recordings were made in the United States, but they are no longer available.

In the 1960s the drought and colonial repression combined hit the culturally flourishing town of Mindelo hard, and many emigrated, including a great number of musicians. Some of those settling in Holland founded the record company "Casa de Silva" (later "Morabeza") and launched what can be considered the first LP with Cape Verdean music at the beginning of the 1960s, "CaboVerdeanos na Hollanda". This started a flood of Cape Verdean recordings abroad, a flood that has continued to flow.[1] Today recordings are also made in Cape Verde, but there is a dearth of proper studios. Many records are produced in Portugal, the United States, and France, where Lusafrica produces mainly Cape Verdean music, with Cesaria Évora as their main star.

Many Cape Verdean musicians and singers are part of the emigrant communities. In Portugal you find, for example, Paulino Vieira, Bana and Titina, and in the United States Ramiro Mendes, Fantcha, and Sâozinha. The Cape Verde musicians in the diaspora devote themselves to cherishing the classical music treasure, and at the same time feeding it into the flows of world music.

Where does it all come from?

We have found that the *morna* in particular, but also the *coladera* and the new *funaná* function as icons in the construction and maintenance of an all-Cape Verdean identity. If one wants to discuss why these musics attained this position, the question can be approached in two different ways. On the one hand, one can ask what the roots of these musics are, and what influences shaped them, as I have briefly done above. On the other hand, one can ask what needs these particular music styles answered. I am especially interested in how the *morna* expression of heart-breaking *sodade* has become identified as the expression of the Cape Verdean soul.

There are parallels between the *fado* with its *saudade*, and the *morna* with its *sodade*, both full of longing and nostalgia, perhaps because both Portugal and Cape Verde have lived with the sea as their destiny. The Brazilian *modinha* has also been suggested as a relative to Cape Verdean *morna*, possibly mutually influenced. The Argentinean tango, like the Portuguese *fado*, had a more distinct working class and urban character, however, than the *morna* which was part of an emergent national-

---

1. Gonçalves 1998, p. 186.

ism, foregrounding the indigenous language. To my knowledge no direct links are suggested between the Argentinean tango and the *morna*.

But we can also in a comparative perspective focus on the functions, instead of on the roots and cultural diffusion. Interestingly, there is at least one other country outside the Latino-Iberian sphere, where nostalgia has become identified with the national character, and expressed in music. This is Finland with its very own version of tango, which rose to prominence at about the same time as the *morna*, in the post-war years, and has retained its position since.[1] The longing and lamentation of loss in Finnish tango (*kaipaus*) fulfilled a need during the war, when tango became a favoured music for the boys on the front. In Cape Verde the much more enduring loss was the inability of the arid islands to feed its population, and the recurrent famines, which in the 20th century alone had cost more than 80,000 people's lives.[2]

Special circumstances made for the fast-growing popularity of the Finnish tango. When the Finnish wartime prohibition of public dancing was lifted as late as in 1948, dance places were built at a rapid rate and a demand exploded for danceable music that people liked. The Finnish tango fitted the need and the mood. Singers had no choice but to sing tango to be in demand. Conversely, in Cape Verde with difficult communications between the islands it was an advantage that the melodious *morna* did not require large dance arenas, but could be transmitted by radio and records to all the islands. Much later, in the 1980s and 1990s the *funaná* could spread as dance music beyond São Tiago when communication lines had improved, and also the technical equipment, which made playback possible for big dance events. At the same time, the lack of big halls in Cape Verde has hampered the music scene.

The Finnish nostalgia can seem hypocritical in present-day fairly affluent "Nokialand", and today the Finnish tango mainly laments the longing for lost or not-yet attained love.[3] But separation is perhaps as important as economic suffering, and in both countries more than 300,000 people have migrated to find work elsewhere. It is well known from other contexts as well that the importance of asserting one's identity grows with separation and distance, as does the tendency to express this belonging with traditional cultural markers. Both *sodade* and *kaipaus* are perfect palliatives to soothe homesickness.

In spite of any possible comparisons the differences remain. Perhaps the most distinguishing characteristic of Cape Verdean music was pointed out by Cesaria Évora in her reply to my question why the music meant so much in her country: "We have nothing else".[4]

Interviews

Cesaria Évora May 20, 2000, in Uppsala, Sweden.

Cesaria Évora July 28, 2000, in Mindelo, São Vicente, Cape Verde.

Euclides Carvalho, Radio Morabeza, July 28, 2000 in Mindelo, São Vicente, Cape Verde.

---

1. When I interviewed composer Manuel de Novas in July 2000 he told me eagerly about his stop as a sailor to a Finnish port, where he found that people danced tango, fascinated to find so far north a parallel to the *sodade* of Cape Verde.
2. Anderberg 1995, p. 172.
3. For an interesting penetration of the themes of the Finnish tango, with some references to the Argentine tango, see Kukkonen 1996.
4. Interview with Cesaria Évora May 20, 2000.

Manuel Veiga, Instituto Nacional de la Pesquisa Cultural, July 17, 2000 in Praia, Sâo Tiago, Cape Verde.

Carlos Gonçalves, Radio Comercial, July 18, 2000 and July 21, 2000 in Praia, Sâo Tiago, Cape Verde.

Dulce Almada Duarte, Commissâo Nacional para a Lingua Cabo-Verdiana [The National Commission on Language in Cape Verde], July 21, 2000 in Praia, Sâo Tiago, Cape Verde.

Moacyr Rodrigues, July 24, 2000 in Mindelo, Sâo Vicente, Cape Verde.

Eduardo da Silva, fisherman and musician, July 25, 2000 in Pontinha da Janela, Santo Antâo, Cape Verde.

Manuel de Novas, July 30, 2000 in Mindelo, Sâo Vicente, Cape Verde.

References

Almada Duarte, Dulce, 1998, *Bilinguismo ou disglossia? As relaçôes de força entre o crioulu e o portuguêes na sociedade cabo-verdiana.* Praia, Cabo Verde: Spleen-Ediçôes.

Anderberg, Irene, 1995, "Kap Verde. De törstiga öarna", in *Jord och vatten i södra Afrika, Afrikagruppernas årskrönika*, pp. 172–75. Stockholm: Afrikagrupperna.

Anderson, Benedict, 1983, *Imagined Communities. Reflections on the Origins and Spread of Nationalism.* London: Verso.

Découverte des îles du Cap-Vert. Paris: Ministère de la Coopération et d'Action Culturelle and Praia, Cape Verde: Archives historiques nationales.

Carreira, António, 1972, *Cabo Verde. Formaçâo e extinçâo de uma sociedade escravocrata (1460–1878).* Lisboa: Centro de Estudos da Guiné Portuguesa.

—, 1982, *The People of the Cape Verde Islands. Exploitation and Emigration.* London: C. Hurst & Company. (Original title: "Migraçôes nas ilhas de Cabo Verde" 1977.)

Davidson, Basil, 1989, *The Fortunate Isles: A Study in Transformation.* London: Hutchinson Education.

Eriksen, Thomas Hylland, 1993, *Ethnicity & Nationalism. Anthropological Perspectives.* London: Pluto Press.

Ferreira, Manuel, 1973, *A aventura crioula: ou Cabo Verde, uma sintese cultural e étnica,* Series Coleçâo temas portugueses 2. Lisboa: Plátano.

Fryer, Peter, 2000, *Rhythms of Resistance. African Musical Heritage in Brazil.* London: Pluto Press.

Gonçalves, Carlos Filipe, 1998, "Kap-Vert Band", in *Découverte des îles du Cap-Vert,* pp.163–91. Paris: Ministère de la Coopération et d'Action Culturelle and Praia, Cape Verde: Archives historiques nationales.

Hall, Robert A., 1966, *Pidgin and Creole Languages.* Ithaca, New York: Cornell University Press.

Hall, Stuart, 1990, "Cultural Identity and Diaspora", in Rutherford, Jonathan (ed.), *Identity, Community, Culture, and Difference*, pp. 222–37. London: Lawrence & Wishart.

Jansson, T., 2002, "Kreolspråk", in *Nationalencyklopedin*, Vol. 11, p. 394. http://www.ne.se/jsp/search/article.jsp?i_art_id=231335

Kukkonen, Pirjo L.H., 1996, *Tango Nostalgia. The Language of Love and Longing.* Helsinki: Helsinki University Press.

Lira Folk & Världsmusik (Sweden), Dec. 1999–Jan. 2000.

Lobban, Richard A. Jr., 1995, *Cape Verde. Crioulo Colony to Independent Nation.* Nations of the Modern World: Africa. Boulder: Westview Press.

Manuel, Peter, 1988a, in Lobban and Halter (eds), *Historical Dictionary of the Republic of Cape Verde*, African Historical Dictionaries, No. 42. Metuchen, New Jersey & London: The Scarecrow Press.

—, 1988b, *Popular Musics of the Non-Western World. An Introductory Survey.* Oxford and New York: Oxford University Press.

Martins, Vasco, 1989, *A musica tradicional cabo-verdiana I (A Morna).* Praia, Cape Verde: ICL.

Meintel, Deirdre, 1984, *Race, Culture, and Portuguese Colonialism in Cabo Verde*, Foreign and Comparative Studies/African series XLI. Syracuse, New York: Maxwell School of Citizenship and Public Affairs, Syracuse University.

Monteiro, Vladimir, 1998, *Les musiques du Cap-Vert.* Paris: Éditions Chandeigne–Libraire Portugaise.

Mortaigne, Véronique, 1997, *Cesaria Évora. La voix du Cap-Vert.* Série "Afriques". Paris: Actes du Sud.

Rodrigues, Moacyr and Isabel Lobo, 1996, *A morna na literatura tradicional. Fonte para o estudo histórico-literário e a sua repercussâo na sociedade.* Praia: Estudos e Ensaios, Instituto caboverdiano do livro e do disco (ICL).

Sandahl, Sten, 1993, text for CD *Music from Cape Verde*, produced by Svenska Rikskonserter/ Caprice Records).

Silva Andrade, Elisa, 1996, *Les îles du Cap-Vert de la "Découverte" à l'independence Nationale (1460–1975).* Paris: L'Harmattan.

Smith, Anthony, 1991, *National Identity.* Harmondsworth: Penguin Books.

Tomlinson, John, 1999, *Globalization and Culture.* Chicago: The University of Chicago Press.

Veiga, Manuel (ed.), 1997, *Insularité et littérature aux îles du Cap-Vert.* Paris: Éditions Karthala.

A note of thanks

There are many to whom thanks are due for help in the preparation of this paper, and unfortunately none that I can blame for the result. Thanks to Eva Jørholt who gave me the idea, and the first collection of Cape Verdean music; to Helena Tolentino who so generously gave of her time to organise all the right contacts on Cape Verde; to Antonio Lourenço who travelled with me to Cape Verde, and helped translate the interviews; to Onesimo Silveira for arranging music experiences and interviews; to all those who gave of their time for the interviews; to Cesaria Évora for opening her house to us; to Irene Anderberg for her guidance on Santo Antâo: to Joaquim Morais of the National Library and Ausenda da Silva at the Instituto do Patrimonio Nacional for giving advice on sources; to Joanne Hoffman for sharing some insights from her fieldwork as an ethnomusicologist; to Chico Serra and his family for a relaxed luncheon with useful small talk; to Noel Pinto and his wife for sharing with us memories of the classical period of the *morna* and *coladera*; to the staff at the Ralph Rinzler Folklife Archives and Collection at the Smithsonian Institution in Washington D.C. for giving me access to the complete set of tapes from the Cape Verde session of the 1995 Folklife Festival in Washington DC; to Maria de Lourdes Varela da Veiga for trying to teach me Kriolu.

Gender, Ethnicity and Politics in Kadongo-Kamu Music of Uganda

Analysing the Song Kayanda

Sylvia Nannyonga-Tamusuza

The song *Kayanda* was composed by Willy Mukaabya of the Festak Guitar Singers and produced by Kasajja and Sons Studios in 1988.[1] It is a song with a long narrative, more than 150 lines. The song had limited broadcast on Radio Uganda, the only radio station that existed at the time *Kayanda* was released. Even when new radio stations were opened up in the late 1990s, *Kayanda* was not broadcast. I did not hear this song until 1996 when a friend in the United States of America sent me a dubbed copy. As of 2002, *Kayanda* is not broadcast on any of the more than fifteen radio stations existing in Uganda. The probable reason is that *Kayanda* in allegorical ways touches upon sensitive gender, ethnic and political issues in Uganda. To explore this we need to remind ourselves of some ethnic terms, in order to put the song *Kayanda* in its context.

Buganda is the region of the Baganda people (Muganda for individuals), the largest ethnic group and one of the oldest kingdoms in Uganda. The kingdom, headed by the Kabaka (king) is located in southern Uganda. Luganda is the language of the Baganda people. The term Kiganda denotes that which belongs to the Baganda people, for example Kiganda music and Kiganda culture. Sometimes Ganda is used as synonymous with Kiganda. Banyarwanda (Munyarwanda for individuals) means people from Rwanda. Barundi (Marundi for individual persons) means people from Burundi. As people from Rwanda and Burundi are foreign to Buganda and all come from west of Buganda, they are clustered as the same people by the Baganda. In a number of cases, the terms "Banyarwanda" and "Murundi" are used interchangeably. Actually the Baganda may refer to any foreigner from west of Buganda as Munyarwanda or Murundi.

A music programme presenter on Radio Uganda, who requested anonymity, attributed *Kayanda*'s limited broadcast to its politically loaded and sensitive message. He said, "we have to be careful not to lose our jobs because of political songs like *Kayanda*". This presenter related the lyrics of the song to ethnic and power structures in Uganda:

> *Kayanda,* is about an immigrant Murundi who came to Buganda as a shamba-boy [gardener], but eventually gained a lot of power and became the boss. Similarly, there are many Barundi and Banyarwanda among us who have continued to claim that they are Baganda. We have married the Barundi and Banyarwanda and now they are marrying our daughters. We have given them our property to inherit and some have just grabbed away our wealth. *Kayanda* is a direct social critique; I would not be comfortable to broadcast it.[2]

---

1. Information on the cassette cover does not indicate the date when the song was published, but the composer Willy Mukaabya told me it was released in 1988. When I asked him why he did not indicate the date, he told me that "customers do not want old songs; without a date one cannot tell how long the tape has been on the market". Mukaabya, interview May 29, 2000.
2. Anonymous interview, June 20, 1998.

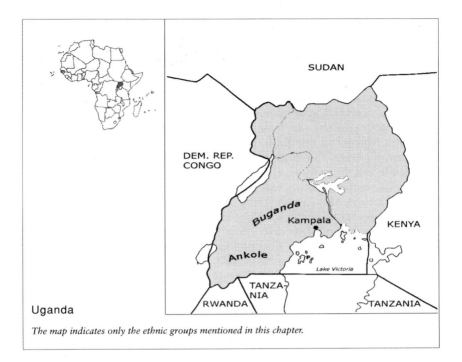

The map indicates only the ethnic groups mentioned in this chapter.

Kayanda is a song of the *kadongo-kamu* popular music that manipulates the inherent ambiguity of language and music to define political, gender, and cultural identities among the Baganda. *Kayanda* brings together musical and dramatic aspects, a style that characterizes *kadongo-kamu* music of the 1980s, spearheaded by Matiya Luyima as in his famous composition called *Nakakaawa*. We will return to the music, but let us first summarise the story of this long narrative song.

The story of *Kayanda*

The story of *Kayanda* revolves around a central character, Kayanda, who is a Murundi immigrant. Kayanda came to his master Mukaabya's home as a gardener to pick coffee, fetch water from the spring well, and chop firewood for the lady of the house. In the song, Kayanda is projected as a man with a powerful personality. He is outgoing and virile. These attributes render Kayanda a threat to his boss, Mukaabya, who is cold and impotent. Kayanda befriends the master's wife who seeks Kayanda's love and consolation in the absence of her husband who is always away on business trips. Kayanda's love is articulated by his reference to the wife of the house as *Mugole*, a title given to a newly wedded beloved wife. Kayanda is the only character who refers to Mukaabya's wife as Mugole. The other characters and even Mukaabya himself call her *mukyala* (wife). According to Kayanda, Mugole was no longer a wife of his master, but Kayanda's bride.

Above all, Mugole wants to have a child; in Buganda, child-bearing defines the identity of a woman. The result of the affair between Kayanda and Mugole is a baby girl named Nakiyimba. However, Mukaabya assumes that Nakiyimba is his child until he learns about Kayanda's and Mugole's love affair.

Discovering that Kayanda has a relationship with Mugole, Mukaabya summons the Resistance Council I (RC I), which consists of the village leaders, to mediate.[1] At the end the case is decided against Mukaabya despite the fact that it is proved that Mugole had deceived her husband and that Nakiyimba was his daughter. Mukaabya is declared guilty of neglecting his wife and embarrassing the Baganda people by allowing Kayanda, a Murundi, to run his home affairs. Moreover, the RC respects Kayanda as a powerful man because he has a child while Mukaabya has none.[2] Kayanda's inferior status as an immigrant Murundi is compensated by his progenital productivity. Mukaabya decides to send Kayanda away. However, Kayanda says that he can only leave if he is compensated for his nine years' work. Mugole sides with Kayanda and threatens to go with him if he is sent away.

During the session, another case comes up. The contenders include Kijjambu (a rich Muganda man), Mukyala Kijjambu (a wife of Kijjambu), and Kijjambu's driver. In the song, Mukyala Kijjambu is caught having a "drink" with the driver in Colline Hotel in Mukono town.[3] This case too, is decided in favour of the wife, Mukyala Kijjambu. The RC also blames Kijjambu for neglecting his wife, with resultant loss of power and authority over his household. The song ends with fighting between Kayanda and Mukaabya, and Kijjambu and his driver. *Kayanda* widens the space for interpretation and construction of meaning as the song ends without resolution of the conflict.

Kadongo-Kamo music

In many ways *Kayanda* defines the Baganda's cultural identity and in order to examine how this is done, one needs to understand how *kadongo-kamu* as a genre came into being. First, it has roots in the coming of the British colonisers and Christian missionaries, who brought not only their religion, but also their music and culture. In schools, churches, army, and police establishments, the colonisers and missionaries introduced pianos, guitars, western drums and brass instruments, which later became the base for the "new" music of the 1950s. Eventually, the European music replaced the Kiganda "traditional" music at political and cultural ceremonies. Peter Cooke has reported that, "by the 1960s the Kabaka [King] had established his own Western-style military band which played for parades of his private police regiment".[4] As a result, performers of "traditional" musical instruments became fewer and mainly performed at special court ceremonies.

Second, from 1946, Kampala, the administrative headquarters of the Buganda kingdom housing the Mengo palace, developed into an industrial, educational, and business centre.[5] Kampala lay along the railway line connecting Mombasa, Kenya's main port and Kasese, bordering the present Democratic Republic of Congo (DRC), formerly Zaire. As a result people migrated from all corners of Uganda and outside the country to Kampala. Kampala's strategic position attracted not only business people, but also musicians from Kenya and especially the DRC, who have shaped the city's "popular" music since the 1950s. Further, when the national radio station was established in 1953, Latin American and Caribbean music became popular. In

---

1. Resistance Council (named Local Council after 1996) is a political structure introduced by President Yoweri Kaguta Museveni when he took power in 1986. The structure has five levels, RC I, RC II, RC III, RC IV, and RC V. Each level is constituted of nine people, of whom one as a minimum must be a woman.
2. The Baganda assume a partrilineal system; the child belongs to the father's clan.
3. A "drink" in this case refers to having an intimate relationship with Kijjambu's driver. The driver and Mukyala Kijjambu were on their way back from a funeral rite, a trip actually authorized by the husband.
4. Cooke 1996, p. 440.
5. Elkan 1960, p. 15–16.

his song *Twalyako Bye Twalya* ("We Ate What We Could"), Elly Wamala sings that in the 1950s, people danced to calypso. As people of different cultures and music of different styles settled in Kampala, the Buganda's cultural identity began to be re-defined.

Third, agitation for nationalism grew in the 1940s and the desire to consolidate Buganda's then fading power through reconstructing through Buganda's cultural identity became more crucial. The development of *kadongo-kamu* music in the late 1940s and early 1950s was one of the means sought for the revival of the crumbling cultural identity. However, this music had to be defined in a way that would accommodate the new identity, which was a hybridisation of foreign and Kiganda cultures, especially in urban areas. Music was to act as a vehicle for identity formation and cultural patterning in a new and diversified society. The Baganda were to turn to music as a means of expression for values and meanings and as a basis for new community life.

Music and instruments in the playing with identities

The innovated Kiganda music adapted a European guitar, played by one person, while imitating the Kiganda style of playing the *ndongo* (lyre). The style of playing the *ndongo* involves singing in a narrative style, while accompanying oneself. The *ndongo* is a plucked eight-stringed instrument that can be played as a solo or in accompaniment with other instruments. As a matter of fact, the term *kadongo* is a diminutive for the *ndongo*. *Kadongo-kamu* refers to a solo guitar.

Kayanda was performed with the following instruments: solo voices, three electric guitars (solo, rhythm, and bass guitars), and keyboard. According to the composer, he intended that each instrument should imitate a *Kiganda* instrument. The solo guitar outlines the vocal melody; the rhythm guitar imitates the *ndongo* (lyre), which takes an accompanying role to the voice, while the bass guitar simulates the *ngoma* (drums) and the keyboard imitates the *madinda* (a log xylophone).

Kayanda, like other *kadongo-kamu* music, adapts *baakisimba* drum rhythms on the bass guitar. These rhythms are played without sacrificing the distinctive speech-based rhythms of the specialized Kiganda genre. *Baakisimba* is at the very heart of the Baganda's culture; it is a music and dance genre, as well as a name for a drum set. One can dance *baakisimba* with the accompaniment from *Kayanda*. The use of drum rhythms in *Kayanda* reflects the Baganda identity because of the importance of the drums in general terms, and *baakisimba* rhythms in specific terms. The drum is the "king" of all instruments; it is sounded during war time, when one is dead; when a child is born; at a wedding ceremony and in all ritualistic ceremonies of the Baganda. Further, *baakisimba* is a space where gender relations are articulated among the Baganda. Before the abolition of the Buganda kingdom in 1967, there were clear gender roles in performance of *baakisimba*. The women were the main dancers, while the men performed the music. The drum as a symbol thus constructs both gender and cultural identities in Buganda.

The drum symbolises Buganda itself. The adaptation of guitars to play in a Kiganda style closer to that of the *ndongo* (lyre) also contributes to a reconstruction of the Baganda's cultural identity. The identity of the foreigners in the story is constructed by the use of a Western diatonic scale as opposed to the Kiganda anhemitonic pentatonic scale.

Kayanda adapts a "traditional" tune, *Omugongo*, as an ostinato played on the rhythm guitar in the accompaniment. *Omugongo* is a tune popularly played on the *ndongo, ndingidi* (one-string fiddle), and *madinda* (log xylophone). It is important to note that while there are a number of one-string fiddle players, there are few good lyre players today. Appropriation of the *Omugongo* tune, therefore, facilitates the preservation of the traditional tune. Although the tune is in diatonic scale as opposed to the anhemitonic scale typical of Kiganda music, it is still possible to identify it as *Omugongo*. Moreover, the singers employ the *ggono*, a vocal style characteristic of Kiganda indigenous songs. The singers employ a nasal and throaty tone with vibrato, usually produced by singing microtones at the end of a phrase. Although the composer does not use this tune for the melody of the song, its repetitive nature in the accompaniment clearly foregrounds the Kiganda musical style.

Lyrics, language and hidden meanings

The Luganda text in this song strengthens the identity for the Baganda given the large number of languages that are spoken in Uganda. The Kabaka (King) of Buganda stressed that, "one of the major pillars of culture is language, and these young kids who come to major cities of Buganda have lost a certain amount of their culture".[1] The lyrical narration of *Kayanda* refers directly to the lives of the Baganda by making use of the Luganda language and employing images familiar in the Kiganda historical, cultural, political, and social settings. These narratives are presented in a folkloric style of story telling that has special meaning for the Baganda. In *Kayanda*, as in Kiganda traditional music, the song text is the "soul of the song".[2] The melodies have limited variations because the composers invest mainly in the text. *Kadongo-kamu* being strongly defined by the narrative and ostinato styles to give prominence to the lyrics may be boring to one who does not fully understand the language.

Kayanda uses a language with hidden meanings. It is common among the Baganda to use a hidden language when addressing issues that are obscene or when they do not want to address an individual directly, and this is also adopted in their music. Willy Mukaabya, the composer and one of the performers of *Kayanda* declared that "we, the composers are like messengers of God, through whom He communicates with His people. Our listeners usually get more meaning than what we intended to communicate."[3] Likewise, Jody Berland has observed that production of meaning in a song is located in the "activities and agencies of audiences".[4] Therefore, there are as many meanings that can be constructed from a piece of music, as there are listeners. Hence, attempting to understand a song in relation to the initial motives of the composer only provides one of the many possible meanings. A case in point is when Mukaabya sings: "*Kayanda oliir'otya mu sowaani yange?*" ("Kayanda, how dare you eat from my plate?"). Although the translation of the text refers to Kayanda being accused of eating from Mukaabya's plate, Mukaabya can be interpreted as accusing Kayanda of having sex with his wife. Moreover, when Kayanda answers back: "*Ndina eyange*" ("I have mine"), some members of the audience may be made to believe that the song is actually referring to the plate.

Kayanda has well spelled out and developed characters that build up a clear and flowing story. In a live performance, action on stage with fully costumed actors and actresses adds greater communication to the message, which is missing if one listens

---

1. Acan-Oturu 1995, p. 21.
2. Gray 1992, p. 99.
3. Mukaabya, interview, May 29, 2000.
4. Berland 1990, p. 42.

The cassette jacket of Willy Mukabya's "Kayanda", produced in Uganda. The composer is in the picture.

only to the audio recording.[1] Through sound, language, and drama, *Kayanda* connects with old cultural identities, while at the same time adapting to new identities.

The socio-cultural history illustrated by *Kayanda*

The composer told me that his personal experience and the historical information he gathered from his parents informed his composition. In order to understand *Kayanda*, therefore, one needs to understand the historical context from which it arose. *Kayanda* is deeply rooted in Uganda's social, political, and cultural history. John Tosh has observed that history can

> ... serve as a collective memory, the storehouse of the experience through which people develop a sense of their social identity and future prospects. [That] history provides knowledge from which 'we' decide who 'we' are, where we are coming from and where we are going.[2]

Uganda, like many other African countries, is an amalgam of diverse peoples, "each with a history, a culture, a tradition, a language and an identity which reflected all these features."[3] They were put together under British colonisation. Uganda is divided into two major language groups: the Nilotics in the north and the Bantu in the south.[4] The Baganda belong to the Bantu groups.

When Speke and Grant came to Uganda in 1862 in search of the source of the Nile, Buganda was under the rule of Kabaka (king) Mukaabya Mutesa and had an advanced political, social, and cultural base in comparison to that of other ethnic groups.[5] Moreover, the Baganda had a tradition of superiority over the surrounding peoples. Their kings extracted tribute from the Soga and other peoples on the eastern

---

1. Although I have never had the opportunity to attend a live performance, I was lucky to obtain a video recording. I must note however, this video was not a professional recording, so it is not in circulation. Mukaabya told me that it is impossible to perform the song again because many of his cast are dead. "I cannot replace people like Muwaya who acted as Kayanda. Muwaya died in 1990." Mukaabya, interview May 29, 2000. Further, apart from the Festak Guitar Singers, Mukaabya's group, no other group has performed the song.
2. Tosh 1984, p. 1.
3. Segal et al., 1976, p. 8.
4. Mutibwa 1992, p. 1.
5. Note that Mukaabya, is also a character in *Kayanda*.

border, as well as from the Kooki on their western border, and occasionally from the Nyoro.[1]

The British used the Baganda's strong political, social, and cultural base to colonise the rest of Uganda with less resistance. The policy of employing Baganda for this purpose is often referred to as "Buganda sub-imperialism".[2] As a result, the Baganda became most privileged, gaining wealth and more power over the other ethnic groups in Uganda.[3] Their superiority made them begin to despise other ethnic groups both within and outside Uganda.

Since Buganda was an agricultural region, the British introduced coffee, cotton, and rubber which became the cornerstones of the economy of the British administration. This resulted in giving the Baganda even higher status.[4] In order to boost the coffee and cotton production, the colonialists assisted the Baganda to recruit labourers for their farms from poorer parts of Uganda, Ruanda, Urundi and Kenya.[5] As a result, the Baganda peasants who themselves were exploited, took part in the exploitation of immigrant labourers.[6] Among the labourers, the Banyarwanda and the Barundi were highly discriminated, exploited, and abused by the Baganda. They were never allowed to dine with the master's family, and they had to build their huts at the edge of the master's land. Their low social status was clearly defined and established.[7]

Narrating to me his experience with these immigrant labourers, popularly called the *bapakasi,*[8] Mukaabya, (the composer of *Kayanda),* said they were indeed of a low class. Mukaabya was born in 1959 and raised at Kabunyata, Kikusa in Bulemeezi County. Mukaabya vividly remembers that:

> Because of their hard work and submissiveness, many Baganda women were attracted to the *bapakasi.* Women would leave their legal Baganda men and elope with the Banyarwanda and Barundi. Although the Baganda men were very proud and greatly despised the Banyaranda and Barundi, they were attracted to the beauty of the Barundi and Banyarwanda women. These men consoled themselves with the Kiganda proverb: *Nnyoko abanga omunyoro nakuzaala ku kika.* ["It does not matter whether your mother is a foreigner, as long as your father belongs to a clan of the Baganda."][9]

Accordingly, no Muganda man would permit his daughter to marry a "foreigner". And since unmarried girls and women were seen as property for the fathers and brothers, the men determined which man would take their daughter or sister. Kagwa writes:

> Women were looked down upon and in many respects completely segregated. They were not permitted to touch things that men were doing. According to the creation story it was Nambi Nantutululu, the wife of Kintu, who on account of her disobedience brought Mr. Death with her and destroyed several of Kintu's children. It is thought that this had a great deal to do with the suffering of women.[10]

It is evident that men constituted the Buganda hegemony; the Baganda women were just as voiceless as the foreign Banyarwanda and Barundi.

The Buganda's hegemony could not last forever. The Buganda monarchy already met resistance after the conversion of the King's subjects into colonial servants. The commoners began to challenge the ruling oligarchy in Mengo palace and demanded

---

1. Richards 1969, p. 43.
2. Mutibwa 1992, p. 3.
3. Richards 1969, p. 46.
4. Mutibwa 1992, p. 7.
5. Richards 1969, p.46. See also Mutibwa 1992, p. 7.
6. Mutibwa 1992, p. 7.
7. Richards 1969, p. 68.
8. The term *bapakasi* was simultaneously used to refer to the Barundi and Banyarwanda immigrant labourers.
9. Mukaabya, interview, May 29, 2000.
10. Kagwa 1934, p. 161.

change in the sharing of power in the kingdom. A dramatic outburst took place in the 1940s against the Kabaka and the Buganda government.[1] The conflict between the Baganda subjects and their king was an opening for other ethnic groups to question Buganda's power.

In 1962, Buganda lost power to Milton Obote, a Langi from northern Uganda, when he became the prime minister and led the country to independence. Obote worked towards abolishing Buganda monarchism and eventually succeeded in deposing the Kabaka and turning Mengo palace into an army barracks in 1966. After making himself president in 1966, Obote abolished all monarchy structures in 1967. However, in 1971, through a *coup d'état*, the army commander Idi Amin from northern Uganda and of Kakwan and Nubian ancestry, overthrew Obote's government. He ruled Uganda for nine years. After intervention by Tanzanian troops Amin was ousted from power in 1979, and was succeeded first by Yusufu Lule, then by Binaisa, both Baganda. Obote had another turn in 1980, but was ousted violently in 1985 by Bazilio Okello, an Acholi from northern Uganda. In 1986 Yoweri Kaguta Museveni, a Munyankole from Ankole in western Uganda became the president through what has been called either a popular uprising or a *coup*. Museveni is the longest ruling president in Uganda, having been in power for 16 years (as of 2002).

Although President Museveni reinstated Buganda Kingdom in 1993, it took on a different structure in a politically, socially, and culturally changed Buganda. Museveni restored the Buganda kingdom, "on condition [that the Kabaka] stick[s] to cultural affairs and stay[s] out of politics …".[2] In this case, Kabaka, who culturally had power, was made impotent and had to depend on the central authority controlled by Museveni (once regarded as a *mukopi*, a commoner, Kayanda, among the Baganda royalties). In 1995 when the Baganda agitated for federalism, which would recreate a political Kabaka, the anti-federalists contended that federalism would only rob the unity of the people of Uganda.

With the breakdown of the monarchy system, cultural norms controlling the behaviour of women began to change. With more women attending school, the traditional attitude of restricting women to the kitchen began to change.

Kayanda represents the voice of the subverted Buganda hegemony, both in political and social terms. The once powerful Buganda has lost its power to the "strangers". The song challenges the traditional male-dominated society, while promoting the contemporary gender ideology of women's emancipation. Although *Kayanda* dwells at length on marital infidelity it simultaneously critiques "political infidelity". *Kayanda*, speaks out a history that would probably not be openly discussed in the present day Buganda.

Political identities in *Kayanda*

While the song *Kayanda* points as far back as the mid-sixties when transformations in Buganda's political structure began to take place, it connects directly to the period after President Museveni took power in 1986. Dixon Kamukama notes that Museveni, a Munyankole, had been publicly labelled "Munyarwanda" by Obote and the supporters of his party.[3] Obote had questioned Museveni's holding power because of the fact that he is not Ugandan but came to Uganda as a refugee.[4]

---

1. Mutibwa 1992, p. 11.
2. Boorstein 1999.
3. Kamukama 1997, p. 40.
4. Onyango-Obbo 1997, p. 13.

The Banyarwanda and Banyankole of Ankole (western Uganda) have a close ethnic relationship. According to "Uganda, a Historical Dictionary" the Banyarwanda

> ... are Bantu speakers ... and include Hutu agriculturists, the majority of whom are ethnically related to the Bairu ... of Ankole ... and cattle-keepers Tutsi minority who traditionally formed the ruling group and who are [also] closely related to the Bahima [of Ankole].[1]

Moreover, historically, there have been many waves of Banyarwanda and Barundi immigration from Rwanda and Burundi to Uganda through Ankole since the nineteenth century. Consequently, with intermarriages and assimilation, it may be difficult to establish a pure Munyarwanda or Munyankole identity. In addition, it is "impossible ... to distinguish between natives of 'British Ruanda' ... those living over the Ugandan border in Bufumbira county, and those of the main territory of Rwanda administered by Belgians: the political boundary as elsewhere cut across the ethnic distribution of population."[2] But most important, characterization of Museveni as a Munyarwanda, "a foreigner", is a political issue.

Although, Kayanda is a name also used by the Banyarwanda and Barundi, in the song, it specifically refers to a Murundi. Since anyone from west of Buganda is a *mupakasi* (sing. for *bapakasi*), a "foreigner", a Munyarwanda, a Murundi, Kayanda can be seen as a symbol for Museveni. The question is: how does Kayanda symbolize Museveni? Kayanda adapts an accent characteristic of Barundi when speaking Luganda. The Barundi do not pronounce certain syllables in Luganda, but instead, they create their own. Further, they use an intonation quite different from that of the "indigenous" Baganda. The composer told me that he cast Muwaya to take Kayanda's part because he was a Murundi and could easily transfer the Lurundi/Lunyarwanda accent of speaking Luganda into the song. Although Kayanda's pronunciation does not affect the understanding of the text, anyone who knows Luganda can tell that he is not a Muganda. And if one had ever heard a Murundi or a Munyarwanda speaking Luganda, one would not doubt that Kayanda is a Murundi or Munyarwanda. Similarly, as an interviewee said, "when Museveni speaks Luganda, you cannot mistake him for a Muganda, but definitely one from western Uganda."[3] Moreover, adapting an accent foreign to the Baganda and yet singing in a *ggono* Kiganda vocal style, *Kayanda* opens a discussion on Buganda's cultural identity, with language as its core.

The Baganda's attitude towards Museveni is divided. Some Baganda see him as a Munyarwanda or a Murundi, a foreigner like Kayanda, voiceless like the Baganda women. As such he is supposed to accept his low position and should not dine with the Baganda (an allegory for involving himself in the political affairs of the country), and he should build his hut at the edge of Buganda land. On the other hand, immigrants and some Baganda, especially the culturally marginalized like women and peasants, refer to Museveni as the saviour Uganda has been looking for since independence. In the song, Mugole and Mukyala Kijjambu represent Museveni's supporters, symbolised by their love for Kayanda and Kijjambu's driver respectively, rather than their legal husbands, Mukaabya and Kijjambu.

If Kayanda is taken as a symbol for Museveni, his hegemony is articulated when Kayanda refuses to leave when Mukaabya wants to send him away. Kayanda even threatens that if he were chased away, Mugole would commit suicide. Kayanda's

---

1. Pirouet 1995, p. 68.
2. Powesland 1954, p. 30.
3. Anonymous interview, June 20, 2000. I interviewed a number of people, and all agreed that people from different regions outside Buganda have a different way of speaking Luganda and usually it is possible to tell the region where one comes from.

position in this case, shows that Mugole cannot survive without Kayanda. To assert his power, Kayanda has the wherewithal to speak out loudly that Nakiyimba, the daughter, belongs to him and he will have to go with her back to Burundi. Mugole asserts herself when she sings:

> You are sent away? You are not going anywhere. People don't appreciate when they are assisted! Whenever you [Mukaabya] go for your business trips, it takes you months before you return home; please leave my Kayanda alone. He is my custodian in this lonely home, he is the only one who understands my sorrows, Kayanda.[1]

Kayanda's power, symbolized by his ability to win Mugole's heart and eventually produce a child, relates to Museveni's power over Buganda and the entire country.

Kayanda and Mugole's relationship could be seen as a reference to the alliance of politicians with some prominent Baganda people, and the song *Kayanda* has been used as a commentary on politics in Uganda as it has unfolded even after the song was written. Although the Baganda lost their power before independence, they still have a strong influence on who is to be in power and prospective presidential candidates must establish alliances among the Baganda for success. Buganda influence has its roots in its long time political domination during the colonial time and also the strategic geographical position. The Baganda surround the capital city and the main administration centre, Kampala, with its rich hinterland widely supplied with transport and communication systems.

Mugole's decision to leave Mukaabya and Mukyala Kijjambu's feeling that she has a right to go for a "drink" with the driver project women's increased personal, social, economic, and political power as exhibited under Museveni's regime. Kayanda's outgoing character and his ability to "handle women" articulate Museveni's regard for women. Museveni is the first President to incorporate many women in political decisions and as a result, he is popular among women. It is during Museveni's era that "women have made considerable advances, holding important decision making posts not only in their villages but also in central and local government."[2] The present Vice-President, Dr. Specioza Wandira Kazibwe is the first woman in Uganda's history to hold such a high political position and one of the only two in Africa as of 2001. Further, in 1996, out of 270 Members of Parliament (MPs), 51 (ca. 19 per cent) were women, yet between 1962 and 1986 (before Museveni's regime) only five women were MPs. Moreover, in 1996, "two cabinet posts out of 21, and five ministers of state out of 31 were women in Museveni's government."[3] Although this progress may seem modest, it is a breakthrough for women in Uganda. *Kayanda* narrates a socio-political situation in which women are wielding more public power in Uganda's political sector.

As in *Kayanda*, where Mugole decides to opt for Kayanda instead of Mukaabya (her legal husband), many Buganda women decided to vote for Museveni instead of Ssemwogerere (a fellow Muganda) in the 1995 elections. *New African* magazine reports that it was the "women's caucus of the Constituent Assembly that nominated Museveni to be its presidential candidate in the 1995 elections".[4] Museveni's governance system whereby every village is required to have an executive committee composed of nine people, one of whom must be a woman, was the basis for his sup-

---

1. *Bakugobye? Toyina gy'olaga. Abantu temuyambika baganda bange, wano ogenda mu mirimu gyo omala myeezi tozze waka; nze nneerekeerera Kayanda wange, ye mukuumi mu maka muno, yamanyidde ku nnaku yange, Kayanda!*
2. "Museveni for President", *New African*, 1995, p. 28.
3. Onyango-Obbo 1996.
4. Constituent Assembly (CA) is a body that was elected to negotiate or discuss the 1995 Uganda Constitution.

port in the 1995 elections.[1] Ssemwogere was seen as not being capable of ruling Uganda—this can be related to Mukaabya's impotence.

Using "Mukaabya", as a character, *Kayanda* foregrounds the political and cultural identities of the Baganda people. King Muteesa Mukaabya was the most powerful king who reigned in the nineteenth century. His symbolic value for Buganda lies in the power he had over the kingdoms of Bunyoro, Ankole, and Toro. In the song, Mukaabya seems to stand for the Buganda monarchy. As in the song, Mukaabya's impotence points to the present King, Ronald Muwenda Mutebi, a Muganda and a king without political power. Mukaabya's inability to produce children can be seen as a symbol of the King's powerlessness.

Ending the song with fighting and no concrete resolution, illustrates Buganda's political conflicts to which no clear answer is yet available. Among the Baganda, some people are agitating for federalism, which it is hoped will restore the King's power, while others advocate for the need to build Uganda as a nation and forget about ethnic clusters. There are struggles between those who want to identify themselves as the "Baganda", and others who believe in a "Ugandan" identity.

Gendered voices in *Kayanda*

In her study on Kiganda radio songs Hellen Nabasuuta Mugambi asserts that through the songs "artists are constantly recreating and manipulating gendered structures derived from myth and history to mediate perceptions of womanhood into contemporary discourses."[2] I have interviewed men and women on their reception of *Kayanda,* and my research indicates that men and women tend to identify differently. Among those I interviewed, women tended to like Kayanda's character more than men. To the women, *Kayanda* voices an identity they have long struggled to achieve. "I love the song because it shows that women can also be free; we can now say what we want", said Mrs. Musisi.[3] On the other hand, Fred Kanyike regrets that "the song is sending a wrong message to the women, they will begin not to respect us."[4] The women's emancipation is an invasion of men's traditional and long-guarded space.

In Buganda, gender is a prescribed and fluid identity, which is contingent on biological, social, and cultural structures. The historical construction of gender is dependent on whether one belongs to royalty or the commoners' class. The gender socialization within the palace assigns both the princes and princesses a man gender, and the commoners—both male and female—a woman gender. However the woman gender assigned to the commoner males is only situational. They retain a man gender outside the palace contexts. What then are the social and cultural constructions of men and women in Buganda as articulated in *Kayanda*? *Kayanda* characterizes a male-dominated society of the Baganda. Foremost, the characterisation of more than six men and only three women in the song re-establishes a gender imbalance. Further, the women are depicted negatively; Mugole is weak while Mukyala Kijjambu is passive. Mugole is portrayed as one who cannot survive without Kayanda. Moreover, the only woman in the jury is bypassed. We never get to hear the woman's verdict on her fellow women. As a matter of fact, in Buganda, women were expected to be voiceless when men talked. Although they have some voice today, many

---

1. "Museveni for President", *New African*, 1995, p. 28.
2. Mugambi 1994, p. 47.
3. Mrs. Musisi, interview July 20, 1998.
4. Fred Kanyike, interview November 19, 1999.

men try to suppress them whenever they can get a chance. In the song the men, except Mukaabya and Kijjambu, are projected as strong and authoritative. Although Kayanda is considered culturally an outcast because he is a commoner, his being a man with the ability to have a child makes up for his social deficiency.

Although Mugole and Mukyala Kijjambu get the sympathy of the RC jury, the male voice from the council betrays the deep-seated sentiments of the male jury members. The voice states that:

> But you My Car [a title for rich men] are very funny.
> How dare you entrust your wife to a driver?
> Why doesn't she drive herself, doesn't she have hands?
> Then, give her money for transport if she has to go somewhere.
> And you Mukaabya you are not right in this case.
> How dare you leave your wife for a full year?
> There is no reason why Kayanda would not have seduced her.
> Remember how weak-minded women are.
> They must be guarded like fierce dogs.[1]

The text presents a woman as perceived in the Baganda male community, with a weak mind, one that needs to be guided in her decisions. Further, the last two lines of the judgment in particular re-emphasise the women's position in the Kiganda society despite their movement towards emancipation. Equating a woman with a dog portrays her as property; for dogs have owners. Moreover, the view of the jury that Mukaabya should have "guarded" Mugole, reaffirms a woman as property, which must be guarded.

In a related situation, Mukaabya argues that Kayanda had no right to take over his wife because he did not contribute to the bride price. He sings:

> Kayanda leave my wife alone,
> You never had a share in the bride price.[2]

Indeed, women were and are still commodities that can be bartered in exchange for another commodity or service. John Roscoe notes that "when the king engaged a new drummer, he gave him a woman, a cow, and a load of bark cloth."[3] In the present day, although it is no longer common that a man pays bride price for a wife, there is a new version of commodification of women. Under the guise of "gifts" for the parents (*ebirabo bya bazadde*), during the introduction ceremony (*okwanjula*), proposing men are expected to bring a lot of food, clothes, and money to the girl's parents.

Kayanda articulates the constructed identity of a Muganda woman as a procreator. Childbearing and domestic work define a typical woman; inability to satisfy those roles disqualifies her. In her struggle to establish her constructed identity as a woman, Mugole resorts to all means to get a child. In Buganda, if a marriage is barren, the woman is the first to be blamed. The Baganda have a saying that "a useless

---

1. *Naye nammwe ba "My Car" mulimba nnyo, omukyala w'awaka omuwa otya driver?*
   Lwaki teyeevuga talina mikono ggye?
   gyalaga muwe ezimutwaala?
   Ate no Mukaabya mukino olimba nnyo,
   oleeka oty'omukyala omwaka mulaamba?
   Lwaaki Kayanda takulivvule?
   Emmeeme y'abakyala omanyi nnyangu.
   Alina kukuumwa bukuumwa ng'embwa enkambwe.
2. *Kayanda nze nviira ku mukazi wange*
   Essente eza muwasa tekuli zizo.
3. Roscoe 1911, p. 30.

persons like a lazy woman who is barren; such a woman does no work and cannot produce any children".[1] In order to assert herself, Mugole had to have a secret relationship with Kayanda who promised that he could make her have a child. Although the child was to be fathered by Kayanda, Mugole was ready to keep this secret and claim that the child belonged to Mukaabya.

Although Mugole was not satisfied with Mukaabya's relationship, she had to stay with him. Mugole's identity as a proper woman is contingent on the fact that she is married and lives under Mukaabya's roof. A woman who is not married under a man's roof is branded *nnakyeyombekedde* (a "woman house-owner, master-less woman"), one who threatens men's position and thus, subverts the constructed identity of a Muganda woman.

On another level, the song promotes the contemporary subverted woman identity. Although the revolution for women's emancipation in Buganda can be traced as far back as the early 1950s,[2] Museveni's regime has been a great eye opener for women's liberation. The women in *Kayanda*'s story evade the social structure that constructed them as subordinate subjects to men. In particular, Mugole wants a child but her husband is impotent so she finds a way of circumventing this obstacle. The woman also asserts her freedom by defending Kayanda when Mukaabya decides to send him away. She argues that Kayanda had been a good companion to her in the absence of her austere and distant husband. Mugole is ready to go with Kayanda and leave Mukaabya, here symbolising the exploitative Baganda men.

However, the chaotic conclusion of the song leaves Mugole with an empty victory and an uncertain future. First, although, Kayanda is loving and caring, he has no ancestry and social status. Second, being a refugee and a *mupakasi*, Kayanda has no means to look after himself, Mugole, and the child, Nakiyimba. Third, now as a divorcee, Mugole would find it difficult to cope with social ideals and expectations of the Baganda. By creating such an ambiguous ending, the artist opens up spaces for multiple interpretations.

My discussion is informed by the view expressed by Coplan that:

> Popular music ... provides a multiplicity of meanings, accommodation and a range of manipulation, interpretation and choice, and supplies a measure of solidarity in an environment characterized by social insecurity, dislocation, and differentiation.[3]

I argue further, that meanings in any piece of art are fluid. *Kayanda* is the "product of an on-going historical conversation in which no one has the first or the last word."[4] It is this infinite signification, along with the rich language and dramatisation, that constitutes the aesthetic success of *Kayanda*.

Discography

(sorted by authors of the song tracks)

Luyima, Matia, n.d., "Embaga ya Nakakaawa". Album: *Sente-Entebbe*. Performed by the Super Singers. Kasajja and Sons Studios Ltd.

1. *Nantaganyula: ng'omunafu omugumba.*
2. In the 1950s women gained more access to European formal education that resocialized and opened them to new possible views on their own gendering. Moreover, this education postponed the age of marriage for girls, giving them more time to pursue activities outside marriage including career building.
3. Coplan 1982, p. 116.
4. Lipsitz 1990, p. 99.

Mukaabya, Willy, 1988, "Kayanda". Album: *Kayanda*. Performed by the Festak Guitar Singers. Kasajja and Sons Studios Ltd.

Wamala, Elly, n.d., "Twalyako Byewalya". Performed by Elly Wamala. Tony Sengo and Goodie Lubuulwa Studios.

Interviews

Mukaabya, Willy, composer of the song *Kayanda*. Interview May 29, 2000 in Katwe, Kampala.

Musisi, Margret. Interview July 20, 1998 in Kisaasi, Kampala.

Kanyike, Fred. Interview November 19, 1999 in Naluvule, Wakiso.

Anonymous interview with radio broadcaster. June 20, 1998 in Kampala.

Anonymous interview with 45-year-old shop attendant. June 20, 2000 in Nyendo, Masaka.

References

Acan-Oturu, Assumpta, 1995, "Ronald Muwenda Mutebi II: King of Buganda", *Image* (January), pp. 19–22.

Berland, Jody, 1990, "Angels Dancing: Cultural Technologies and the Production of Space", in Grossberg et al. (eds), *Cultural Studies*, pp. 38–55. New York and London: Routledge.

Boorstein, Michelle, 1999, "Buganda Struggles to Find Identity", Saturday, July 17. http://search.*washingtonpost*.com/wp-srv/WAPO/19990717/v000221-071799-idx.html

Cooke, Peter, 1996, "Music in a Ugandan Court", *Early Music*, Vol. 24, No. 3, pp. 439–52.

Coplan, David, 1982, "The Urbanization of African Music: Some Theoretical Observations" in Middleton and Horn (eds), *Popular Music*, pp.113–29. Cambridge: Cambridge University Press.

Elkan, Walter, 1960, *Migrants and Proletarians: Urban Labour in the Economic Development of Uganda*. London: Oxford University Press.

Gray, T. Catherine, 1992, "Patterns of Textual Recurrence in Kiganda Song", *International Review of the Aesthetics of Sociology of Music*, Vol. 23, No. 1, pp. 85–100.

Kagwa, Apollo, 1934, *The Custom of the Baganda*. New York: Columbia University Press.

Kamukama, Dixon, 1997, *Rwanda Conflict: Its Roots and Regional Implications*. Kampala: Fountain Publishers.

Kasozi, A.B.K., 1999, *The Social Origins of Violence in Uganda, 1964–1985*. Kampala: Fountain Publishers.

Lipsitz, George, 1990, *Time Passages, Collective Memory and American Popular Culture*. Minneapolis: University of Minnesota Press.

Mugambi, Hellen Nabasuuta, 1994, "Intersection: Gender, Orality, Text, and Songs", *Research in African Literatures* (Austin, Texas), Vol. 25, No. 3, pp. 47–70.

"Museveni for President", 1995, *New African*, July/August, No. 332, p. 28.

Mutibwa, M. Phares, 1992, *Uganda Since Independence: A Story of Unfulfilled Hopes*. London: C. Hurst and Company.

Nanyonga [Nannyonga-Tamusuza], Sylvia, 1995, *Selected Traditional Secular and Sacred Music of the Baganda People: A Comparative Study*. M.A. thesis, Makerere University, Uganda.

Nannyonga-Tamusuza, Sylvia, 1999, "Baakisimba Dance: The Articulation and Negotiation of Power and Gender Relations among the Baganda People of Uganda", *Newsletter for Mid-Atlantic Chapter of the Society for Ethnomusicology (MACSEM)* 23/1, pp. 5–8.

—, 2001, *Baakisimba: Music, Dance, and Gender of the Baganda People of Uganda*. Ph.D. dissertation, University of Pittsburgh.

Onyango-Obbo, Charles, 1996, "Opinion: Boom! Museveni Knocks the Women, but They Ain't Down", *The Monitor*, July 12–15. All the writings in this paper by Onyango-Obbo can be accessed under his web page: http://www.africanewsa.com/obbo/aricle.html

—, 1997, "Of Obote's Hair N'Museveni's Father", *The Sunday Monitor,* July, 27. http://www.africanews.com/obbo/article100.html

Pirouet, M. Louise, 1995, "Historical Dictionary of Uganda", *African Historical Dictionaries,* No. 64. Metuchen, New Jersey and London: Scarecrow Press.

Powesland, P.G., 1954, "History of the Migration in Uganda", in Richards (eds), *Economic Development and Tribal Change,* pp. 17–51. Cambridge: W. Heffer and Sons.

Richards I. Audrey, 1969, *The Multicultural States of East Africa.* Montreal and London: McGill-Queen's University Press.

Roscoe, John, 1911, *The Baganda at Home: An Account of Their Customs and Briefs.* London: Macmillan.

Segal, H. Marshall, Martin Doornbos and Clive Davis, 1976, *Political Identity: A Case Study from Uganda.* Syracuse and New York: Syracuse University.

Stokes, Martin, 1994, "Introduction: Ethnicity, Identity and Music", in Stokes (ed.), *Ethnicity, Identity and Music: The Musical Construction of Place,* pp. 1–27. Oxford: Berg.

Tosh, John, 1984, *The Pursuit of History.* London: Longman.

From Mutant Voices to Rhythms of Resistance

Music and Minority Identity among the Idoma and Ogoni in Contemporary Nigeria

Jenks Z. Okwori

The past like the present is not finite, it is continuously under construction informed by new experiences. The balance between the past, present and the future lies at the heart of the enigma called identity. Memories of the past, exigencies of the present and anxiety over the future are the currents that propel identity articulation. They generate the tensions which foreground the *why*, *when* and *how* groups insist upon their identities.

Though they seem to invoke an origin in a historical past with which they continue to correspond, identities are actually about questions of using the resources of history, language and culture in the process of becoming rather than being: not 'who we are' or 'where we came from', so much as what we might become, how we have been represented and how that bears on how we might represent ourselves.[1]

The above quote positions the thrust of this chapter and frames its dynamics. The aim is a discussion of how two groups in contemporary Nigeria, the Idoma and the Ogoni, use music as a cultural medium both to articulate their identity and their resistance to federal policies they object to as oppression of minorities.[2]

Identity and the narrative of music

Identity is a terrain for negotiating the local and the global, and this negotiation happens via representation, as pinpointed by Hall. Representation implicates the individual or collective in the active exercise of narration. The narrative rubrics within which identities are constructed are located in the exercise of memory. Memory invokes and utilizes the past, the present and the future.

As a process constantly under construction identities are "produced in specific historical and institutional sites within specific discursive formations and practices, by specific enunciative strategies".[3] These formations, practices and strategies belong to the *milieux de memoire*[4] within which ethnic groups are able to reassemble memories, memories that are practices that are always located in the here and now, propelled by the concerns of the moment. "It involves processes of selecting, forgetting—wilfully as well as unconsciously—and re-assembling narratives that are passed down in written form, orally, and in bodily practices."[5] In this chapter I will

---

1. Hall and Du Gay 1996, p. 4.
2. This study is based on a research project which has been carried out since 1988 on how cultural forms are mobilised in order to articulate identity in order to resist oppression.
3. Hall and Du Gay 1996, p. 4.
4. Nora 1994.
5. Richards 1998, p. 9.

examine the narrative of music, which significantly encapsulates these oral and bodily practices.

The Caribbean after World War II provides a powerful example of the use of
music for both resistance and the articulation of identity by an oppressed people.
West Indian migrants to England finding themselves at the lowest level of the British
economy and the target of racism articulated their experiences through music thereby developing a pan-Caribbean consciousness. In the 1980s rap offered poor blacks
in America what reggae had offered in Jamaica a decade earlier: a political and economic critique, and the music also helped to forge a sense of identity and pride in
the local community.[1]

Similarly, the Idoma and Ogoni of Nigeria continue to use music to project their
existence. These two peoples live far from each other, and neither their structure nor
their political goals are identical. But they are the only groups that have systemati-
cally organised resistance against their oppression as minorities. The two formed
what may be called resistance organisations in 1990: the Idoma National Forum and
the Movement for the Survival of the Ogoni People (MOSOP).

The Idoma and Ogoni peoples—apart and alike

The Idoma who are about a million people are located in the middle belt area of
Nigeria. Slightly over half of these live in Idoma territory, the remaining are workers
and labourers in major Nigerian cities. They share Benue State with the Tiv ethnic
group. Both the Idoma and Tiv are largely agriculturists but the Tiv are numerically
stronger. There is really only one urban centre Otukpo, which serves as the headquarters of the Idoma people. The Idoma have a strong communal spirit validated
by festivals and ancestral worship in which music plays a very prominent role.

The Ogoni on the other hand are found in the south. Numbering some 400,000
people, they are an oil producing community. However, there is nothing here to
show for the decades of oil exploration. Here the strong communal spirit is under-
scored by the need to resist the chronic exploitation of their oil resources without
commensurate benefit to their community. For them, music is both a unifying and
liberating factor.

What are now known as Idoma or Ogoni are colonial creations from 1946–
1948. Prior to this period they existed as kindred groups, with each kindred group
overseen by the council of elders. There was a strong family bond which forbids
marriages between clan members. The kindred groups were descendants from the
same mother or father. Both these peoples have a history of long migrations before
settling in their present locations. In both communities women are very visible, and
take part in communal decisions. They do not dissolve their identity in marriage, instead, they keep their names and their bodies are returned to their families when they
die. The Idoma and Ogoni speak completely independent languages. In fact the language is the basis of their common identity and this was the basis upon which the
colonial authorities brought their kindred groups together as nations. The peoples
began to be called Idoma and Ogoni after 1946–48.

The Idoma and Ogoni have their unique languages, and they live far from each
other, but they are both victims of the transatlantic slave trade, and they were both
raided constantly by their more powerful neighbours. They are products of constant

---

1. Thomas and Wells 1995, pp. 177–80. Their article is a review of Dick Hebdige's 1987 book *Cut'N Mix: Culture, Identity, and Caribbean Music.*

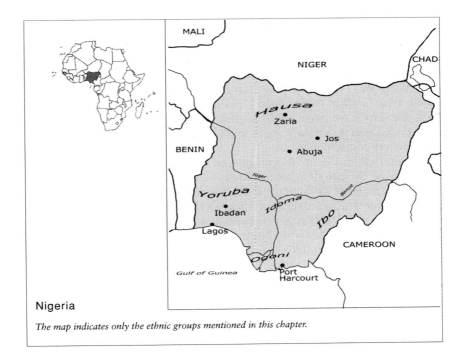

Nigeria

The map indicates only the ethnic groups mentioned in this chapter.

wars with their neighbours as well as internally. In war they are numerically weak, and this increases the role of rituals for their existence as a group. Music is essential to their burials, their festivals, their performances as well as their religious expression.

The Idoma rallied together to demand a state of their own as a way of liberating themselves from the hegemony of the Tiv majority in Benue state. So trenchant was their campaign that the state house of assembly then under the control of the Tivs passed a resolution removing Idoma from Benue state in 1990.

The Ogoni on the other hand are known internationally for their campaign to control the oil resources of their land, and their fight against northern domination. International attention was focused on the Ogoni by the execution of the so-called "Ogoni nine" (including the well-known author Ken Saro-Wiwa) in what has been termed worldwide as judicial murder.

It should be noted that there is much more than what I have called "resistance music" in the lives of the Idoma and Ogoni. There is not among them a type of music called and known as resistance music. But they are unique among the minorities in Nigeria, in that they have been able, from the early 1990s, to use their music to service their identity projection and resist domination.

Prior to the late nineties, the Idoma and Ogoni had believed in the Nigerian nation. There was not much discussion of Idoma identity or Ogoni identity as such. But when it became manifestly clear that their domination would be perpetual unless they did something about it, the conscious resort to articulation of identity began. The first movements and meetings began in 1990 both for the Idoma and Ogoni. MOSOP was formed in 1990, and the Idoma National Forum was formed in the same year. The two organisations set out to reclaim their respective identities as a way of forging unity and resisting domination. This sparked off the agitation, which significantly included mobilizing people by means of music.

Drawing on tradition

Unlike most other ethnic groups who have either lost their music and performance traditions to the larger ethnic groups or to Christianity, the Idoma and Ogoni continue to hold on strongly to their performances side by side with modern cultural flows in some cases. They have found a way of drawing from their rich performance tradition even in their contemporary performance behaviour. In the two places music is the vehicle for carrying the soul of the departed into ancestorhood, music forms the axis upon which their rituals and festivals are based. Their poetry and even story telling are couched in music.

Music is traditionally an integral part of daily living. It is a crucial part of the propagation of the people's belief system or cosmology which recognises three planes of existence: the world of the living, the dead, and the not yet born. The belief is that these three worlds are separated but can be kept linked through performances of certain kinds of music. In engaging in ritual music, they believe they are maintaining a symbiotic relationship with the three worlds for the effective existence, of, especially, the world of the living. In the absence of any meaningful solution to incomprehensible phenomena, they believe that ancestors who have become gods, by virtue of their death can intervene in the world of the living to make it function properly.[1]

Death is not seen as only an end but also a progression into another plane of existence. This is a crucial journey in which the dead change dimension through the playing of certain kinds of music, "the drumming, singing and dancing providing festive echoes for the spirit along the subterranean alley-way of transition."[2] To negotiate the two worlds the living and the dead, "the ancestors are believed to travel back to the living, through the mediant persona of the protagonist(s) to partake and celebrate with their living offspring, in a re-invigoration of their relationship."[3]

By so doing the dead are able to "empower the living through the performance of memory."[4] Richards elucidates this empowering process by drawing from Dennis Scott's play *An Echo in the Bone*:

> Performance is kinesthetic memory or history written onto the body, for the dance steps, songs, and drum patterns that are used in the nine-night wake ceremony, central to this drama, have been transmitted from generation to generation. Their repetition provides an opportunity for the individual participant to experience his/her personal history in relation to the collective history of the village.[5]

The musical situation provides an opportunity for the people to rehearse their lives thereby holding them up for reflection and mediation. In this way the values of existence, the language, the norms and mores, the attitudes and symbols which make the individual Idoma or Ogoni are revalidated and reinvigorated. The interesting point here is the way in which, at each period, music responds to the circumstances of the moment.

In the olden days the music addressed issues of law and order, of training in farming, of passing secrets of war and rituals, and of discussing survival strategies. In contemporary times when these functions have diminished, music is being used to articulate identity and organise resistance. The musical type and style that have been

---

1. Okwori 1998, p. 5.
2. Illah 1983, p. 15.
3. Illah 1983, p. 8.
4. Roach 1969, p. 34.
5. Richards 1998, pp. 10–11.

*Gamji Performers, one of the groups which draw on tradition
even as they perform contemporary songs.*

used for identity articulation and for resistance are the ritual and ritually derived musics.

When it comes to rituals, where music plays a prominent part, the Idoma or Ogoni do not regard the musician and his art as separate from the rest of the society. "His music is not abstracted from its context, nor regarded as a thing apart, but rather is thought of only as a part of a much wider entity, i.e., the total framework of belief and behaviour."[1] He sees himself in terms of his relatives and his community. His joys and travails are shared by the community members for whom he is merely performing a social or religious function as the case may be. It is very much as Nketia notes of the musician in Akan society in Ghana:

> He is not treated or regarded in a class apart from the rest of the members of his society. Nor can he himself find means of expressing his musicianship by working in isolation from everybody else. On the contrary, it is as a member of a group that it is believed he can make his distinctive contribution ... in ordinary life he is like everybody else a farmer, trader, carver, or fisherman who depends more on these for his living than music.[2]

However, the conditions that engender the initial use of music have not only altered but the music itself has changed. It is necessary to examine the phenomena that produced and continue to produce the shifting contexts in Nigeria.

One powerful factor of change was the missionary activity to Christianise and "civilize" the people, which paved the way for the human and material looting of Africa and its subsequent colonization. These combined forces created the present or contemporary definitions of statehood, community and the individual and the consequent tensions they continue to generate. For example, the needs for cash-paid jobs, which can only be found in the cities, have meant the relocation of people from their communities. The process of separation and continuous contact with other cul-

1. Merriam 1973, p. 278.
2. Nketia 1975, p. 83.

tures has redefined the sense of music. Added to this is the fact that both in the cities and communities, the cultures of other parts of the world constantly interact with the local.

Nigeria was put together in 1914 by the British colonizers for British interests. Akinjide writes about how Lord Lugard, the Governor General of Nigeria did it:

> Lugard said the North is too poor and they have no resources to run the protectorate of the North. That they have no access to the sea; that the South has resources and has educated people. …Therefore, because it was not the policy of the British Government to bring the taxpayers' money to run the protectorate, it was in the interest of the British business and the British taxpayers that there should be an amalgamation. But what the British amalgamated was the administration of the North and South and not the people of the North and South … between 1914 and 1960, that is a period of 46 years, the British allowed minimum contact between the North and South because it was not in the British interest that the North be allowed to be polluted by the educated South.[1]

Thus by colonial fiat, over four hundred nationalities were bound together. This structure was passed to the Nigerian leaders at independence in 1960. In the period leading to independence, sensing the danger of the colonial division of Nigeria, the minorities articulated their fear of perpetual domination at the Constitutional Conference in London, in 1953. This led to the setting up of the *Willink Commission of Inquiry into Minority Fears in Nigeria* (1957/58). The commission proposed no changes but left the minority problem for incoming nationalist governments.

In Nigeria today, after the democratic election and return to civilian rule in 1999, and despite a federal constitution, the centre remains absolutely powerful. It has continued unbridled access to and control of the resources of the Nigerian state. For example, oil which accounts for 87 per cent of Nigeria's foreign exchange earning constitutes the national resource in Nigeria. At present all the oil produced in Nigeria comes from the Southern part of the country, in the area where the Ogonis, a small community of about 400,000 people are located. Decades of oil exploration have not only polluted and devastated the land, but the area remains grossly underdeveloped, poor and neglected. The area has since the fifties been wrecked by the "eternal blaze", the gas flaring from the oil wells, as well as oil spills and saturation which have contaminated both land and water making fishing and farming impossible. According to Ake:

> What is at issue is nothing less than the viability of Nigeria, for oil is the real power and the stuff of politics in Nigeria as well as what holds the country in a fragile unity of self-seeking.[2]

The promise of independence had created an illusion of statehood and of one Nigeria. This illusion was to be shattered by decades of military dictatorship and brutal repression of dissent, which kept the voices of the minorities timid and suppressed. It remained a graveyard peace, a silence pregnant with meaning. As different military dictators succeeded each other and as the resources of the Nigeria state kept being misappropriated by a section of the country the mutant voices became restive. What sounded the final clarion call were the events leading to the 1993 transition programme and the subsequent election for the first time of a Southerner as president of Nigeria. When the June 12, 1993 elections were annulled that single act made it obvious that the minorities were in serious danger. If the electoral winner Abiola, who as a Yoruba came from one of the majority groups, could be denied leadership, what would the fate of the minorities be? It became blatantly clear that the resources

---

1. Akinjide 2000, p. 44.
2. Ake 1997, p. 19.

Ken Saro-Wiwa, late leader of the Movement for the Survival of the Ogoni People (MOSOP).

of the Nigerian state would continue to be used to prop up the comforts of the majority, especially the North. The threat was perpetual domination for the minorities.

With the return to civil rule, in May 1999, the people hoped that things would change but this was not to be. Faced with neglect even by a civilian administration, the people began to vent their pent-up anger against a Nigerian state that has neither given them fairness or justice. In the new political equation the majority ethnic groups the Hausa-Fulani, the Yoruba and the Ibo repositioned themselves without responding adequately to the yearnings of the minorities. The revenue allocation formula, which favours those that control government at the centre, has continued to be used.

The Idoma and Ogoni have resisted and continue to resist these oppressions and attempts at perpetual domination. While the Idoma have demanded a state of their own, the Ogoni have agitated for the control of the resources of their land. Both minorities protest against the failure of the majority ethnic groups to respect the rights and identities of the minorities. Saro-Wiwa, the leader of the Movement for the Survival of the Ogoni People (MOSOP) articulated this feeling in 1990 through the Ogoni Bill of Rights:

> Thirty years of Nigerian independence has done no more than outline the wretched quality of the leadership of the Nigerian majority ethnic groups and their cruelty as they have plunged the nation into ethnic strife, carnage, war, dictatorship, retrogression and the greatest waste of national resources ever witnessed in world history, turning generations of Nigerians, born and unborn into perpetual debtors.[1]

1. Saro-Wiwa 1990, p. 4.

Old ritual music with new functions

The Idoma and the Ogoni keep responding to these oppressive situations and chang-ing circumstances just like they used to do before the coming of colonialism and its attendant integration of the peoples of Nigeria into a transnational global space. As an inheritance from the past to which they continue to correspond, music has played a pivotal role in this process of 'retribalisation' or renegotiation of identity. Severed from the homogeneity and communal cohesiveness of old, the peoples have had to reinvent themselves as a way of projecting an identity of liberation.

The ritual performance music is a particularly important locus for the resistance of the Idoma and Ogoni communities. The ritual music is revered and accepted as part of the religious practice. Even though many are Christians, rituals are still be-lieved in, feared and obeyed. There is a strong attachment to ancestors who can only be accessed via ritual music, and solutions to incomprehensible phenomena are found in rituals. Even learned Christians go back to rituals for promotion in their jobs, to win elections and for protection against enemies and evil forces. Since rituals employ music, ritual music has a strong hold on the people and has a great capacity to move them to action. It is interesting to note that the two groups have employed music in similar ways and for the same reasons.

When it comes to identity articulation and agitation, everyone goes back to their community's music and performance system. In Ogoni oil workers are mainly out-siders, in Idoma where there is no industry the number of non-ethnics present is min-imal. In their cultural life there is of course a lot of borrowing from other cultures including the west. But when it comes to ritual, they follow the procedures as they are believed to have been passed down from generation to generation. Of course be-lief and following of the rituals are no longer the same. From 1990, the conscious attempt to reclaim the original ritual tendency as a way of identity articulation be-came a passion, which was picked up by musicians some of whom were deliberately used to promote the messages of identity and resistance.

Music provides a comfortable environment for these articulations, for not only has it served such functions in the past, the very basis for its previous usage still per-sists albeit in different forms today. In music "intractable traces of the past are felt on people's bodies, known in their landscapes, landmarks and souvenirs, and per-ceived as the tough moral fabric of their social relations."[1] In music, especially ritual music, the Idoma and Ogoni find a participatory group activity which enables peo-ple to come together for a common purpose.

There are three broad areas of aesthetic importance in contemporary Idoma and Ogoni music presentation. These are in the delivery style, the quality of sound and the techniques of delivery. There are of course differences between the Idoma and the Ogoni ritual performances. Their languages are different, their leg movements, choreographic styles, gestures and so on. Yet the emotional and psychological use to which the rituals are applied is similar.

The musical mode of presentation involves the elaborate use of body movements, facial expressions and costumes during performances. By employing colourful and flamboyant costumes, musicians bring an aliveness, which establishes an image as well as communicates a philosophy. The costumes validate the symbolic colours of the people, for example, the Idoma colours and cloth which is black and red is a strong sign of identity articulation, which provides a rallying point for projecting the

---

1. Werbner 1998, pp. 2–3.

Idoma demand for a separate state of their own. The costumes add to the total visual experience of music making and presentation.

To communicate with their audience performers work up a highly emotional and physical involvement, through movements, stretches, gestures and rhythmic vibrations. Apart from creating the atmosphere to enjoy the music, this physicalisation enables the audience to enter the performance as active participants rather than mere spectators. The audience will scream, clap, leap, embrace and bump into each other. They will exhort and interject the performance with ululations, hand clapping and foot stamping sometimes urged on by the performers. Even the instrumentalists are expected not to merely play but to perform their playing of instruments. At times an instrumentalist comes forward to give a solo rendition of his instrument by showing his dexterity in moving, squatting, leaping and swirling around while keeping his beat and rhythm. The audience shows their appreciation by clapping, ululating and applauding.

In a context where music is inextricably involved in the discussion of survival strategies and of life, functionality takes precedence over mere aesthetics. The sounds of music are closely linked with the imitation of nature and are produced by manoeuvring the mouth, cheek, tongue and throat or by manipulating timbre, including shading and texture. When they alternate percussive timbres with the lyrical or the raspy or when they juxtapose instrumental with vocal textures in the process altering pitch and dynamic levels or when straight tones are alternated with vibrato ones in which grunts, moans, hollers and screams are woven, musicians bring intensity to their performance. This intensity invites the audience to enter the performance both physically and emotionally.

The audience expects variety as well as unique performances. Musicians respond to this demand by being highly improvisational. This enables the individual musician to show off his style, his innovations and dexterity. All in all this means that no two performances are the same as the involvement of the audience and their reactions to the performance dictate the nature of the performance itself.

Song interpretation among the Idoma and Ogoni is structured by time, text and pitch. Time is manipulated by the musicians through the extension of the duration of notes during climaxes. Sometimes words or phrases and entire sections of songs are repeated by adding cadenzas to the vocals and instrumentation. As handclaps or hand-clicks, tapping, and instrumentation gradually build up, the density of textures increases.

The call and response structure is a main feature of songs performed by contemporary Idoma and Ogoni musicians. It provides the baseline within which improvisations are done and helps the musicians to generate musical change. It also enhances the participation of the audience since they can easily pick up the chorus, which usually forms the response.

These musics are characterised by rhythmic complexity. Music making entails a lot of syncopation and production of polyrhythms, which are achieved by playing different repeated patterns on various instruments. This complexity enhances the intensity of the overall music experience as each repetition creates additional rhythmic tension. Also as one part repeats, another is freed to embark on melodic and textual variation.

The management or manipulation of pitch is another striking feature of these musical performances. When voices of different ranges are not being juxtaposed, polar extremes of a solo voice are emphasized. Most times, bends, passing of tones and melismas are used to vary pitch. Other forms of melodic embellishment commonly used are trills, suspense and nonsense syllables.

Idoma gospel singing and identity

One of the contemporary forms of music among the Idoma and Ogoni can be located in Christianity. Since the coming of missionaries and the subsequent demonisation of indigenous artistic forms of expression, the converts though abandoning the traditional and cultural systems which sustained their music have carried with them their musical traditions into the church. The "African Church" or "Indigenous Church" came about as a result of the introduction of African music behaviour into church service. Through this, local situations, idioms and cultural wisdom are domesticated into ecclesiastical postulations. Peter Otulu, one of the greatest Idoma gospel singers, in response to accusations that he was an alien preaching in an alien way, responds in one of his classic songs, *Odiya num gwije*:

> People ask me why I sing
> I am not a fool
> I know why I sing
> (My songs give me an identity)
> (It establishes who I am)
> I was lost but God found me
> I am alive today by His grace
> So why shouldn't I thank Him?

Gratitude to God is expressed in the context of roots, an identity, and a source without which the singer would have been a nobody. The sense of loss articulated by the song is in terms of not doing things or living according to the dictates of Christianity as propounded by the missionaries, yet his rebirth as a result of knowing God is precisely because he has an identity that establishes who he is. This is an identity that establishes first his historical being and his Idoma-ness which of necessity he needs in order to practise Christianity. To call attention to the liberating potentials of Christ, Otulu, draws the attention of Christians to the fact that one must first fight one's problems before seeing those of others in the gospel song *Aam 'oche oha, ami yoon*:

> You who are watching someone else
> And not looking at yourself
> Someone squats to blow the fire
> And you bend to see his arse
> As you bend someone else is watching yours
> Defend yourself before assuming other people's problems
> God says we shouldn't look at others
> We should look at Jesus

In using the idioms Otulu stamps an Idoma identity not only on the church but also on their conception of Christ and salvation. The interesting thing in this exercise is how the Christians negotiate a Christian identity and an Idoma identity at the same time. The Christian identity encourages the Idoma believers to seek deliverance by consciously detaching themselves from the forces of darkness within which all cultural practices are rooted. "The underlying programme here does not put the stress so much on the creation of certain spiritual communalism, but on post-nostalgic, individual self-actualisation through an active emancipatory process of self-construction in which, to achieve fulfilment, one has to free oneself from past dependencies."[1] Yet the believer remains part and parcel of his community and sharing in its hopes and aspirations. To this end he must also project an identity of belonging. This dual identity features prominently in Christian music where the instruments, idioms and dances from the demonised practices are employed in praise worship while at the same time drawing attention to what the people must do. Even though salvation lies in Christ, one must put one's house in order, that is, one must fight for one's rights.

J.O. Adah, another prolific musician sees Christianity and Western civilization generally as a bad omen. To Adah:

> A true Idoma must behave like his people
> A real Idoma must live like one
> We must not forget our tradition
> Let's not follow (the whites') modernity
> And abandon our home

Adah then goes on to explain that the reason people flock to the church is that they wish to subvert the rigours of tradition. He blames the church for moral laxity and denigrating the people's culture. Adah's fight to protect Idoma culture from dying underscores a larger quest for the survival of the Idoma nation. Thus in addition to political domination, the people should also be resisting foreign values.

Tom Abah, calls the people's attention to the crucial value of unity without which the Idoma cannot present a solid resistance:

> Idoma listen to this song
> Why can't we progress
> Why do we wallow in suffering and poverty
> It's enough, enough, enough
> What is it? What is it?
> Idoma my fatherland
> Enough is enough
> Idoma listen and hear

If Tom Abah's music was a lament then Bongos Ikwue's *Ainya* ("Thank you"), was a celebration of identity. Bongos is a very successful musician and businessman in Nigeria, also well educated. His pride in Idoma is unmistakable as he not only expresses joy at being an Idoma, but also shows his gratitude. Beyond all these is the sense of return to roots to rediscover oneself and join hands to build Idoma:

> Thank you, thank you
> Thanks Idoma my fatherland
> This entire world is a joke
> If it is good for you don't jubilate that others don't have
> Come home, come home
> So that we can farm
> Come home, come home

He draws our attention or the attention of the Idoma to the transient nature of life, hence the necessity to discover home, return to it and develop it. Farm, is a metaphor for development as it involves clearing the land, tilling, sowing, tending, harvesting before eating. He also calls to the Idoma who have made it that they should spread their wealth and not use it to oppress their fellow Idoma.

---

1. Werbner 1998, p. 35.

Ogoni reactions to exploitation

As can be seen from the above examples, most of the music of Idoma offers a critique of the people's lack of unity or enjoins them to come together to pursue a common goal. This is a clear recognition of strength in unity. The Ogoni on the other hand are faced with the crisis of environment and resource exploitation. Thus their music differs in texture and temper. Sir Kingdom Kombo, in *MOSOP Nubue*, pathetically summons angels Gabriel and Michael to intervene in the plight of his people. Hear him:

> Angel Michael who would you send
> To lift us out of this problem.
> They drove all of us from our houses

He goes on to say that neither angel Michael nor Gabriel could answer because God has already given the power to act to man to save himself. The salvation of the people lies in their hands, in their resolve to resist and fight their oppression. Tracing the genesis of Ogoni crisis there is an earlier popular song among the Ogoni:

> The flames of Shell are flames of hell
> We bask below their light
> Nought for us save the blight
> Of cursed neglect and cursed Shell

The people's reaction to the exploitation of their resources and the attendant environmental degradation was to form the Movement for the Survival of Ogoni People (MOSOP). Under this organised grouping they were able to not only articulate their grievances but to wage war on Shell and the Nigerian government their collaborators in oppression. As Ken Saro-Wiwa, points out in his introduction to the booklet, *The Ogoni Nation Today and Tomorrow*:

> It is ironical that the discovery of oil on our land has brought us nothing but misery, hunger and pain. By contrast, oil brought prosperity, wealth and plenty to those who controlled the government. ... We do not preach hate. We do not ask that our people nurse the injustices of the past. ... But we do ask that the disgrace of the past should be our armour against the future.[1]

MOSOP succeeded in mobilizing all the Ogonis not just by the mere intensity of the people's oppression. Ken Saro-Wiwa was able to motivate his people to instigate mass hysteria and frenzy. Ken Saro-Wiwa began, interjected and ended all his addresses with a song:

> Get up, get up, get up and fight
> Ogoni get up and fight
> We would no longer agree
> That the world
> Should cheat us

In moments like this music invests the listener with a mix between full possession and full awareness filling the participant with an intoxicated sensation, a sense of lift, excitement and determination that helps to assert the self, define the I, and projects the source of origin (birth or belonging) so necessary for finding meaning in life.

---

1. Saro-Wiwa 1990, pp. 11, 22.

Nowhere is this more poignant than among the Ogoni, where even the usual traditional dance in celebration of victory or success has been converted to an instrument of struggle. The *Eedee Bari Bii Kor Dance Club* have this lead in their album, dedicated to Ken Saro-Wiwa who was framed by the military government for murder and executed without proper trial along with other Ogoni/MOSOP activists in 1995:

> Ogoni/Khana seek Wiwa, the promised light of God.
> They have killed Wiwa for us
> God should come and deliver us
> They hanged him with a rope
> They tied a rope round his neck
> And stretched him to death
> Like someone with no name
> Like someone without people
> People where are you

The song describes the details of the execution as a way of instigating anger and revenge. In addition, it reminds us of the fate of an Ogoni in Nigeria and underscores the relevance of recalling the past to the service of the present.

As the *Eedee Bari Bii Kor Dance Club* perform across Ogoniland or as their music blares away from tape recorders, the voices whip up sentiments about the loss, the despair, about the displacement, the dislocation, about poverty, about estrangement, about a very deep sense of individual and community loss and crisis. We are reminded of what De Boeck wrote on music in the Congo: "In the song, individual and collective experiences of the crisis are expressed by means of reference to death, ancestral land, and thus to roots."[1]

The group not only describe the problem, but are also offering suggestions for a way forward. In *Follow our footsteps* the Ogoni people are encouraged to take action instead of being complacent, while those who reside outside Ogoniland are encouraged in *Come let us go home* to return home and be interested in what is going on there. In *Things to do* the Club spell out what the people need to do to liberate themselves. They insist that the people have no option but to fight in whatever way they can.

Sir Kingdom Kombo's recent music titled *Reward* laments the situation in which some Ogonis betrayed their people by collaborating with the state and the forces responsible for their predicament:

> Why do you suffer your brother because of your position
> Them a looting them a shooting them a killing
> Yee you must get your reward
> Everything you do here on earth you must get the reward
> Mama don't you see now what you have done
> Papa don't you see now what you have done
> The things you have done have turn back to you
> Them a gonna live after you
> No running place
> No hiding place
> Whosoever lies against his brother
> It must come back to him
> Whosoever killed his brother
> He must get to be killed

---

1. De Boeck 1998, p. 26.

Ogoni land flowing with milk and honey
They come with uniform of brutality they took away my brother man
Suffer them in prison yard
Kill them and put them in graveyards

This song counters the government propaganda that Saro-Wiwa committed murder and had to pay for it. Sir Kingdom captures the soul of the Ogoni by insisting that:

We were born as Ogoni
And that's what we want
Ogoni will move forward
Ogoni will never surrender
Kenule will never surrender
Ogoni will no longer hide
We must unite to move forward

Concluding remarks

In music according to De Boeck the "memory of the individual draws upon collective, culturally embodied idioms and images, collective social memories cannot be properly understood without an analysis of individual memories, vivid with existential immediacy."[1] This very privileging of individual memory vivid with existential immediacy is fundamental to the way the two minority groups of this study negotiate their identities via music. The present day individual Idoma or Ogoni is a product of two worlds: the world of the community struggling to hold on to a fading past and distorted cultural system, and a globalised world imported via satellite, Hollywood movies and music.

Among the Idoma and Ogoni, masquerade performances are occasions for exhibiting musical prowess and dexterity. As the physical representations of the (dead) ancestors, the masquerades are meant to capture the state of being of the ancestors, that is reflect their context while in existence. However, the construction of the knowledge of the ancestor is done by the individuals who inhabit the world of today. Therefore, some of the masquerades of today have as part of their regalia signs of modernity: aeroplanes, motorcars, motorcycles, television, radio and so on. In some instances white rubber masks can be seen during communal performances. Even the concept of ancestorhood is thus being negotiated in the light of modernity.

While the masquerade essentially retains its ancestral aura, its mediatory role in communal conflicts, moral education, law and order has been lost to modernity. Instead it has become a cultural icon, a symbol which links one to the source by narrating histories and values via music and thereby generating a nostalgia for the past, ancestors and roots.

In addition to rendering old forms in the context of the moment, some musicians have *funkified* or *reggaefied* or *discofied* traditional songs. Thus you have reggae music in Idoma or Ogoni. However, there does not seem to be any take-over of the resistance spirit of the Jamaican reggae. By and large this kind of global influence is interpreted as a way of making the local available to a global audience.

In virtually all music for the Idoma and Ogoni, however, the overriding quest for identity unites the forms. Music remains an existential matter. The Idoma and the Ogoni are unique in Nigeria in their use of music, significantly in the form of rituals, but with a new political content. This is not a playing with identities, but a battle for survival.

---

1. De Boeck 1998, p. 39.

Discography

Bongos Ikwue, 1987, *Ainya*. EMI Records, Ibadan.

Eedee Bari Bii Kor Dancing Club, 1997, *Esaa Khana Gbi Wiwa*. Audio Cassette, Khana Studios, Port Harcourt.

Eedee Bari Bii Kor Dancing Club, 1997, *Nyone me for*. Audio Cassette, Khana Studios, Port Harcourt.

Eedee Bari Bii Kor Dancing Club, 1997, *Nu yaagoh dap doo*. Audio Cassette, Khana Studios, Port Harcourt.

J. O. Adah, 1985, *Alinme*. Audio Cassette, EMI, Ibadan.

Peter Otulu, 1992, *Igblenyi ka'awanda*. Audio Cassette, Pamel Studios, Kaduna.

Peter Otulu, 1992, *N'gweije; Aam 'oche oha, ami yoon*. Audio Cassette, Pamel Studios, Kaduna.

Sir Kingdom B. Kombo, 1998, *Culture ba King*. Audio Cassette, King studios, Eleme.

Sir Kingdom B. Kombo, 1998, *Reward*. Audio Cassette, King studios, Eleme.

Sir Kingdom B. Kombo, 1998, *Esaa Lee*. Audio Cassette, King studios, Eleme.

Sir Kingdom B. Kombo, 1998, *MOSOP Nubue*. Audio Cassette, King studios, Eleme.

Tom Abah, 1995, *Idoma Oladam*. Audio Cassette, El Shaddai Studios, Makurdi.

References

Abah, Oga Steve, 1997, *Performing Life: Case Studies in the Practice of Theatre for Development*. Zaria: Shekut Books.

Ake, Claude, 1997, "Shell, Oil and Nigeria", *Panafrica*, Vol. 2, No. 2, February, pp. 17–19. London.

Akinjide, Richard, 2000, "The Amalgamation of Nigeria Was a Fraud", *The Guardian on Sunday*, July 9, pp. 44–45.

Anyidoho, Kofi, 1989, *The Pan African Ideal in Literatures of the Black World*. Legon: Ghana University Press.

De Boeck, Filip, 1998, "Beyond the Grave: History, Memory and Death in Postcolonial Congo/ Zaire", in Werbner, Richard (ed.), *Memory and the Post Colony: African Anthropology and the Critique of Power*. London: Zed Books.

Gilroy, Paul, 1995, *The Black Atlantic: Modernity and Double Consciousness*. Cambridge: Harvard University Press.

Hall, Stuart and Du Gay, Paul (eds), 1996, *Questions of Cultural Identity*. London: SAGE.

Harper, Peggy, 1981, "The Inter-Relation of the Arts in the Performance of the Masquerade as an Expression of Oral Tradition in Nigeria", *Black Orpheus*, pp. 1–5, University of Lagos Press.

Illah, John S., 1983, "The Performing Arts of the Masquerade and Its Changing Status in Igala-land", M.A. thesis, Ahmadu Bello University, Zaria.

Merriam, Alan P., 1973, "The Bala Musician of Northwestern Congo (formerly Zaire)", in d'Azevedo, Warren L. (ed.), *The Traditional Artist in African Societies*. London: Indiana University Press.

Nketia, J.K., 1975, *Music of Africa*. London: Victor Gallancz Limited.

Nora, Pierre, 1994, "Between Memory and History: Les Lieux de Memiore", in Fabre, Genevieve and Robert O'Meally (eds), *History and Memory in African-American Culture*. Oxford: Oxford University Press.

Okwori, Jenkeri, 1998, *Ije: The Performance Traditions of the Idoma*. Zaria: ICRC.

Richards, Sandra, 1998, "Echoes in the Bone: Performing Memory, Performing Power in African (Diasporic) Festivals", paper presented at the opening of the "Echoes in the Bone ..." Workshop, Institute for the Advanced Study and Research in the African Humanities, held at Northwestern University, Illinois, USA, 15–17 May.

Roach, Joseph, 1996, *Cities of the Dead: Circum-Atlantic Performance.* Columbia: Columbia University Press.

Saro-Wiwa, Ken, 1990, *The Ogoni Today and Tomorrow.* Port Harcourt: Saros International Publishers.

Thomas, Deborah A. and Diana E. Wells, 1995, "The Black Atlantic and Double Consciousness and Cut 'N Mix: Culture, Identity, and Caribbean Music", *Identities: Global Studies in Culture and Power,* Vol. 2, No. 1–2, pp. 177–80. Basel: Gordon and Breach.

Werbner, Richard (ed.), 1998, *Memory and the Post Colony: African Anthropology and the Critique of Power.* London: Zed Books.

Multipartyism, Rivalry and Taarab in Dar es Salaam

Siri Lange

Taarab music no longer respectable
For those who grew up with the old taarab music school, the rate at which the popular brand of music along the East African coast has deteriorated, is very disturbing indeed.[1]

This article is concerned with the popularisation of *taarab* in Dar es Salaam during the 1990s.[2] *Taarab*, or *tarabu* as it is called in colloquial Swahili, was developed in Zanzibar in the late 19th century. It is essentially "a form of sung poetry with instrumental accompaniment" modelled on Egyptian orchestras.[3] Traditionally, this music is performed for a seated audience by large string orchestras, and it is central for musicians, singers and listeners alike to express poise and dignity during performances. Popularised *taarab* in Dar es Salaam on the other hand, has been transformed to dance music. The poise and dignity are no longer there, as a shocked journalist reported in the Tanzanian paper *The Guardian* in March 2000:

> Take the example of this lady, who out in the streets on any other day will pass for a very respectable person but who in a taarab evening at the Vijana Social Hall will leave you wondering whether she has got any morals at all. (...) The same lady and others of her sort in the hall will embrace men or any object including pillars and begin doing scenes normally done in the confines of one's bedroom as part of the crowd cheers.[4]

The journalist and other adherents to classical *taarab* strongly condemn modernised *taarab* and the new identity that this musical form has developed. In their view, *taarab* has become "degenerated" and it is "polluted with obscenities". The journalist appeals to a government body, the National Arts Council, to address the situation seriously and tame the situation before it gets out of hand.[5] He chooses to ignore the fact that the party in power sponsors the very troupe that is in fact leading in this development. This article looks into the processes behind this musical change, processes that have encouraged the development of, what seems to me, a new category of *taarab*. My main argument is that the changes that *taarab* has gone through in Dar es Salaam not only have to do with popular taste, but are a direct result of recent political changes and the ruling party's tradition of appropriating popular cultural forms for their own benefit.

---

1. Mgaya 2000.
2. An earlier version of this article was published in 2000 (Lange 2000).
3. Topp Fargion 2000, p. 39.
4. Mgaya 2000.
5. Mgaya 2000.

With the introduction of multipartyism, the party which earlier held a monopoly of political power CCM *(Chama Cha Mapinduzi)*, established a cultural troupe to campaign for them. This group, Tanzania One Theatre (TOT) was modelled on privately owned cultural troupes that offer four-hour long variety shows to paying urban audiences in social halls. One of the most popular items of the shows in the early 1990s was a simplified version of *taarab*. To attract fans to their new group, TOT launched a more sophisticated and modernised form of *taarab*. By appropriating popular taste, CCM hoped to win continued support under new political circumstances.

The independent cultural troupes face difficult dilemmas now that the ruling party has to a large degree withdrawn not only their control over the cultural field but also their support to it. This paper explores the reaction of the most famous of the "old" troupes, Muungano Cultural Troupe, to the establishment of Tanzania One Theatre—and the kind of rivalry that has developed between the two. *Taarab* is at the core of this rivalry. The troupes compose songs with highly controversial sexually charged lyrics, which are used for mutual, public insult. The article draws on participant observation with Dar es Salaam based cultural troupes in the period 1992–2000 and focuses on the large-scale contests that were arranged between the two troupes in Dar es Salaam, Morogoro and Mwanza in 1997.[1] Before we look at this case however, I will provide a short history of *taarab* and the background of the privately owned cultural troupes in Dar es Salaam.

A short history of *taarab*

The history of *taarab* dates back at least to the 1880s. Most *taarab* historians see Sultan Seyid Bargash of Zanzibar as the progenitor of the form.[2] Before Bargash came to power, he spent some years of exile in India "where he was exposed to and greatly impressed by magnificent palaces and court life".[3] When he later came to power, he decided to develop a new court culture in Zanzibar where music would be a central element. A Zanzibari musician, Muhammed Ibrahim, was sent to Cairo for musical training.[4] This man later organised and taught a small musical group that performed for the Sultan in his palace. It was this elitist band that provided the model for the popular string musical clubs that developed in Zanzibar in the late 19th century. The new musical form came to be known as *taarab*. A number of different explanations for the term exist. Kelly Askew suggests that it come from "the Arabic abstract noun *tarabun* meaning joy, pleasure, delight, rapture, amusement, entertainment, music".[5] Werner Graebner on the other hand, holds that it comes from *tariba*, an Arabic verb denoting "to be moved or agitated".[6]

Small *taarab* clubs—modelled directly on the Zanzibari ones—were formed in Dar es Salaam in the early 20th century, but it was only from the 1930s that *taarab* became big in the city.[7] The popularisation of *taarab* owes much to Siti binti Saad who was of slave origin. She revolutionised *taarab* not only by abandoning Arabic

---

1. During my first fieldwork I was a member of Muungano Cultural Troupe for nine months, and I have since kept in close touch with this troupe. I am grateful to Norbert Chenga for letting me do my research with his troupe, and I wish to thank all the artists for their warm hospitality and friendship.
2. For an analysis of the musical characteristics of *taarab* on Zanzibar see (Kirkegaard 1996).
3. Askew 1997, p. 155.
4. Askew 1997, p. 155.
5. Askew 1997, p. 148.
6. Graebner 1994, p. 350.
7. Graebner 1994, p. 353.

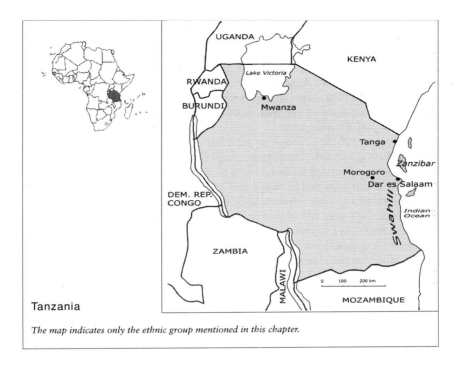

Tanzania

The map indicates only the ethnic group mentioned in this chapter.

and singing in Swahili instead, but also by "adding drums to the orchestra, and moving performances out of private men-only clubs into more public spaces".[1] In 1928 she went to record her songs in Bombay and the records were distributed all over East Africa.[2] Although becoming increasingly "swahili-ised", *taarab* clubs still had Egyptian orchestras as their models and they carefully imitated the style of these bands.[3] The most famous Dar es Salaam based *taarab* orchestra for example, established in the 1930s, called itself Egyptian Musical Club. The orchestras were also inspired by the radio broadcasting of Indian film music, by Latin American rhythms and by mainland dance music.[4]

In contrast to modern dance music, which often focuses on gender antagonism, classical *taarab* songs are romantic. One reason for this is that *taarab* traditionally was performed during weddings.[5] Furthermore, Indian films seem to have been an important inspirational source for the romantic songs. In the 1970s Jan Knappert identified ten dominant themes in *taarab* songs: "the nature of love, the pangs of love, departing, parting, reunion, desertion, unrequited love, the fickle woman, infidelity, the love for a child".[6] Kelly Askew, who collected nearly one thousand songs in the early 1990s, adds some more themes to the list: "general insult songs, insult songs aimed at a former lover, songs of lamentation and hardship, and political songs (often in praise of political leaders)".[7] Among the 66 *taarab* songs that I collected by Muungano and TOT, there are none about "the nature of love" or "the

1. Plane 1996, p. 73.
2. Anthony 1983, p. 137; Askew 1997, p. 159.
3. Anthony 1983, p. 133.
4. Askew 1997, p.159; Kirkegaard 1996.
5. Askew 1997, p. 151.
6. Quoted in Askew 1997, p. 151.
7. Askew 1997, p. 151.

love for a child", nor are there any songs praising political leaders.[1] Almost all the songs, 51 in total, are in fact songs which are full of hate directed against rivals who are told to keep away. This is indeed a dramatic change from what Knappert reports from the 1970s, and from the classical *taarab* clubs that are still operating in Zanzibar. In my view, we are looking at a new sub-genre of *taarab*, developed through the rivalry between the two major cultural troupes in Dar es Salaam. The new sub-genre is not only characterised by the themes of the songs, but also by changes in musical structure and performance style.

In classical *taarab*, the musicians perform on a stage with their audience sitting in front of them on chairs. The listeners may dance or walk up to the performers to tip them, but are supposed to then return to their seats. It is in no way dance music. This format, which was used by the "pure" *taarab* clubs that existed in Dar es Salaam, was considerably changed when *taarab* was incorporated into the variety shows. When tipping, fans take the opportunity to dance in front of the singer, displaying not only the notes, but also their clothes—and by the use of dramatic body language they make it clear that the song speaks for them. During popular songs the floor may be so crowded that the seated audience can neither see the singer nor the band. During my fieldwork in 1995, Chenga would regularly try to stop the audience from doing this. "This is *taarab*, not a disco" (*Hii ni tarabu, siyo disco*) he would reprimand them. When I came back in 1997, however, he had given up his tough line. He told me that after all, the group made a living from the fans and that they therefore had to let them do as they pleased.

In fact the troupes own popularising of *taarab* was to "blame" for the participatory actions of the audience. Compared to what we may call "classic" or ideal *taarab*, the new popularised version was made more rhythmic and danceable. This was done by incorporating *ngoma* beats—rhythms from mainland traditional music. Jayson Kami, who writes some of Muungano's *taarab* songs under a Muslim pseudonym, calls this "Tabora style" in contrast to the styles of Tanga and Zanzibar. The musicians talked about this incorporation of *ngoma* into *taarab* as "rapping"—probably referring to the sampling technique often used in rap. In 1997, Muungano went a step further by letting the bass and drumset "come in front" (*mbele*) of the music as they phrased it. They also let some of the *taarab* songs end with a small section of *Kipinda Nkoi*—the Congolese music and dance style that was at its height that year. This of course spurred the fans to dance even more. Compared to both *ngoma* and *musiki wa dansi* (dance music) however, popular *taarab* dancing is more individual—perhaps reflecting an increasing acceptance of greater individualism.[2] Before we look closer at the TOT—Muungano rivalry we will consider the historical background of these troupes.

Cultural troupes in Dar es Salaam

Dar es Salaam, with its population of about three million people, is the only city in Tanzania large enough to support commercial, full-time cultural troupes. These troupes put on four-hour long shows with nationalised "traditional" dances, acrobatics, theatre plays and above all—*taarab* songs. They perform in the social halls of the various Dar es Salaam suburbs from Thursday to Sunday, entertaining an ethnically and religiously mixed audience of adults and children. The troupes also reg-

---

1. All the songs are written by men, while the great majority, 44, are performed by women.
2. A person who dances alone during *Muziki wa dansi* is regarded as either drunk or a very odd person.

The ecstatic athmosphere at a taarab competition in Dar es Salaam
is recorded in the paper Nipashe.

ularly tour the country, bringing this basically urban performance style out to a wider audience.

The presence of multi-ethnic commercial cultural troupes in Dar es Salaam is an unintended result of the socialist cultural policy after independence. The cultural policy was directed towards building a national culture and using traditional art forms to educate the masses about the *ujamaa* policies.[1] A National Dance Troupe was established in the 1960s, performing nationalised *ngoma* with lyrics in Swahili praising the leaders and their work. The term *ngoma* denotes both traditional instruments (especially drums) and a traditional musical event where music, dance and mime form an integrated whole. Nationalised *ngoma* however, was transformed to fit the international convention of staged "folklore". As part of the *ujamaa* policies, neotraditional dance troupes performing this kind of *ngoma* were established at all schools and at most parastatal institutions and companies.

During the 1970s, some of these companies assumed patronage over full-time artists who performed commercially, and it did not take long before troupes were formed independently of any institution, being run on a purely businesslike basis.[2] In 1984 there were more than forty such groups in Dar es Salaam,[3] but many did not make it in the competition and at the beginning of the new millennium there were less than ten. The troupes have contracts with bars and social halls in the suburbs to perform on certain days and they depend on the collection at the door for their survival.[4] The smaller troupes have around fifteen employees while the larger ones have

---

1. See the following works for more details: Lange 1995 and 1999; Lihamba 1985 and 1994.
2. Songoyi 1988, p. 31.
3. Lihamba 1991, p. 274.
4. The tickets for Muungano shows were 300 Tsh. for adults in 1992 and 1000 Tsh. in 1997 and 2000, equivalent to 75 US cents and 1.70 US$ respectively in those years.

as many as fifty or sixty. Muungano Cultural Troupe, which was started by Norbert Chenga in 1980, has from the very beginning been one of the more successful. Their success is a result of careful adaptation to the taste of their audiences. Over the years, the group has incorporated ever new genres and expanded their show from a one-hour dance performance to a four-hour long variety show.

According to the owner Norbert Chenga, the group started up with four *ngoma* only. But when one of the other troupes, DDC Kibisa, introduced comedic skits to give the dancers time to change costumes, Muungano quickly followed their lead.[1] Acrobatics (*sarakasi*) were introduced in 1984, and the comedic skits were gradually developed into full-length plays. In 1985 the cultural troupes of Dar es Salaam incorporated a simplified version of *taarab* into their variety shows. I use the word "simplified" for several reasons. First, none of the variety troupes could afford string instruments—which are central in classical *taarab*. Second, the troupes did not hire specialised *taarab* singers but used "all round" artists who were generally already hired by the group to dance *ngoma* and/or to act as well. Up to 1992, theatre was the most popular item of a cultural show.[2] This changed when TOT entered the scene and challenged Muungano's leading position with their *taarab* of a much higher standard.

TOT came into being as a direct result of the decision of the government to open up for multipartyism. The ruling CCM party felt the need to have a cultural troupe to campaign for them—and TOT was to be their "secret weapon". Rumours had it that the initiative was supported economically by the Chinese government.[3] Up to 1992 there had been no need for CCM to have their own troupe, as all the cultural troupes in the country had been performing *ngoma* songs that supported CCM, its leaders, and the political system in general. The artists fulfilled this role partly because they believed in *ujamaa* in the early years, partly to win the goodwill of the government. This goodwill was needed to get renewals of their permit to perform, to get paid assignments for performing at celebrations of various kinds, and if lucky, even tours abroad. With time the political propaganda songs simply became a convention of the nationalised *ngoma* genre.

With the nation preparing itself for a new era of multipartyism, the CCM party feared that they would lose this support. The fear was partly ungrounded. When I asked the Muungano artists in 1992 whether they would stop singing about CCM now that multipartyism had been introduced, most of them said that they would continue to sing about CCM until they saw which party would win. Muungano did, however, stop their habit of playing the CCM tune at the end of every show. CCM asked Captain John Komba to be the leader of their cultural troupe. Komba was a perfect choice. Not only did he have a high position in the party—he was charismatic and had for years been the leader and star solo singer of the Army Cultural Troupe (*Jeshi la Wanainchi*). Komba recruited artists from the already existing cultural troupes, among them Muungano—to Chenga's great dismay. The artists were more than willing to move to this new troupe, which due to the generous economic backing from CCM, could offer much better terms and had higher standards in costumes and musical equipment.

TOT was established as a propaganda tool, but the CCM seemed to have learned a lesson from their thirty years of experience with political use of the arts. It was not *ngoma* or a propagandistic choir that came to profile the troupe, but *taarab* songs

1. Plane 1996, p. 67.
2. Survey conducted in 1992, Lange 1995, p. 115.
3. Askew 1997, p. 367.

with sexy and scandalous lyrics.[1] Captain Komba recruited two talented artists from the Zanzibari *taarab* orchestra Culture Musical Club, Khadija Kopa and Othman Soud. Before their first official performance on July 17th 1992, TOT released some of their songs on the radio,[2] and the troupe's name was soon on everybody's lips. TOT's *taarab* was new and modern, making extended use of electronic instruments. There was no doubt that TOT's glamorous appearance and their exciting new *taarab* quickly won them many hearts. Norbert Chenga, owner of Muungano Cultural Troupe, soon felt the position of his troupe endangered. He realised that if they were to keep up with TOT, they too would have to develop their *taarab* section and the group therefore hired professional singers and string musicians.[3]Incidentally, Captain Komba fired his two greatest stars, Khadija Kopa and Othman Soud after they had gone on a private concert tour to Dubai. Norbert Chenga promptly recruited them and from here a fierce rivalry started—a kind of rivalry Muungano had never had during their decade-long co-existence with the other cultural troupes of the city.

Still, the Muungano-TOT rivalry falls into a long tradition of competitive performance in East Africa.[4] The Sukuma in the north of Tanzania and the Ngoni in the south are both well known for their competitive dance societies. Dance rivalry has been a central feature on the Swahili coast for centuries[5] and the competitive urban Beni dance associations of the colonial times were a continuation of this practice.[6] In Tanga and Zanzibar several *taarab* clubs have a history of fierce rivalry,[7] and the same is true for dance bands in Dar es Salaam.[8]

Rivalry and fans

In 1994, two years after TOT was started, the first contest between the two rival troupes was arranged. This was seen as a major event in the cultural life of the city, and one of the Asian-owned video enterprises in town, Tajin & Habib Partners Limited, decided to produce a video about it for sale. The video must have been an economic success, because the company followed up with video productions of the 1996 and 1997 contests as well. Tajin & Habib Partners Limited in fact sponsor the competitions and in return get a percentage of the collection at the door as well as the full rights to the video production.

Both troupes, but especially Muungano, depend upon sponsors to raise enough capital to arrange the contests. The contests are expensive endeavours for the troupes, for several reasons. First, the groups forfeit income because they stop performing for some weeks or even a full month before the contest and therefore loose income. They do this to rehearse new material, but also to build up suspense among their fans. Second, it is of major importance for their success to look their best. Ideally, all the costumes should be brand new for the competition day. This means new costumes for the two or three *ngoma,* new track suits for the acrobats and above all;

---

1. I have not come across TOT *taarab* songs with overtly political content. Muungano on the other hand, performed a *taarab* song praising Mwinyi in 1992.
2. *Sunday News* 1992.
3. The new focus upon *taarab* changed social relations within the group. During my first fieldwork in 1992, Muungano was characterised by an egalitarian air and wages depended on a large degree on seniority—the artist's age and his/her number of years with the group. *Taarab* stars on the other hand, are way above the other artists in social status, and their wage is at least three times higher.
4. Gunderson and Barz 2000.
5. Glassman 1995; Lienhardt 1968.
6. Ranger 1975.
7. Askew 1997; Topp Fargion 1993.
8. Graebner 2000, p. 303.

beautiful dresses and shoes for the *taarab* section and matching shirts for the musicians.

CCM decided to sponsor both troupes for the competitions that were held in 1994 and 1995—before the first multiparty election in October 1995. According to one of the artists, Muungano got 500,000 Tsh. in 1994 and something between one and two million in 1995, in a competition whose purpose was to celebrate the jubilee of the CCM. After the election however—when CCM had secured another five years in power—CCM support to Muungano dried up. The group went through a hard time economically and Chenga had to fire twelve of the artists in 1996.

The last few weeks before a competition, the troupes actively use the Swahili newspapers to draw attention to the forthcoming event. Before and during the 1997 contests, I found 23 articles in 12 different papers, all focusing on the Muungano—TOT rivalry. [1] The papers presented the competition as a clash not only between two cultural troupes—but also between two strong leaders, and the two of them did their best to insult each other publicly through the papers. Captain Komba took advantage of the weak financial situation of Muungano. He claimed that the competition was really only to help Muungano get money for paying the wages that they had been unable to pay for months. He also said that for TOT to compete with Muungano was in fact to disgrace themselves as the latter had no chance of succeeding. [2] Komba further attempted to insult Chenga by jokingly suggesting that he could join TOT as his troupe did not have a snake dancer. [3]

More serious however, were Komba's claims that Chenga had gone to a medicine man to make the TOT singers tremble and cause the troupe's brand new equipment to break down on the competition day. "Why should he shave completely bald, is he a DJ or rapper? He was told to do this by his *mganga*, [4] but I'm a Ngoni, now we will compete so as to see who is greater of him and me". [5] Chenga, on his part, said that despite the fact that TOT had new and expensive equipment, no one in the troupe knew how to use it properly. He added that TOT could win if the competition between them was only on costumes, but that they could not beat Muungano's fifteen years of experience. "(W)hen they want to compete with us, it is like a child competing with its father", he told the journalists. [6]

The troupes use every method to win this media war and make journalists write favourably about them. TOT for example, offered journalists free transport, accommodation and meals if they would come to see them in Morogoro where they were under training. Muungano has no means to give the journalists a treat like the Morogoro trip offered by TOT, but beers and monetary gifts to journalists who write about them are part of their regular expenses, documented along with other expenses in their account books. As most other professionals in Tanzania, journalists are underpaid, and seem to want a little extra before doing an article.

The relationship between TOT and Muungano is often compared to that of the two rivalling Tanzanian soccer teams Simba and Yanga. Like the sport clubs, TOT and Muungano have loyal fans who come to every show and who love to talk about their favourite troupe. The relationship between the two troupes is also described as *utani*, the kind of joking relationship that exists between specific ethnic groups in the country. The joking relationship allows members of these groups—who often

---

1. See for example Dar Leo 1997b; Katona 1997.
2. Zahor 1997.
3. Saullo 1997.
4. *Mganga* is translated as both medicine man and witchdoctor.
5. Dar Leo 1997a. All citations from these newspapers are translated from Swahili by the author.
6. Zahor 1997.

have a former history of hostility—to insult and tease each other in public, but it is also an important institution in times of difficulty, as it is often the joking partners' role to assist the bereaved during burials. That Muungano and TOT have adopted a kind of joking relationship, may explain why the two leaders may insult each other and accuse one another of using witchcraft one day, and greet each other in a friendly way the next day.

The competitions are held on two separate stages, one for each troupe, and they perform in turns. The fans sit or stand in front of the group they support, and few of them move to the rivals' side to have a closer look at *their* performance. Rather, they will shout out when they think it is time for the other group to halt and give the floor to their own group. As part of their boasting, members of both troupes will claim that they have won supporters from the other side during the competition. And the competitions are really about winning the hearts of the fans. There are no formal judges. As in traditional Sukuma dance competitions mentioned earlier, the de facto winner is the group that secures the largest following.[1] To win new fans during a competition also means more money coming in from the normal shows, as fans, if they have the money, go to every show that their favourite troupe put on in their neighbourhood. But the artists are painfully aware of the fact that if they do not do well, the fans can change sides there and then. Losing a substantial number of fans may in the long run mean an end to the group.

The competitions are basically similar in content to the regular shows, but the atmosphere cannot be compared. While the audience at regular shows sit quietly for most of the performance, only to invade the floor at the time of *taarab*, the venue will be boiling during competitions, even before the show itself has started. Groups of fans run around in the hall shouting, singing and waving the flags that they have been provided with by the troupes. When the *taarab* stars arrive, they flock around them and ceremoniously follow them backstage. The performance starts with dance music to warm up the crowds. The groups then show a few *ngoma* each, before acrobatics (Muungano only), followed by theatre plays by both troupes and TOT's choir (*kwaya*).[2] The highlight is no doubt the *taarab* section, which takes around two hours, the same time as all the other genres taken together.

The mortar and the pestle

The troupes compete in all genres, but the rivalry itself is articulated through *taarab* alone. The *taarab* songs are simply perfect for the task, as these songs, according to one informant, basically aim at "saying nasty things about others and getting away with it". A synonym for popularised *taarab* is *mipasho*. This is the word used by the comperes when introducing this part of the show. The word *mipasho* (plural form) is based on the verb *kupasha*, which means "to tell, inform, publicise".[3] The information conveyed is given in a clandestine way, as is the case with many traditional ngoma songs. *Taarab* is the art of figurative language, and while fans of *taarab* appreciate this and take pride in decoding the songs, other people find the songs all too complicated and malicious. Fans, women first and foremost, typically use the songs for their own private purpose. During shows, they make the songs their own by singing along, dancing on the stage and showering the artist with money. They

---

1. Elias Songoyi, University of Dar es Salaam, personal communication 1997.
2. For the Tanzanian *kwaya* tradition, see Barz 1997.
3. Johnson 1939.

may even dance provocatively in front of a seated rival. Outside the performance context they may hum "their song" in the presence of someone they want to tell off, or they may put on a cassette and let it do the work.

Taarab stars frequently use their songs to communicate in public their ill feelings about fellow artists, be they members of their own troupe or a rival one. Names, however, are never mentioned, one has to know the inside of the conflict in order to grasp the intended meaning of the song. This also goes for the songs used by Muungano and TOT against each other. Apparently the first songs that were deliberately composed as part of their rivalry were *Mtwangio* [The Pestle] and *Salaam za mtwangaji* [Greetings to the Mortar]. It all started when TOT released *Mtwangio* in 1994:[1]

"Mtwangio"	"The Pestle"
Yategeni masikio	Lend me your ears
Mpate kunisikia	Please listen to me
Kubwa langu kusudio	My aim today
Leo nawaambia	I tell you
Nausifu mtwangio	Is to praise the pestle
Mimi nnaotwengia	That I pound with
Kwa kutwanga namba wani	It is number one in pounding
Sifa nina watolea	And I praise it
Si thubutu asilani	I will never
Mwingine kuutumia	Use another one
Wa mwingine sitamani	I don't desire any other
Huu nimeuzoea	I am accustomed to this one
Ukweli nawaambieni	I'm telling you the truth
Si utani ndugu zangu	I'm not joking, my friends
Uingiapo kinuni	When this pestle
Huu mtwangio wangu	Enters my mortar
Unatwanga kwa makini	It pounds carefully
Kwenye hiki kinu changu	In this mortar of mine
Nakamilisha usemi	I now end what I had to say
Nilosema ya hakika	And what I have said is for sure
Mtwangio wangu mimi	This pestle of mine
Kweli umekamilika	Is really complete
Hata kwa masaa kumi	Even for ten hours
Hutwanga bila kuchoka	it pounds without tiring
Chorus:	Chorus:
Mtwangio twanga	Pestle keep on pounding
Usichoke	Don't tire
Mtwangie twanga	Pestle keep on pounding
Bila wasiwasi	Don't worry
Mtwangio wangu	My pestle
Kinu kimekuridhie	The mortar is satisfied with you

The female singer praises her pestle, and it does not take a lot of imagination to see that the mortar and the pestle represent the male and female organs. The Muungano artists and fans on both sides however, also read the song as saying that TOT was

---

1. I am grateful to Jayson Kami, Muungano Cultural Troupe, for assistance in translating these two songs.

the best troupe in town, and that there was no need for others. Muungano could not let this insult remain unanswered. They soon came up with a song called *Salaam za mtwangaji* [Greetings to the Mortar].

"Salaam za mtwangaji"	**"Greetings to the Mortar"**
Salaam za mtwangaji	Mortar, I'm bringing you greetings
kinu nakuletea	From the pestle
Kinu kimejaa maji	The pestle says
Mtwangaji anakwambia	You are full of water
Kazoea cha mtaji	I am used to another
Kulichochongwa kwa mutwa	Made of special wood
Sifa ulizotaraji kinu	The praise that you expected
hakija fikia	You will not get
Kimeezekwa saruji	You are covered with just a thin layer
kibovu wakitambua	of cement, and already broken
Heri jiwe ufaraji	Better then, one made of stone
kuliko kinu bandia	Than a fake mortar
Wachekwa hujitambui	You are a laughing stock
siri yako twaijuwa	We know your secret
Mtwango umezilai	The pestle is suffocated
Mashaka wajionea	And doubtful
Kinu chako hakifai	Your mortar is of no use
hawezi kukitwangia	He cannot pound in it
Vishindo na kujidai	Boasting and full of pretensions
aibu kimejitia	Shaming yourself
Chele limezidi tui	The rice has too much coconut milk*
Limekuwa mashondea	It has become really awkward
Kinu kama hujijui	Mortar, if you don't know
Mtwango umekimbia	The pestle has run away from you
Chorus:	Chorus:
Wataisha watwangaji	It will be the end of mortars
kupata si kwenda	One does not get by running after it
Kinu kimejaa maji	The mortar is full of water
Mitwangio yatoka mbio	The pestles are leaving in a hurry

* The Swahili cuisine features rice cooked with coconut milk.

Although the second song is a reply to the first one, it is noteworthy that they do not use the symbols in the same way. In the TOT song, the pestle (or penis) that is praised for its good work represents the troupe itself, and the mortar, the female part could be both the artist herself and the fans of the troupe. In the Muungano reply on the other hand, TOT is the mortar, (the vagina) that is no longer able to satisfy the male part (penis) representing the fans. While TOTs *Mtwangio* was performed for almost a year, *Salaam za mtwangaji* did not stay for long. It was too open, the language considered dirty, and people simply thought it was too much.

In 1996, Muungano composed a new song against TOT, *Homa la jiji* [Fever of the City]. In the song, the ego says to her rival that the time is hers, she's the expert, and the one who makes fever in the city. Muungano performed this song for some time with great success, but were taken aback by TOT who strategically released their answer—"*Cloroqini*" [Chloroquine]—during that year's competition. The song simply says, again in figurative language, that if Muungano is the fever, then TOT is the chloroquine to put an end to that fever.

Struggle for survival under multipartyism

The newspaper *Mtanzania* declared Muungano winner of the 1997 competition in Dar es Salaam. This was without doubt a jewel in the turban of the troupe, but it does not help them much. The rain poured down the full day of the competition and the whole thing was an economic disaster for the two groups and their sponsors. In Morogoro too there were far less people than during the previous year's competition.

All their hope was turned to the last and final contest that would take place in Mwanza city by Lake Victoria, a couple of days train ride from Dar es Salaam. Due to economic problems, bad planning and a whole set of unfortunate circumstances, Muungano arrived too late for the contest and the audience was furious and felt cheated. Komba took advantage of the situation for all its worth, spelling out that TOT had been in town for several days.[1] The two troupes agreed to have their competition the following day, and thousands returned to the stadium.[2] As if their earlier problems were not enough, the loudspeakers of Muungano caught fire during the competition—forcing them to leave the stage to their rivals while they had their equipment repaired. This was food for the press. *Majira* claimed that Khadija Kopa had been crying when this happened and that she had accused TOT of using witchcraft against them:

> Those TOT are really witches, we lost our way many times when coming here and now our equipment has burned. Aha! Now they have finished us.[3]

The paper then reminded its readers that "three weeks ago, before this competition started, the leader of Muungano, Norbert Chenga was recorded to say that the equipment of TOT would burn during their show", indicating that the spell had been returned.[4] One of the other papers that reported on the event did not only indicate this, but brought it into the open:

> The equipment that was burned were four speakers. So the curse that Chenga had made to wish the equipment of TOT burn on the day of the competition, turned against himself and his group.[5]

People I talked to did in fact say that Komba must have been to a stronger *mganga*. While the use of medicine men is a central aspect of Sukuma dance competitions[6]— done in the open—the urban troupes are more discreet about the matter and usually deny that they rely on such traditional practices.[7] After this defeat in Mwanza— which was yet another great economic blow to Muungano—Chenga gave up his earlier tough and proud line. He said that it was wrong to compare Muungano and TOT as the latter had economic power due to its relationship with CCM while Muungano had nothing. In *Heko*, Chenga announced that he was ready to campaign

---

1. Mwambona 1997a.
2. Edmondson 1999, p. 285.
3. Mwambona 1997b.
4. Mwambona 1997b.
5. Msungu 1997.
6. Elias Songoyi, personal communication.
7. Use of magic is also widespread among soccer teams, see Berget 2000.

for CCM so that his troupe could get money, and he declared that he himself was a CCM supporter. The journalist suggested that he could find another political party. Chenga replied that the other parties had no money (*uwezo*): "We have tried various times, but neither NCCR, CUF or Chadema have been able to be favourable".[1]

This willingness to campaign for any political party that is ready to pay does indeed say a lot about the relationship between politics and the performative arts in Tanzania. The artists are simply used to having a patron. In the case of Muungano, they supported the CCM through their arts for almost fifteen years, and interviews revealed that many of the artists came to see this as their role in society.[2] In fear of losing customers who support opposition parties, Muungano no longer sing praise-songs about CCM politicians, but they have kept the *ngoma* songs that praise the nation itself.

According to *Heko,* Chenga said that he wanted "the government to give the same space to all the cultural groups so that they all can have the same economic means and be able to give good entertainment to the citizens".[3] But CCM does not support TOT in order to give the Tanzanian people "good entertainment". TOT is a propaganda tool—the group uses popular arts and music to propagate an image of CCM as a "modern" party. While the cultural troupes of the one-party era used *ngoma* songs with blunt propaganda, TOT makes use of *taarab*'s rich potential for hidden meanings to perpetuate CCM. American anthropologist Laura Edmondson— who went with TOT on one of their campaigns to Kagera—reports that the group performed almost exclusively *taarab*:

> They chose *taarab* songs with open metaphors that could easily be interpreted to fit the campaign; for example, they sang a popular song cautioning the listeners that they are deceiving themselves by "jumping around," and also a song about being careful what they put in their mouth. Although such songs would typically be heard as cautions against infidelity, in the context of a rally, the songs warned the observers against being "unfaithful" to CCM. The singers held green CCM flags as they sang, apparently to insure that the connection would not be missed.[4]

Ironically, *taarab*, together with popular theatre, has won its popularity in Dar es Salaam exactly because it was able to evade the propaganda role that *ngoma* was forced into.[5] CCM, through TOT, follows the popular taste and appropriates *taarab* as they earlier appropriated *ngoma*. To conquer *taarab* may have been especially important to CCM in their attempt to win women supporters. The main opposition party before the 1995 election, NCCR Mageuzi, was said to have a large following among women. When the police used tear gas against the party's chairman Augustine Lyatonga Mrema in Moshi during one of his campaigns, a group of women in Dar es Salaam marched to the Danish Embassy to deliver a protest petition.[6]

Although Muungano is not aligned to any political party, the songs between the two rival troupes are also interpreted politically and they may also be used metaphorically outside of the performance context. In October 2000, an angry group of people approached a local CCM politician, Kitwana Kondo of the Kigamboni ward in Dar es Salaam, to express their discontent with him. They did this by chanting Muungano's latest hit *"Mtu mzima ovyo"* [A Wicked Person].[7] Not only did the lyr-

---

1. Msungu 1997.
2. Lange 1995, p. 46–48.
3. Msungu 1997.
4. Edmondson 1999, p. 240.
5. Lange forthcoming.
6. *Daily News* 1995.
7. Herbert Makoye, personal communication, 20 October 2000.

ics of the song express what these people wanted to say, the fact that it had been composed as part of the rivalry between Muungano and CCM's own cultural troupe probably was significant.[1]

CCM neglects Muungano in the years between elections, but they are careful to keep them at their side during election time, to avoid the group being mobilised by the opposition. Before the election in October 2000, the group was paid two million shillings to campaign for CCM in Dar es Salaam. Meanwhile, TOT accompanied President Benjamin Mkapa on his tour of the up-country regions.

Conclusion: A new category of *taarab*

Traditionally, *taarab* audiences both in Zanzibar and Dar es Salaam were Muslim and belonged to the elite. Alcohol was unheard of, and during concerts, the audience would sit and listen, much like audiences at classical music concerts in the West. When a simplified version of *taarab* was incorporated into the variety shows that were arranged in social halls and bars of Dar es Salaam in the mid-1980s, the musical form won new hearts. Since the song texts are secular, Christians have no problems to identify with the music, and the genre quickly became among the most popular items of the shows. In this setting, it is not uncommon to see people tip *taarab* singers with bottles of beer. However, the greatest transformation of *taarab* in Dar es Salaam came with the introduction of multipartyism and CCM's decision to establish their own cultural troupe. Through their rivalry, TOT and Muungano have pushed the rich metaphoric potential of *taarab* a step further and they have gradually developed the music, incorporating both traditional mainland *ngoma* rhythms and styles from modern dance music. The songs have become more erotically charged, the music has been transformed to dance music and the audience participation has increased accordingly – becoming, in many people's eyes, ever more "obscene".

In a recent publication, Janet Topp Fargion argues that there are three categories of *taarab* along the Swahili coast:

> Three categories of *Taarab* can be identified and described: first, an orchestral form modelled on Egyptian forms of urban secular music serving the more affluent, frequently Arab-oriented sectors of the society; second, a counter-style known as *kidumbak*, in practice modelled on local *ngoma*, developed by peoples of African descent as a result of exclusion from the orchestral form, politics, and more recently by economic limitations, and third, *Taarab ya wanawake* (women's *taarab*), which leans aesthetically toward the orchestral model, but in practice it also leans toward the Swahili-izations of *Taarab* more fully realized in *kidumbak*.[2]

Popular *taarab* in Dar es Salaam has certain characteristics in common with both *kidumbak* and women's *taarab* in Zanzibar. For example, the word *mipasho* (sing. *mpasho*), which is now used as a synonym for popular *taarab* in Dar es Salaam, was first used in the 1970s when a fierce rivalry developed between some of the women's *taarab* groups on Zanzibar. Apart from "backbiting" *mipasho* songs, however, the women's groups on Zanzibar and the professional Dar es Salaam based variety troupes have little in common, and there is little doubt, in my view, that we are looking at a new category that should be added to the above list. I have suggested that we call this new sub-genre *popular taarab* in contrast to orchestral or classical *taarab*. *Taarab* is indeed a musical form that has the potential of taking very different forms

---

1. The song was composed in response to TOTs *Mambo iko huku* [The Things Are There].
2. Topp Fargion 2000, p. 40.

when transformed to fit different needs and tastes. In Zanzibar, increased tourism has entailed a new "traditionalist" form of *taarab* where small orchestras play acoustically on old instruments in hotels and restaurants.[1] In Dar es Salaam, multi-partyism and the ruling party's appropriation of popular culture has pushed *taarab* in the opposite direction—towards a more electronic sound and more audience participation.

References

Anthony, David Henry, 1983, *Culture and society in a town in transition: A people's history of Dar es Salaam, 1865–1939*. Ph.D. thesis, University of Wisconsin (unpublished).

Askew, Kelly Michelle, 1997, *Performing the nation: Swahili musical performance and the production of Tanzanian national culture*. Thesis submitted for the degree of Ph.D., Harvard University (unpublished).

Barz, Gregory F., 1997, *The performance of religious and social identity: An ethnography of post-mission Kwaya music in Tanzania*. Thesis submitted for the degree of Ph.D., Brown University (unpublished).

Berget, Trond, 2000, "Fotball og hekseri", *X*, pp. 30–31. Oslo.

Daily News, 1995, "Dar women oppose use of force against Mrema", *Daily News,* 29 July. Dar es Salaam.

Dar Leo, 1997a, "Komba amshuku Chenga kunyoa upara", *Dar Leo,* 16 October. Dar es Salaam.

—, 1997b, "Pambano la TOT, Muungano kesho: Komba, Chenga watambiana", *Dar Leo,* 17 October. Dar es Salaam.

Edmondson, Laura, 1999, *Popular theatre in Tanzania: Locating tradition, woman, nation*. Thesis submitted for the degree of Ph.D., University of Texas at Austin (unpublished).

Glassman, Jonathan, 1995, *Feasts and riots: Revelry, rebellion and popular consciousness on the Swahili coast, 1856–1888*. Portsmouth: Heinemann.

Graebner, Werner, 1994, "Swahili musical party. Islamic taarab music of East Africa", in Broughton, S. (ed.), *World music. The rough guide*. London: Rough Guides.

Graebner, Werner, 2000, "Ngoma ya Ukae: Competitive social structure in Tanzanian dance music songs", in Gunderson, F. and G. Barz (eds), *Mashindano! Competitive music performance in East Africa*. Dar es Salaam: Mkuki na Nyota Publishers.

Gunderson, Frank, and Gregory Barz (eds), 2000, *Mashindano! Competitive music performance in East Africa*. Dar es Salaam: Mkuki na Nyota Publishers.

Johnson, Frederick, 1939, *A standard Swahili-English dictionary*. Oxford: Oxford University Press.

Katona, Michael, 1997, "Waimbaji taarab wapigana vijembe", *Uhuru,* 20 October. Dar es Salaam

Kirkegaard, Annemette, 1996, *Taarab na Muziki wa densi. The popular musical culture in Zanzibar and Tanzania seen in relation to globalization and cultural change*. Thesis submitted for the degree of Ph.D., University of Copenhagen (unpublished).

Lange, Siri, 1995, *From nation-building to popular culture: The modernization of performance in Tanzania* (revised cand. polit. thesis). Bergen: Chr. Michelsen Institute.

—, 1999, "How the national became popular. Nationbuilding and popular culture in Tanzania", in Palmberg, M. (ed.), *National Identity and Democracy*. Pretoria: Human Science Research Council.

---

1. Annemette Kirkegaard, this volume.

—, 2000, "Muungano and TOT: Rivals on the urban cultural scene", in Gunderson, F. and G. Barz (eds), *Mashindano! Competitive Music Performance in East Africa*. Dar es Salaam: Mkuki na Nyota Publishers.

—, (forthcoming), *Managing modernity. Gender, state and nation in the popular drama of Dar es Salaam, Tanzania*. Thesis to be submitted for the degree of Ph.D., University of Bergen.

Lienhardt, Peter, 1968, "Introduction", in H. b. Ismali (ed.), *The medicine man: Swifa ya nguvumali*. Oxford: Clarendon Press.

Lihamba, Amandina, 1985, *Politics and theatre in Tanzania after the Arusha Declaration 1967–1984*. Thesis submitted for the degree of Ph.D., University of Leeds (unpublished).

—, 1991, "The role of culture", in Hartmann, J. (ed.), *Re-thinking the Arusha Declaration*. Copenhagen: Centre for Development Research.

—, 1994, "Theatre and political struggles in East Africa", in Osaghae and Eghosa (eds), *Between state and civil society in Africa*, pp. 196–216. Dakar: CODESRIA.

Mgaya, Gabby, 2000, "Taarab music no longer respectable", *The Guardian*, 20 March. Dar es Salaam.

Msungu, Vedasto, 1997, "Baada ya mambo kumwendea vibaya Mwanza—Chenga asema yuko tayari kuipigia debe CCM", *Heko,* 4 November. Dar es Salaam.

Mwambona, Chris, 1997a, "Mpanbano na TOT—Muungano Cultural Troupe waingia mitini Mwanza", *Majira,* 3 November. Dar es Salaam.

—, 1997b, "Spika ya Muungano yaungua katika mpambano na TOT", *Majira,* 5 November. Dar es Salaam.

Plane, Mark William, 1996, *Fusing oral and literary practices: Contemporary popular theatre in Dar es Salaam*. Thesis submitted for the degree of Ph.D., University of Wisconsin (unpublished).

Ranger, Terence O., 1975, *Dance and society in Eastern Africa 1890–1970*. London: Heinemann.

Saullo, Saullo G.H., 1997, "Tunakwenda kuwachangia pesa Muungano", *Hoja*, 17–23 October. Dar es Salaam.

Songoyi, Elias M., 1988, *Commercialization. Its impact on traditional dances*. B.A. thesis. University of Dar es Salaam.

Sunday News, 1992, "Tanzania One Theatre launched with pomb", *Sunday News,* 17 July. Dar es Salaam.

Topp Fargion, Janet, 2000, "'Hot kabisa!' The mpasho phenomenon and taarab in Zanzibar", in Gunderson, F. and G. Barz (eds), *Mashindano! Competitive music performance in East Africa*. Dar es Salaam: Mkuki na Nyota Publishers.

Zahor, Rashid, 1997, "Muungano, TOT: Nani atavishwa mkanda kesho?", *Uhuru,* 17 October. Dar es Salaam.

Contributors

Simon Adetona Akindes is assistant professor of Instructional Technology in the Teacher Education Department at the University of Wisconsin-Parkside. With a background in literature, political science and international affairs, his research focuses on cultural studies of technology, educational technology, and popular music. He has published three educational books, as well as numerous articles on computers in education and society, and on politics and culture.
E-mail address: akindess@uwp.edu

Ndiouga Adrien Benga works at the Department of History at University Cheikh Anta Diop in Dakar, Senegal. His present work is on urban contemporary processes in a long perspective, and also on urban violence, street arts and the individualisation process.
E-mail address: nabenga@refer.sn

Johannes Brusila is curator of the Sibelius Museum at the Department of Musicology at Åbo Academy University, working in the fields of ethnomusicology and popular music studies. He has done several periods of fieldwork in Zimbabwe and written his licentiate thesis on the music industry of Zimbabwe. His current work for his Ph.D. has the working title "The Discourse of World Music in the Light of Three Zimbabwean Case Studies: The Bhundu Boys, Virginia Mukwesha and Sunduza". He has also written several articles on world music as a cultural and industrial phenomenon.
E-mail address: jbrusila@abo.fi

John Collins has been involved in West African music as musician, bandleader, recording engineer, producer and journalist since the late 1960s. He has written seven books on West African music and has been involved in numerous television and radio productions. He is a professor at the Music Department of the University of Ghana at Legon, leader of the *Local Dimension* highlife band and Acting Director of the Boloor African Popular Music Archives Foundation (BAPMAF).
E-mail address: jcollins@ug.edu.gh

David B. Coplan is professor and chair in social anthropology at the University of the Witwatersrand in Johannesburg. He has worked and lectured widely in the United States, Africa, and Europe. His best known book is *In Township Tonight: South Africa's Black City Music and Theatre* (1986), but he has also worked extensively on the performance culture of Lesotho migrant mine workers and their women in South Africa, and published a major study, *In the Time of Cannibals: The Word Music of South Africa's Basotho Migrants* (1994).
E-mail address: 031david@muse.wits.ac.za

Annemette Kirkegaard is associate professor at the Department of Musicology at the University of Copenhagen. Her Ph.D. thesis from 1995, "Taarab na Muziki Wa Densi", is on popular musical culture in Zanzibar and Tanzania seen in relation to globalisation and cultural change.
E-mail address: kirkegd@hum.ku.dk

Siri Lange is a social anthropologist affiliated with the Chr. Michelsen Institute in Bergen, Norway. Her Ph.D. thesis, completed in 2002, is concerned with popular culture, urbanisation, gender and the state in Tanzania and has a special focus on popular drama and Swahili "soaps".
E-mail address: siri.lange@cmi.no

Sylvia Nannyonga-Tamusuza is a lecturer in music at Makerere University in Uganda. She is currently pursuing her Ph.D. studies in ethnomusicology at the University of Pittsburgh, Pennsylvania, USA on "Bakisimba Dance Music: Articulation and Negotiation of Power and Gender Relations among the Baganda of Uganda." She has also taught courses and lectured on music and dance from Uganda in the US.
E-mail address: jusy@imul.com

Jenkeri Zakari Okwori is a senior lecturer with the Department of English and Drama, Ahmadu Bello University, Zaria, Nigeria. He has taught a range of courses and researched into indigenous performance and music forms. He is a recipient of several awards and fellowships, including the Kola Ogungbesan Memorial Prize for the Best Graduating Student in the Department of English and Drama, 1982, and an African Humanities Institute Fellowship, Ghana and Northwestern University, Illinois.
E-mail address: drjenks123@yahoo.com

Mai Palmberg has been co-ordinator of the research project "Cultural Images in and of Africa" at the Nordic Africa Institute since 1995. Trained as a political scientist she has published on diverse topics, such as the liberation struggle in southern Africa, US policies in Africa, development theory, AIDS in Africa, the Africa image in Swedish schoolbooks, the new South Africa, and human rights and homosexuality in southern Africa.
E-mail address: mai.palmberg@nai.uu.se

Christopher Waterman is professor, chair and acting dean of the Department of World Arts and Cultures at the University of California, Los Angeles (UCLA). An anthropologist, ethnomusicologist and bass player, he specializes in the study of popular music in sub-Saharan Africa (particularly Nigeria) and the Americas. Waterman is author of *Jùjú: A Social History and Ethnography of an African Popular Music* (University of Chicago Press, 1990) and co-author with Larry Starr of the forthcoming *American Popular Music from Minstrelsy to MTV* (Oxford University Press, 2002).
E-mail address: cwater@arts.ucla.edu